RACIAL CULTURE

RICHARD THOMPSON FORD

racial culture

A Critique

PRINCETON UNIVERSITY PRESS

Princeton and Oxford

Published by Princeton University Press, 41 William Street,
Princeton, New Jersey 08540

In the United Kingdom: Princeton University Press,
3 Market Place, Woodstock, Oxfordshire OX20 1SY

Library of Congress Cataloging-in-Publication Data

Ford, Richard T. (Richard Thompson)
    Racial culture : a critique / Richard Ford.
        p. cm.
    Includes bibliographical references and index.
    ISBN 0-691-11960-0 (alk. paper)
        1. Multiculturalism. 2. Intergroup relations.
3. Multiculturalism—Law and legislation. 4. Discrimination—
Law and legislation. I. Title.

HM1271.F67 2005
305.8'00973—dc22   2004041465

This book has been composed in Adobe Garamond

Printed on acid-free paper. ∞

pup.princeton.edu

Printed in the United States of America

10 9 8 7 6 5 4 3 2 1

To Richard Nicholas "Cole" Ford

CONTENTS

PREFACE

At one point the working title of this book was *Racial Cultures: A Reluctant Critique of Identity Politics*. After I gave a lecture based on the then half-finished manuscript, an impertinent member of the audience asked, "why call it a *reluctant* critique? You didn't sound all that reluctant to me." But I *have* been reluctant to advance this critique for most of the three or so years it has been in the works. More to the point, it was reluctance that kept me from writing something like this earlier. I am no longer reluctant to advance the arguments the book contains, so I dropped the subtitle (although I imagine many will be reluctant to read them, so perhaps I could have left the subtitle alone.)

This book began almost accidentally, when I was asked to write for and speak at a symposium on Race at the Turn of the Century at the University of California, Los Angeles, Law School. The theme of the symposium inspired me perhaps, and, in a millenarian frame of mind, I wrote a short "thought experiment" in which I asked what might be wrong with multiculturalism from the perspective of the proponents of left antiracism. The resulting lecture received a telling combination of enthusiastic applause, angry glares and crossed arms. It also received a thoughtful response by the moderator of our panel, Leti Volpp of American University Law School. Hers was a sympathetic but critical response that asked some difficult questions. They were questions I felt I had good answers to but I could not offer them at the time; the earlier panelists ran over their allotted time and, fortunately for all concerned, the symposium organizers had their priorities straight: we had to break it up and go to lunch.

Haunted by *l'esprit de l'escalier*, I returned to San Francisco and sat down to write. Three-and-a-half years later, I emerged with a manuscript and contract to publish the book you now hold. A lot happened in between, some of it much more important than the book. But some of what happened made the book what it is and this my editors tell me is the place to give credit and blame where they are due. As I mentioned, the book started life as an embryonic thought experiment at the UCLA Law Review's Race at the Turn of the Century Symposium. I gave lectures based on drafts in various stages of development and received invaluable comments at (these listed in chronological order): The European Law Center at Harvard Law School, a faculty workshop at the University of Southern California Law School, the Center for the Study of Law and Culture at Columbia Law School, a faculty workshop at Harvard Law School, a constitutional law seminar at Georgetown Law School and the Yale Law School Legal Theory Workshop. It goes without saying (but still it must be said) that I received characteristically excellent, constructive and critical comments from several faculty workshops at Stanford Law School.

I received typically excellent assistance from the finest academic law library staff in the nation at the Stanford Law School. My ability to craft vague and inaccurately phrased requests for obscure volumes ("I remember Ed Ruscha once said something about the country becoming colorblind.") was no match for Erika Wayne's research skills: almost without fail the desired volume would appear in my faculty box a few days after the poorly phrased request. Archivist Maggie Kimball at Stanford's Special Collections and University Archives took an interest in the project and guided a lawyer with no training and little experience in archival research through the seemingly endless files of past university presidents, deans and academic senates.

Ian Malcolm at Princeton University Press took an interest in this project very early on, offering advice, encouragement and editorial suggestions long before a contract was signed—indeed before the project was far enough along for anyone to know whether it would be publishable.

Many busy people took an interest in the project and contributed their valuable time and even more valuable knowledge and insight, resulting in a vastly superior end product to what might otherwise have emerged. Anyone who knows this group of scholars will also know that many of them will disagree—some vehemently—with part, much or all of what I argue herein. They nevertheless offered their insight and support in the sprit of friendship and intellectual encounter, reminding me (as if I needed reminding) that I have one of the best jobs a capitalist economy has ever produced. They include Bruce Ackerman, Jack Balkin, Rick Banks, Paul Brest, Elizabeth Bartholet, Marcus Cole, Dick Craswell, Kimberlé Crenshaw, Tino Cuellar, Michelle Dauber, Owen Fiss, Barbara Fried, Katherine Franke, Gerald Frug, Lani Guinier, Tom Grey, Pam Karlan, David Kennedy, Duncan Kennedy, Robert Post, Deborah Rhode, Reva Siegel, Kathleen Sullivan, Chantal Thomas, Kendall Thomas, Mark Tushnet, Leti Volpp, Bob Weisberg and Kenji Yoshino. Thank you.

In a group of extremely generous mentors, commentators, correspondents and critics, a few still manage to stand out. Mark Kelman read and responded to numerous drafts and always had the time and patience for yet another conversation about the implications of statistically and economically rational discrimination for left antiracism—a now central topic of inquiry in antidiscrimination law that he was central in developing. Randall Kennedy reviewed a draft of the manuscript for Princeton University Press, and was kind enough to share his observations. With characteristic insight and toughmindedness, he encouraged me to persevere with the project while pushing me to improve it—his comments guided me to transform the project from an intriguing but relatively inaccessible monograph to what I believe is a deeper, better-supported and more readable scholarly intervention.

Janet Halley was inspiration, friend, critic, mentor and (perhaps to her chagrin) a de facto editor for the manuscript. Her own fearless, rigorous and resolutely antidogmatic work in the intersection of feminism, sexuality, antidiscrimination law and jurisprudence awakened me from my dogmatic slumbers and inspired me to put hand to keyboard in service of this project. Her encouragement sustained my determination to complete the project through the numerous "dark nights of the soul" that scholarship generally and antidogmatic scholarship in particular entails. Her review of the manuscript for Princeton was a road map for my crucial final revisions: sympathetic but relentlessly critical, she pushed me to follow my intellectual convictions through to their conclusions and resisted my many less-than-courageous attempts to soft pedal uncomfortable conclusions or downplay ideologically "dangerous" but unavoidable implications of my arguments. And, recognizing that in both battle and in intellectual endeavor, an empty stomach is the enemy of courage, she also offered gourmet meals and a well-stocked bar during all of my numerous visits—working and social—to Cambridge and Dighton, Massachusetts.

My wife Marlene participated in countless (and, no doubt, endless as well from her perspective) conversations about this project, offering razor-sharp legal analysis, sociological insight, impressively complete and accurate historical knowledge from memory, wise cautionary counsel and, most of all, inspiration, companionship, patience and love. All references to German culture, correct spelling and usage of German vocabulary and placement of umlauts are to her exclusive credit.

I did not inflict as many conversations about the book on my mother, Nancy Ford, but her influence was nevertheless profound. She has consistently endeavored to pass on to me her rare combination of courage, forbearance, patience and steadfast conviction. Her sympathy for the victims of injustice and yet her unwillingness to default to excuses for herself and her own; her connection to her own distinctive upbringing and community and yet her openness to new experiences and her insistence on both loyalty and evenhandedness have inspired me for as long as I can remember. Her unwavering belief in my ability (which has, over the years manifested itself in the distinctively motherly forms of both praise and censure), her unconditional support and her love, formed the foundation for whatever good I have accomplished.

As I consulted volumes in my personal library, I was struck by the number that were marked with my father's handwriting. Some contained simple dedications: "To Rich from Dad, Christmas 1992." Others, yellowed and dogeared, contained marginal notes in his distinctive hand. Although he did not live to see me begin this manuscript, it is still the case that Richard Donald Ford, perhaps more than anyone else, contributed to it. No doubt he would have profoundly disagreed with some (perhaps much) of what I write here (a professor and dean of the School of Health and Social Work at California State University at Fresno for almost thirty years and member of the National Association of Black Social Workers he would, for instance, have had kinder things to say about the NABSW's support for race-matching in adoptions than I do) and he would have enjoyed to no end letting me know it. Nevertheless, if anything herein is worth the candle, it is ultimately to his credit.

RACIAL CULTURE

Preamble

The title of this book, *Racial Culture*, is a riddle. Racial culture? Does the title refer to the culture of a racial group, such as "black culture"? Does the text promise to examine one racial culture or perhaps a multiplicity of racial cultures? Does it explore what makes a racial group also a cultural group, ask what makes a cultural practice also a racial practice, limn the distinction between race (blood, ancestry, skin and bone) and culture (collective institutions of meaning, identification and expression)? Does the book then explore the range of actual and potential legal interventions in the life of a race and a culture? Is the book to grapple with the role of law in shaping, facilitating or hindering the expression or development of identities that are based on the cultural commonalities shared among members of various racial groups?

Or do these pages analyze the culture of a society that is organized around the idea of race; does it refer to *our* collective racial culture and ask what role law plays in producing this "culture of race" and its corresponding identities? Is the book about a culture of race, racism or racialism, a collective structure that produces the concept of race and in which that concept is salient?

There are stakes involved in getting the answers right. Thebes is in peril, and what seemed like good answers in act 1, may lead to blindness in act 3. Stay tuned: the Sphinx may well have the last laugh.

. . . . .

A lot of ink and paper have been devoted to something called multiculturalism, a.k.a. identity politics, alias: the politics of recognition. In a sense, this book is another two-hundred-plus pages of ink and paper devoted to the same protagonist. Some of the issues this book addresses—affirmative action, gay rights, transracial adoption, the racial categorization of the federal census—are staples of the literature on multiculturalism. There's a multiculturalist position and an anti-multiculturalist position on the issues. Most of the literature

1

is one or the other. The book is a critique of a type of multiculturalism, what I'll call "difference discourse," and that would seem to put me in the "anti" camp. What's left to say?

There are several potentially distinguishing features of my critical position. One is that, unlike some other critics, I'm sympathetic to many of the ends "multiculturalists" seek to achieve. My critical reactions stem primarily from a suspicion that the costs of multiculturalist policies *for the groups that they are supposed to help* have been obscured by wishful thinking. For instance, I support affirmative action, but I worry about the effects of the "diversity" justification for race conscious university admission as articulated by the Supreme Court in *U.C Regents v. Bakke* and more recently in *Grutter v. Bollinger.* I worry because the notion of "diversity," when it comes from the Supremes, is a court order that covers both the universities and their minority race students. As to the latter: to put it crudely, if diversity is the reason you got in to school, you better get off your chair and show us some diversity. There are other, better and less treacherous reasons to support affirmative action, reasons that "diversity"—an idea whose vogue is directly attributable to the variant of multiculturalism that I call "difference discourse"—displaces and obscures. Similarly I'm all for the idea of mixed-race or "multiracial" identities and the social flexibility they suggest. But I worry that the check-every-race-you-please census reform misses the point of governmental racial categorization (to monitor the enforcement of civil rights law, which itself properly focuses on ascriptive racial status, not on a metaphysics of ancestry or the unplumbed depth of subjective identity) and encourages individuals to think that their identities, self-image and self-esteem depend on the imprimatur of government.

Second, whereas most scholars' discussions of multiculturalism—pro and con—take as given the idea that "culture" can be usefully distinguished from ideology, norms, behavior and taste, mine does not. Rather I interrogate claims to cultural difference and often find such claims difficult to distinguish in principle or in practice from ideological differences, difference in tastes or difference in opinions.

Finally, my central focus is on law and legal institutions. I hope to uncover the effects of law—not only what the text of various laws and their advocates say the laws do, but also their unintended side effects, hidden messages and covert agendas. I believe that law can do and has done a great deal of good in alleviating social injustice. But I'm also certain that law and in particular specific legal forms (such as rights) have their limits, and we push those limits to our peril. I'm primarily concerned about the effect that ideas about group difference have in the context of legal rules. I hope to offer a new way of looking at these issues, one that is informed by a willingness to ask whether some of the typical concerns of multiculturalism are beside the point, others tell only part of the story and still others are right on the mark, but often involve stakes that the bulk of for-or-against multiculturalism literature doesn't capture.

Much of *Racial Cultures* is a critique of proposals to extend the reach of civil rights so that they would prohibit "cultural discrimination" or "coerced assimilation." A critique of a civil rights proposal perhaps naturally gives rise to some suspicions: the book is an apologia for the status quo or it is informed by a naive belief that racism and other illegitimate hierarchies are relics of the past that no longer demand redress. But the argument of this book is *premised* on the conviction that racism and other status hierarchies are a real and present threat to America's nobler, democratic and egalitarian aspirations. I do not critique civil rights generally; only a particular interpretation of our civil rights tradition that I will argue is counterproductive for the cause of social justice and bad policy more generally.

I also suggest that the strategies of some minority group members—particularly the obsession with group difference—participate in producing the conditions that make life hard for them. I do not say that the victims of the bigotry are to blame for their situation, but rather that some of the reactions of the victims—however understandable—are counterproductive. In this I echo the sentiments of law professor Randall Kennedy who writes,

> Many African Americans have sought to counter white racial pride with black racial pride, and white racial power with black racial power. White racial narcissism began the destructive spiral and is far more potent than black reactions, which are essentially defensive and compensatory responses to white aggression. Victims of oppression are nonetheless quite capable of hurting themselves and others through specious beliefs and mistaken actions.[1]

I would expand Kennedy's comment in one respect: the celebratory discourse of group difference does not simply react to or even mirror majority group bigotry—in many case it employs precisely the same description of group difference that the bigots employ. Rather than rejecting group stereotypes, the celebration of group difference endorses them and simply insists that the stereotypical characteristics are unfairly undervalued by a "hegemonic" majority culture.

Some readers might object that a critique of a well-intentioned, even if misguided, expansion of civil rights is a poor use of time and energy. Difference discourse is not primarily responsible for keeping illegitimate status hierarchy alive; why not attack a fundamental social injustice? My answer: The difference approach is not only ineffectual; it is harmful. The ideology of

group difference is not simply a poor solution to racism and other status hierarchies; it actively contributes to illegitimate social hierarchies. I have written
a great deal elsewhere about the ongoing, institutionalized and systematic
evils of American racism, as have others far too numerous to name. Here I
focus on the obsession with difference, not because it is the worst of the cul-
prits but because it is passing as a Good Samaritan.

Difference Discourse

The book analyzes a series of claims, proposals and practices that I name "difference discourse." It takes aim at a set of moral and legal arguments that promote what I dub "rights-to-difference." These arguments hold that a just society could and should prohibit discrimination on the basis of the cultural
difference (thereby establishing a "right-to-difference") for the same reasons it
should prohibit discrimination based on statuses such as race. I discuss them,
not only because they are influential proposals that either have been or may
well be implemented, but also because these arguments are emblematic of a
more general set of social beliefs about race, identity, culture and justice.
These more general beliefs—the ideology of difference discourse—have profoundly influenced substantive policies and underwritten litigation victories.
I argue that the rights-to-difference line of argumentation is doubly wrong:
the reasons that underlie legal prohibition of discrimination based on status
do not apply to cultural difference generally; moreover "rights-to-difference,"
however justified, are likely to have socially deleterious consequences unasso-
ciated with traditional anti-discrimination law.

Although, as the title indicates, the central concern of the book is claims
of *racial* culture, I believe the problem the book addresses is characteristic of
more than race relations. It is in play to greater or lesser degrees in many of the
social classifications that inspire modern identity politics and multiculturalism:
ethnicity, sex, sexual orientation, tribal membership. I cite such other "identities" when relevant, with, I hope, due attention to important specificities and
distinctions.

A significant portion of my argument focuses on scholarly literature that
advocates the expansion of civil rights to include rights to "cultural difference"
or "identity correlated traits." The main text will treat the scholarly literature as exemplary or symptomatic of a larger social discourse that pervades
the popular media, public policy and the reasoning of the judiciary as well.
Accordingly it will not deal with any specific scholarly text comprehensively.
Nevertheless, I do wish to describe my critique in relationship to the more
prominent schools of academic thought so as to acknowledge similarities and

to highlight distinctions between my approach and that of others with whom some readers may be familiar. I will deal primarily with the two most important sources of related thought in the academy: political philosophy and legal scholarship.

Political Philosophy

Political philosophers are by and large concerned with the compatibility of multicultural reforms with liberalism—Will Kymlicka's defense of cultural rights in *Multicultural Citizenship* and Brian Barry's critique of same in *Culture and Equality* are good examples. By contrast my central concern is with the capacity of legal reforms (and their related ideologies and narratives) that are premised on the existence and centrality of cultural difference to produce that difference and mandate its centrality. Whereas the philosophers tend to focus on principles and concepts, my concern is with how law-on-the-books affects life on the streets. The central concerns of political philosophy are generally at some remove—although never entirely absent—from my analysis. I focus on the likely social consequences of legal rules, rules that are in turn influenced by and deploy the language and analytics of philosophy.

It's fair to say that "multiculturalism" constitutes a distinct genre within political philosophy. As is true with most scholarly literature, a review of the multicultural literature could borrow a title from a spaghetti western—it includes the good, the bad and the ugly. In the service of intellectual probity, fairness and, most importantly, brevity, I will take its more meritorious and attractive practitioners as representative.

MULTICULTURALISM AND LIBERALISM

Much of the political philosophy literature concerns the implications of group cultural pluralism for liberal principles and liberal ideals of justice. A first rough cut would divide the literature between radical multiculturalism and liberal multiculturalism. Radical multiculturalism would insist that the rights of culturally distinctive groups to retain their distinctive practices and mores should trump the demands of political liberalism: if a group culture requires illiberal institutions such as theocracy, collective ownership of property (thereby effectively prohibiting exit from the group by prohibiting individual control of resources) or institutionalized subordination of women, the cultural traditions of the group should prevail. The radical multiculturalist either rejects liberalism as a general matter, or, more commonly, argues that liberal commitments are themselves culturally specific and therefore applicable only to people raised in liberal cultures.

I am more or less agnostic as to the cultural relativism of radical multiculturalism—it is largely irrelevant to my arguments whether liberal ideals and commitments are universally valid or specific to the culture of the modern West. But the radical multiculturalist rejection of liberalism flirts with contradiction: the conviction that minority cultures have rights to autonomy and self-determination is itself an unmistakably liberal position. Having rejected the universal applicability of liberal ideals, one needs some other principles of justice with which to indict the supposed cultural imperialism of imposing liberalism on illiberal minority cultures. Perhaps the charge is hypocrisy: liberals should adhere to their own principles in dealing with other cultures. But this puts liberals in an impossible bind: they can adhere to liberal principles in their dealings with illiberal cultures as groups only by abandoning them in their dealings with the members of those cultures as individuals. Perhaps this fact is thought to demonstrate the self-consuming nature of liberalism. To me it does not do so; instead it demonstrates the banal point that any normative discourse, liberalism included, has its constitutive limits.

My arguments assume the validity of liberal ideals, defined broadly and generally. Moreover, difference discourse is premised on the validity of liberal ideals: the claim that minorities have rights-to-difference is based on liberal ideals of equality, freedom of choice and self-actualization. For these reasons I have little to say about radical or illiberal multiculturalism.

My own concerns are sympathetic with those of the "liberal egalitarian" critics of multiculturalism, of whom I take the English philosopher Brian Barry, author of *Culture and Equality* to be representative. Like the liberal egalitarians, I worry that multicultural rights may unduly impinge on individual liberties; like them I worry that robust group identification threatens to exacerbate social divisions that we should work to lessen, and like them I worry that multicultural rights will distract attention from the most pressing contemporary social ills that, by and large, concern disparities of wealth and income. Like liberal egalitarians such as Barry, I believe that generally applicable legal rules—be they rights or restrictions on action—are to be preferred to group-specific rules or exceptions. At the same time I believe that group-specific policies and exceptions are necessary in some cases (I will vigorously defend a group-specific view of anti-discrimination law and affirmative action in these pages), but I believe they are necessary in far fewer cases than many proponents of multiculturalist policies would have it.

WHICH GROUPS? ANALOGIES AND DISTINCTIONS

Much of contemporary multiculturalist scholarship presumes that the cosmopolitan mass democracies of the West consist of numerous different "cultures" whose form and substance we must take more or less as given. From this it seems to follow that the central problem of group difference is how to negotiate incompatibilities among the different group cultures. Consider this passage from the introductory paragraph of an essay by political philosopher Chandran Kukathas entitled, "Are There Any Cultural Rights":

> At least since the American civil rights movement, many people have become more aware of the harm suffered by ethnic and cultural minorities laboring under discriminatory practices or inequities. . . . The conditions of the American black and the American Indian, the Canadian Inuit, the New Zealand Maori, and the Australian Aborigine have been the subject of various administrative and legislative initiatives. And the political claims of the Basques in Spain, the French Canadians in Canada, and the Tamils in Sri Lanka have been gaining wider prominence.[2]

Here, social groups defined by race are treated as analogous to geographically insular cultural minorities and certain indigenous or aboriginal tribes. The presumption underlying this statement seems to be that all these groups have a distinctive culture, that it is primarily this cultural difference that distinguishes the groups from each other and perhaps from some ruling class (that is responsible for the "discriminatory practices or inequities") and that therefore the claims of the various groups for cultural rights are the natural offspring of the American civil rights movement.

In this book I argue that this quite widespread idea is profoundly wrong. The simplest statement of my thesis in this regard is that racism (and analogous forms of "status based discrimination"—I'll return to this difficult idea in chapter 2) is different than social conflict arising as a result of cultural difference. Contemporary anti-discrimination law is reasonably well suited to confront at least some limited manifestations of racism. I will argue that it is quite poorly suited to deal with the conflicts and potentials of cultural pluralism.

If we suspend the typical multiculturalist presumption that the word "culture" denotes the most salient social groups in contemporary society and that the most salient examples of social group conflict and illegitimate hierarchy are well understood as conflicts between incompatible cultures, we can begin to develop useful distinctions among group conflicts. For instance, racial difference, as typified by the African-American experience, is not well described as first and foremost a matter of cultural difference. As the philosopher Kwame Anthony Appiah writes, "It is not black culture that the racist distains, but blacks. . . . [N]o amount of knowledge of the architectural achievements of Nubia or Kush guarantees respect for African-Americans. . . . [C]ulture is not the problem, and it is not the solution."[3] The paradigmatic problems of race in the United States involve discrimination that attaches prior to and independent of any evaluation of cultural conflict. Lunch counters in the Jim Crow south refused to serve anyone who *looked* black; racial profiling involves targeting individuals for police interrogation based on *visual* confirmation of racial identity alone; New York taxicabs refused to stop for Hollywood actor Danny Glover, not because he hailed them in a culturally distinctive manner but because of the color of his skin and the texture of his hair. Granted, cultural practices play a role in marking out racial difference, but it is extremely doubtful that that role has begun to approach, much less eclipse the classical and crude function of physical appearance as the primary marker of racial difference.

Moreover, the degree and salience of cultural differences between the races is much less dramatic than between insular aboriginal groups and urbanized cosmopolitans. And the salience of cultural difference for regionally centered ethnic groups such as the Québécois and the Basque is much greater than it is for most racial groups, if only for the simple reason that culture is the *only* thing that distinguishes the Québécois from the Anglo-Canadian majority and the Basque minority from the Spanish or French majorities. Multiculturalism may be the appropriate lens through which to understand such social divisions (and in fairness, many multiculturalists are careful to limit their analyses to such cases).

Indeed, some of the most influential articulations of liberal multiculturalism are, on their own account, simply irrelevant to the argument of this book. For instance, Will Kymlicka, whom I take as representative of a significant strain of liberal multiculturalism, explicitly distinguishes both American blacks and immigrants from the central object of his own concern, what he calls "national minorities":

> [W]hereas racism against blacks comes from the denial by whites that blacks are full members of the community, racism against Indians [a "national minority"] comes primarily from the denial by whites that Indians are distinct peoples with their own cultures and communities. . . . The historical situation and present circumstances of African-Americans are virtually unique in the world, and there is no reason to think that policies which are appropriate for them would be appropriate for either national minorities [such as Canadian First Nations or the Québécois] or recent immigrants.[4]

Blacks, according to Kymlicka, are best served by anti-discrimination laws that guarantee equal access to existing institutions. Immigrants, on Kymlicka's account, can legitimately be expected to assimilate to the culture of their new country, despite having radically different cultures of their own, "so long as [they] had the option to stay in their original culture. . . . In deciding to up-root themselves, immigrants voluntarily relinquish some of the rights that go along with their original national membership."[5] And "the best that refugees" who migrated involuntarily due to persecution at home, "can expect is to be treated as immigrants . . . and hope to return to their homeland as quickly as possible."[6] The bulk of Kymlicka's arguments defend rights for "national minorities," whereas I am mainly concerned with arguments made on behalf of the groups that Kymlicka's definition of national minority excludes—such as racial minorities, immigrants and homosexuals.

Kymlicka is right to distinguish the situation of African-Americans from that of groups defined primarily by cultural difference, a distinction I will insist on repeatedly throughout this book. And I suppose I could simply let the matter drop with this: Kymlicka, like many multiculturalists, is concerned with different groups and different problems than I. His arguments just don't apply to my cases.

But despite his initial caveats, many of Kymlicka's arguments would appear to apply across the board, to any social group with distinctive traits and practices. He does address a portion of his argument to what he calls "poly-ethnic rights," which, for Kymlicka, seem to apply to religious and ethnic minorities who cannot claim the status of "national minority." Many of his arguments for polyethnic rights are parallel to his more robust argument in favor of rights for national minorities and proceed from similar ethical commitments and according to a similar logic.

Moreover, Kymlicka's profered distinction between national minorities (on Kymlicka's definition a very small population of relatively minor significance in a few national contexts) on the one hand, and ethnic minorities and immigrants (obviously a very large and diverse population of profound significance for almost every nation on the planet) on the other, does not withstand scrutiny. Indeed Kymlicka's own arguments belie it: many of Kymlicka's arguments in fact apply with equal force to racial minorities, ethnic minorities, recent immigrants and potentially a host of other social groups. Kymlicka's argument involves (and benefits from) a slippage between a narrowly defined set of "national minorities" and a much broader group of minorities. This slippage is characteristic of multicultural argumentation, as I have suggested above.

Kymlicka's first line of defense for cultural rights holds that rights to group cultural differences are necessary, not because minority cultures (or any specific cultures) are valuable in and of themselves, but rather because access to one's own cultural traditions and institutions is a necessary precondition for the effective exercise of liberal rights. He argues that "people's capacity to make meaningful choices depends on access to a cultural structure."[7] A central difficulty for this line of argument is in defining "culture." In order to convincingly make the argument that access to culture is a precondition of meaningful choice, culture must be understood to be encompassing and robust, as Kymlicka defines it when he avers to " 'societal cultures' whose practices and institutions cover the full range of human activities, encompassing both public and private life."[8]

But, as Kymlicka admits, even on the most robust definition of societal culture (with a correspondingly negligible set of groups to which it applies) it is not clear that meaningful choice requires access to one's own culture—only to *some* culture.[9] For instance, were the French to conquer the United States and impose a Francophone culture in San Francisco, I would not be disabled from making meaningful choices, as long as I had access to the new, Francophone, social, economic and political institutions. To be sure, there would be costs involved in my assimilating to the new culture (such as learning to speak French), but these costs would not be disabling and in any event could be subsidized. In this sense, what is required is not "cultural rights" but rather rights of equal access to whatever institutions are in place—rights against discrimination.

But, having acknowledged this gap in his argument, Kymlicka rejects its implications, arguing that "integration . . . is a costly process and there is a legitimate question whether people should be required to pay those costs unless they voluntarily choose to do so, . . ." and noting that "even where the obstacles to integration are smallest, the desire of national minorities to retain their cultural membership remains very strong."[10] These arguments sound in an entirely different register than those concerning culture as a context of meaningful choice. Here, the function of cultural rights is not to guarantee a meaningful context of choice; instead it is essentially distributive—to avoid imposing psychological *costs* on the members of minority cultural groups. It bears emphasis that in almost every contested case (meaning any case in which there is social or economic pressure to integrate—in other words any case in which cultural rights would be meaningful), the question is not one of *whether* society will impose costs or refrain from so doing—instead it one of *who* will bear the inevitable costs associated with cultural pluralism. If some cultural minorities do not bear the costs of integration, then someone else will bear the cost of their failure to integrate—society as a whole, members of the majority, members of other minority groups or other members of the group in question. Much of this book will focus on these costs—especially the cost to members of the group itself.

On Kymlicka's new rationale for cultural rights, the number of groups with standing to sue is quite large. There is no reason not to include recent immigrants and ethnic and racial minorities, and nonethnic groups with specific practices and mores. If "there is a legitimate question whether" Native-Americans or

French-Canadians "should be required to pay the costs" associated with integration, surely there is also a legitimate question whether American blacks, recent immigrants fleeing political persecution or poverty, white ethnics with rich cultural memories or gay men and lesbians with a distinctive subculture should be required to pay them. At this point the argument of a liberal multiculturalist such as Kymlicka becomes a general argument for rights to difference—the position I will critique extensively in this book.

The slippage between quite insular groups defined by "societal cultures" and fairly diffuse groups with only mild and relatively superficial cultural distinctiveness is characteristic of multiculturalist argumentation. As long as the argument begins and ends with groups defined by the strong version of "societal cultures," I have little to say about it. But, because the number of groups with such "societal cultures" that are also minorities within a nation-state is vanishingly small, I suspect that, in practice, very little will depend on a reference to groups with societal cultures. My suspicion is confirmed by Kymlicka's shift to a distinct rationale for multicultural rights that refers, not to the fundamental importance of societal cultures specifically but to the *psychological costs* of assimilation generally. At this point the argument is essentially one of distributive justice. Multiculturalism and rights discourse do not offer useful insights into questions of distributive justice; this isn't surprising because they do not try to do so; instead they seek to resolve these distributive questions by proxy, with reference to conceptual shibboleths such as "culture" and "self determination."

Legal Scholarship

One can get a representative sample of the rights-to-difference genre in the legal academy from the pages of the *Yale Law Journal* alone. In 1985 Stephen Cutler argued in the *Yale Law Journal* for "A Trait-Based Approach to National Origin Claims Under Title VII."[11] In a 1991 *Yale Law Journal* article Mari Matsuda proposed anti-discrimination protection for accents based on a sophisticated theory of the relationship between racial and cultural difference.[12] In 1995 Barbara Flagg suggested in the *Yale Law Journal* that Title VII should prohibit discrimination on the basis of "personal characteristics [that] . . . intersect seamlessly with [one's racial] self-definition."[13] And in 2002 Kenji Yoshino argued in the *Yale Law Journal* that anti-discrimination law should prohibit demands for assimilation by protecting traits and behavior that are correlated with social identities such as race, gender and sexual orientation.[14] New Haven doesn't have a monopoly on the rights-to-difference approach: Paulette Caldwell may have inaugurated the rights-to-difference genre of legal scholarship in her groundbreaking "A Hair Piece,"[15] which argues that workplace rules forbidding cornrow hairstyles are actionable race and gender discrimination. Juan Perea argues that Title VII should prohibit discrimination based, not on ethnicity, but on "ethnic traits."[16] And William Bratton and Drucilla Cornell propose that Title VII prohibit employers from requiring that bilingual Spanish and English-speaking employees speak only English while on the job, not because all people should have a right to speak their first language but *because of the centrality of Spanish to Latino* identity.[17]

As law reform proposals, these arguments are inspired by the well-justified conviction that traditional anti-discrimination law—which is triggered only by either demonstrable animus on the part of a decision maker or by a policy that has a statistically demonstrable disparate impact on a protected group and is not sufficiently related to a legitimate institutional objective—fails to remedy a great deal of the socially pervasive bias directed at members of historically sub-ordinated groups. To take an example from chapter 1, if an employer forbids its employees from wearing all-braided or "cornrow" hairstyles, many people will (correctly in at least some cases) perceive the policy as racially biased. But a plaintiff who attempts to sue to overturn the policy will lose because courts have (correctly) interpreted the relevant anti-discrimination statutes to exclude discrimination on the basis of behavior or characteristics within the immediate control of the plaintiff. Under the proposed reforms, the plaintiff would win if she could demonstrate that the hairstyle was subjectively "central to her racial identity" or objectively "racially correlated."

Nevertheless, the proposals suffer from practical and conceptual problems. What counts as racially correlated? Is it enough that the plaintiff believes the trait is correlated with her race? Must she show that a perception of racial cor-relation is socially pervasive? Must she demonstrate an objective, statistical correlation? Suppose the trait in question is more problematic than an uncon-ventional hairstyle—suppose someone argues (as some already have) that cer-tain racial or ethnic groups are culturally resistant to mechanical time or have "alternative" modes of interaction with authority figures. Must an institution accommodate habitual tardiness or insubordination because they are arguably correlated with a social identity? If so, will such a legal regime and the result-ing codified account of minority group culture well serve the people it pur-ports to protect? I am concerned with both the practical policy consequences of questionable ideas about group cultural difference and the ideological ef-fects of the group culture idea and the policies it underwrites.

Despite the concerns raised above, *Racial Culture* advocates a narrow but robust form of race consciousness. Justice and sound policy requires a sober accounting of the practices of racism and a realistic assessment of its victims and likely future targets. "Colorblindness" threatens to become blindness, not to race, but to racism; because colorblindness cannot be enforced on the population as a whole, racism will continue to do its dirty work. Colorblindness will keep us from diagnosing and remedying the evil of racism. For these reasons, race consciousness must be robust: we must acknowledge the existence of racial groups—groups produced by racism—in order to craft appropriate remedies and administer remediation.

But because of the difficulties of distinguishing benign from malignant forms of racial recognition, race consciousness must also be narrow. We should limit formal race consciousness to a remedial function. We should limit the formal acknowledgement of race to its most formal and culturally empty definition. This would exclude accounts of the distinctive cultural attributes of racial groups, not necessarily because there are no such things as racial cultures, but because even to the extent that there are, on balance the risks of attempting to acknowledge them in policy and law outweigh any potential benefits.

Legalism

A central theme of this book is the risk of what I will call "legalism": the tendency to describe social conflicts first and foremost in legal terms. People who have no intention of filing a lawsuit regularly speak in terms of their "rights" and in terms of "discrimination" (understood in terms of its legalistic denotation—legally actionable status-conscious decision making—rather than its *Webster's Dictionary* meaning.) It's rare that we think of race, gender or sexual orientation without somewhere in the back of our minds imagining legislation or litigation.

Legalism has, needless to say, helped to usher in profound advances in terms of social justice for minority groups. But it has also cost us something. Legal thinking has "occupied the field" as we say when a federal law displaces a local ordinance; as a result it's hard to think about many issues of social justice without filtering them through formal legal analysis (at which laypersons in the United States are surprising adept), litigation tactics, the language of the equal protection clause or the judicial opinion in *Brown v. Board of Education*. One cost of this occupation of the field is that we may lose sight of the many approaches to a better society, and the many possibilities of a good life that are not embodied in case law and that are not well articulated as a legal entitlement.

But I fear it's even worse than that. My greatest fear is that litigation has become much more than a tool to be deployed to an autonomous end; instead the ability to secure legal recognition is an end in and of itself and the self-esteem and self-conception of many people—especially the more vulnerable groups and individuals in our society—is ever more dependent on the imprimatur offered by civil rights legislation and the published opinions of the federal judiciary.

In this sense this book is a critique of legalism—a style of thinking influenced by law—rather than of law or law reform proposals per se. Thus when I critique "rights-to-difference," for the most part I mean to critique a discourse—a peculiarly legalistic style of argumentation—as much as the actual proposal and its likely consequences.

Ideology

The working title of this book was for a long time, *Racial Cultures: A Critique From the Left*. I decided to drop this subtitle because it seemed to me to beg the question: what is "the left?"—a question which requires a book of its own. By and large my analysis proceeds from commitments characteristic of "the left," but my approach in *Racial Cultures* has been to play the field, ideologically speaking, rather than going steady with one discrete set of influences. If someone has a good idea, I'll climb into the back seat with her no matter which side of the tracks she's from. Hence, some of the arguments I make in *Racial Cultures* echo those made by political conservatives, who have long argued against identity politics in all of its forms. I leave it to the reader to judge the significance of this fact. A conclusion that some at least will almost certainly reach is that the book takes a conservative position.

I do not by and large hold the constellation of policy positions and beliefs that we conventionally associate with political conservatism; indeed my positions on most social issues belong deep in the left wing of the palace. But at the same time I don't think it wise to reject a position simply because something similar has been expressed by people with whom I disagree on other issues. If conservatives have adopted a compelling position, I see no reason to reject it simply because they got there first.

To the extent I agree with conservatives on some points, the agreement is neither wide nor deep. For instance, like anthropologist Peter Wood, I critique the "diversity" rationale for affirmative action.[18] But I critique it for largely different reasons than he and, unlike Wood, I do not oppose affirmative action; in fact one reason I find the diversity rationale troubling is because I do not find it the most compelling justification for a policy I support, but which I believe requires justification.

Racial Cultures is generally suspicious of governmental intervention and insistent on the limits of civil rights and law generally. This I expect will fuel the sense that the book is conservative, or libertarian.

I can expound in more detail about libertarianism because, unlike conservatism—a vaguely defined political leaning which can entail any number of divergent substantive positions—libertarianism has a fairly specific content and a coherent set of ideological commitments. I can't accept the compliment offered by those who would call *Racial Cultures* libertarian however (although I am happy to acknowledge that I have benefited from the thoughtful critiques of governmental overreaching offered by many libertarians) precisely because "libertarian" carries the connotation of a general worldview, a commitment to certain principles, an ideology, that I do not embrace.

Let's say my friend Ayn is a libertarian. This would mean that she has faith in private ordering, free markets, and invisible hand phenomena; faith both in the existence of these things and in their inherent practical and moral superiority over governmental regulation. As a classical libertarian, Ayn would believe that governmental regulation is inefficient and clumsy and therefore unlikely to achieve its goals, and she would also believe that governmental regulation wrongfully impinges on the rights of individuals to make their own decisions and order their own affairs. For her, opposition to state regulatory policy is super justified: regulation doesn't work, produces horrible side effects and violates rights that should be an absolute bar even to regulation that worked brilliantly and had no side effects.

The libertarian's conjoined faith in private ordering and suspicion of government extends to both the economic and the social sphere. Ayn will argue that the minimum wage, laws against hate speech and antisodomy laws are all wrong *for the same reason:* they interfere with the right of individuals to make their own decisions and to order their affairs through voluntary associations.

Because the libertarian's opposition to government regulation is extremely broad and over determined, it cannot follow that anyone who makes an argument that a libertarian might also make is, by virtue of that fact alone, a libertarian. The need for a modifier in the term "civil libertarian" suggests why. Suppose Ayn's sister Nadine is a civil libertarian; this would mean that Nadine opposes a certain species of governmental regulation but potentially also supports a great deal of regulation outside that species. Nadine's arguments against those regulations she opposes (say antisodomy laws and hate speech laws) might sound a great deal like Ayn's objections to a much broader range of governmental regulation. But it would be a mistake to conclude that Nadine's views are identical to Ayn's. Nadine might argue that antisodomy laws violate individual rights but the minimum wage does not because of what she experiences as a principled distinction between the two. It would be a mistake to assume that both Nadine and Ayn are "libertarians" and therefore Nadine's position can be attacked with the same arguments used against Ayn's much more sweeping position.

Now suppose Nadine's friend Ellen opposes governmental regulation of sexual relations between consenting adults, such as antisodomy laws (we might call Ellen a "sexual libertine"). Ellen might use arguments similar to Ayn's and Nadine's to attack antisodomy laws, but it would not do to decide on this basis that Ellen is a libertarian, or a civil libertarian. Ellen may very well favor, not only the minimum wage, but also the criminalization of hate speech and a law outlawing all religion. She might support these, not because she is unprincipled or has failed to understand the implication of her "libertarian" position on sodomy, but because her position on sodomy is not well described as libertarian. Ellen would insist that her reasons for opposing antisodomy laws are context specific—yes, *in this case* governmental regulation violates individual liberties (or simply does harm to consenting adults with no offsetting benefit for society), but in the other cases no equally compelling liberties are at stake and the benefits of the regulation outweigh the costs. Ellen's position on sodomy does not commit her to Ayn's position on the minimum wage; nor does Ellen's position derive from the same ideological commitments as Ayn's.[19]

By the same token my critique of rights-to-difference does not derive from libertarian ideology. The critique is pragmatic and context specific: it holds that regulation that requires a judicial inquiry into the content of group identity, as rights-to-difference would, is likely to have bad side effects that dwarf any corresponding benefits. Embrace of this critique does not make one a libertarian (though if libertarians embrace it, I'm happy to have their support), any more than concern about the side effects of morphine therapy makes one an enemy of modern medicine or opposition to nuclear power makes one a Luddite.

As for ideological valence, I will add two last remarks. There is something odd about the faith that proponents of cultural rights place in government—the same government that is the focus of their sustained and by and large accurate condemnation as far as bias and discrimination are concerned. Unless one believes that legal rights are self-executing or that judges become more enlightened and virtuous than their counterparts in other branches of government by virtue of donning black robes, one should be worried about a rights regime that would give judges sweeping authority to determine and enforce ideas of "correct" or authentic group culture. To worry, one need not be a libertarian, only someone concerned about liberty, nor need one believe that judges are cretins or bigots, only that they are no better, on the whole, than the politicians and private citizens whose decisions they review.

Finally, as many have insisted before me, I would also insist that there is reason to worry that an obsession with group difference will ill serve such traditionally "left" causes as egalitarian distribution of resources and well-designed social programs. As the philosopher Brian Barry points out, "the proliferation of special interest fostered by multiculturalism is . . . conducive to a politics of 'divide and rule'[,] . . . diverting attention away from shared disadvantages such as unemployment, poverty, low-quality housing and inadequate public services and is an obvious long term anti-egalitarian objective."[20]

I would add that the tactical exaggeration of group cultural difference ("strategic essentialism" and such) for purposes of solidarity not only restricts the liberty of group members (that's a large part of the point, I'm afraid), but also makes common social objectives difficult to imagine, much less achieve. If, for instance, every group has to have its own primary school curriculum—a gay high school in New York City, Afrocentrism and Latino Studies at Berkeley High School, et cetera—we effectively achieve a convenient, politically correct form of school segregation and often, academic tracking. Worse yet, privatization is the obvious—perhaps the only feasible—long-term solution to the inevitable proliferation of group-specific curricular demands: I may be happy to have my tax dollars pay to educate all children in the three Rs, but hostile to being required to support the inculcation of cultural values that I do not (and, on multiculturalist epistemology, cannot) understand or appreciate. Here multiculturalism seems the ally of the conservative school–choice agenda, which would privatize the important functions of public education, as against the liberal aspiration of public education for the purpose of common citizenship.

Lexicon

The subject matter of this book presents a difficulty in terminology. As I have already argued, many discussions about race, ethnicity, cultural difference, sexual preference or orientation, gender, and indigenous peoples proceed as if these group identities and the social phenomena surrounding them raise analogous issues, involve similar stakes and demand parallel legal and policy responses. Yet a careful examination of the literature and of social conversations reveals widespread disagreement even among people with generally similar ideological predispositions about which groups are analogously situated to which others, exactly what stakes are involved, and what legal and policy interventions are called for.

The differing perspectives on group difference are often difficult to identify because of a casual use of terminology. The definition of terms such as "multiculturalism" and "identity politics" is generally left to popular intuition and inference. The colloquial use of terms such as "nationalism" and "ethnicity" invites imprecise analogy. The lack of a precise definition of race, gender, and sexual orientation leaves the boundaries and contours of the groups thereby defined a matter of conjecture and debate.

To some extent this is unavoidable, the nature of the beasts. The problematic this book addresses (and does not, I confess, resolve) is how we should think about and deal with social identities whose very nature is the result of how we think about and deal with them. But this is no excuse to leave the situation any more beastly than absolutely necessary. I offer a tentative set of working definitions in the hope that, if they will not tame the beasts, they will at least make the zoo somewhat easier to manage.

Multiculturalism: This term has become a general signifier for all manner of social group conflicts. In a sense, this imperialism of "multiculturalism" is precisely what this book opposes. When I use the term sincerely (meaning when I use it for my own purposes rather than in reference to someone else's ideas) "multiculturalism" will refer to conflicts that *centrally* involve cultural difference. The conflict between Anglo-and French-Canadians strikes me as appropriately multicultural, as do the conflicts of recent immigrants from non-Western nations to the West. Certain conflicts involving religious doctrine, especially those that are ambiguously religious and ethnic, are also appropriately "cultural" such as the ongoing "headscarves affair" in France in which some Muslim families oppose a general prohibition of religious symbolism and attire in French public schools.

To the extent racial and ethnic conflicts centrally involve cultural difference rather than simply atavistic prejudice, they too enter the domain of multiculturalism. But it does not follow that all or even most racial and ethnic conflicts are well described in the language of multiculturalism. When blacks resist job discrimination or lobby for race-conscious electoral reapportionment, these struggles do not sound in the register of multiculturalism; instead, they are struggles against racial domination and better considered as a distinct variety of social encounter. Similarly, the gay rights movement is not primarily multicultural; instead, it is primarily a movement for sexual autonomy, a demand for rights to privacy, perhaps a demand for rights to what social critic Michael Warner has called a "sex public." The conflict here involves moralism and morality, privacy and self-assertion;—all of the positions involved are perfectly cognizable within the cultural frame of the cosmopolitan West.

Identity politics: Identity politics centrally involves group self-consciousness. Any social group whose members identify as a group potentially can develop a political *group consciousness* directed at achieving shared ends. The political actions of a social group *as a social group* are appropriately called "identity politics." What is required is a group identity around which the political efforts centrally cohere. The American civil rights movement was not necessarily a movement of identity politics because the struggle involved rights and concerns thought to be universally applicable rather than of specific concern to a particular group. At the same time, one *could* understand the civil rights movement as "racial identity politics" as well.

The "gay rights" movement *is* a movement of identity politics to the extent it centers on the interests of a group identity—"gay"—rather than a principle or set of policies such as, say, "sexual autonomy." By contrast, what scholars such as Michael Warner[21] and Janet Halley[22] have called "queer" politics, which explicitly rejects gay identity as an organizing concept in favor of a broad-based attack on sexual moralism generally, is not a form of identity politics.

For our purposes, an important feature of identity politics is that it tends to collapse issues that might be better considered independently. In the context of race it collapses issues of race and issues of culture; in the context of sexual orientation it collapses issues of sexual liberty and issues of "culture" loosely speaking (mainly style and affect) and in the context of sex and gender it collapses issues of sex hierarchy ("male chauvinism") and issues of culture (women's "different voice") again loosely speaking.

Identity politics is usefully, if delicately, distinguished from the following:

The Politics of Recognition: Perhaps a subset of identity politics, the politics of recognition is centrally concerned with the social validation of distinctive group differences. These differences need not be cultural differences, although they often are. What is crucial here is not only the practical consequences of a given public policy for a concrete group interest, but also and indispensably the symbolic validation of the group as both different and valuable. An official policy of disdainful tolerance of the group and its practices simply flunks the test of the Politics of Recognition, as does a policy that effectively insulates the practices of the group from censure through generally applicable rules that fail to recognize the group as a group with a distinctive identity. Similarly, the opinion of the Court in *Lawrence v. Texas*, which invalidated laws prohibiting homosexual sodomy, applying a generally applicable privacy right (but did not consider homosexual status worthy of legal recognition), combined with a reinterpretation of constitutional and anti-discrimination law which effectively (but not explicitly) outlawed discrimination against homosexuals, might satisfy the requirements of a pragmatically oriented gay identity politics; it would not satisfy the demands of the politics of recognition.

Obviously these three modes of analysis and political action share much in common and blur at their boundaries. Nevertheless, there is a reason that distinctive names have emerged: at the core, they are animated by distinctive concerns, they reflect distinctive normative aspirations and in some sense they reflect distinctive conceptions of human subjectivity.

Overview of the Book

The book is divided into four chapters.

Chapters 1 and 2 describe the set of ideas, policies, and literature I wish to attack and introduce the book's central thesis: Group cultural difference—racial culture—is a social discourse that produces rather than describes preexisting group cultural differences. I argue that the "recognition" of group difference is not an antidote to the forced assimilation of distinctive social groups. Instead the two—recognition of difference and forced assimilation—are both part of a *single mechanism of oppression*, a whipsaw dynamic that effectively produces and punishes group difference, making assimilation both mandatory and unavailable. By examining the use and effects of the "diversity" rationale for affirmative action, I attempt to demonstrate that a seemingly benign "recognition" of group cultural difference can be a means of forcing group members into confining social roles while simultaneously obscuring the salience of pervasive social bias and discrimination that attaches to those very roles.

Chapter 2 argues that racial and analogous social identities are never autonomously adopted or intrinsic; they are always, at least in part, the effect of this social regulation. It offers several examples of this, perhaps counterintuitive, phenomenon. Chapter 2 suggests that, instead of presumptively protecting the traits associated with groups that have suffered from pervasive social and political oppression (which would reinforce the regulation that produced the identities in the first place), anti-discrimination law should only protect individuals from discrimination based on ascribed group membership or status. I conclude that "cultural difference" conflicts, which concern traits or conduct, are distinct from social struggles concerning racial and other ascribed statuses.

In chapter 3 I build on this conclusion and argue that political solidarity based on a common relationship to oppression and domination is the appropriate focus of (racial) identity politics and legal rights assertion; by contrast cultural claims are more contestable on both descriptive and normative terms and should be left to more fluid domains of conflict resolution such as social dialogue, the democratic process and the market economy. If, as a provisional matter, we sever group identity politics from questions of cultural pluralism, it becomes possible to evaluate both sets of questions differently. For instance, untethered from a civil rights–oriented identity politics, it is not obvious that our thoughts about cultural pluralism should be organized according to the familiar opposition between recognition of difference and assimilation. If we drop or suspend this dichotomy, another ideological conflict implicated in questions of cultural pluralism becomes easy to see: cosmopolitanism versus provincialism. This conflict reveals stakes that were hidden from view by the recognition/assimilation dyad and allows for the possibility of new political alliances and re-evaluated commitments.

Chapter 4 addresses the limits of civil rights law with respect to cultural pluralism and group identity and suggests a direction for reform of anti-discrimination law consistent with my arguments above. The appropriate goals underlying anti-discrimination law are to counter the social and economic isolation of historically subordinated groups, which is produced by the ascription of stigmatized status. Rights-to-group cultural difference are of questionable legitimacy at best when evaluated in this pragmatic, consequentialist manner. The chapter ends by suggesting approaches to cultural difference and the expression of individual identity that would avoid the pitfalls of difference discourse.

1. Difference Discourse

Plaintiff is a black woman who seeks $ 10,000 damages, injunctive, and declaratory relief against enforcement of a grooming policy of the defendant American Airlines that prohibits employees in certain employment categories from wearing an all-braided hairstyle. . . . She alleges that the policy violates her rights under the Thirteenth Amendment of the United States Constitution, under Title VII of the Civil Rights Act . . . in that it discriminates against her as a woman, and more specifically as a black woman . . . plaintiff assert[s] that the "corn row" style has a special significance for black women. She contends that it "has been, historically, a fashion and style adopted by Black American women, reflective of cultural, historical essence of the Black women in American society." The style was "popularized" so to speak, within the larger society, when Cicely Tyson adopted the same for an appearance on nationally viewed Academy Awards presentation several years ago. . . . It was and is analogous to the public statement by the late Malcolm X regarding the Afro hair style. . . . At the bottom line, the completely braided hair style, sometimes referred to as corn rows, has been and continues to be part of the cultural and historical essence of Black American women.[1]

This has long been an easy case for the antiracist left. A large, impersonal, uptight, mainstream, and possibly racist corporation versus a proletarian underdog whose deeply personal mode of self-expression is also the literal embodiment of the soul of a subject people. Milquetoast versus multiculturalism; bureaucracy versus braids: we know what side we're on.

But isn't the argument as the plaintiff Rene Rogers advanced it at least disquieting? Corn rows are "the cultural and historical essence of Black American women"? The theory of racial discrimination and civil rights underlying Rogers's claim raises tough questions for anti-discrimination law. Leaving aside the volumes of critique of racial essentialism as a conceptual matter, I would maintain that the claim of historicism is questionable as a matter of fact: Rogers's own pleadings assert that the style was popularized *in the 1970s* by Hollywood actress Cicely Tyson. Raising the historical point may seem like nit picking, but it does problematize the link between race and the hairstyle: if the style was popularized by a Hollywood actress, how different is it from the coif Farrah Fawcett made famous at roughly the same time?

Very different if we believe that Tyson's and Rogers's braids, unlike Farrah's feathered tresses, made a political statement of racial pride: Rogers's briefs evoke Malcolm X in support of the political importance of the cornrow hairstyle for blacks. But should anti-discrimination law protect politically controversial, if racially salient, behavior advanced through the vehicle of physical grooming? Suppose some black women employed by American Airlines wished to wear cornrows and advance the political message they ostensibly embody, while others thought cornrows damaged the interests of black women in particular and reflected badly on the race as a whole (given the cultural politics of black America in the mid-to late 1970s, there almost certainly were such black women employed by American Airlines and even more certainly there were such black women among its customers). Suppose further that the management of American Airlines, either formally or informally, sought out and considered the opinions of its employees as well as of its customers and made its grooming policies based at least in part on such information. Now Rogers's claim is no longer plausibly described as a claim on behalf of black women. Instead it is a claim on behalf of some black women over the possible objections of other black women.

Rogers and her supporters might object: "What business is it of other black women whether *we* wear braids—no one will be forced to wear them." But this individualistic account of the stakes of the case flatly contradicts the proffered rationale for conceiving of the hairstyle as a legal right: cornrows are the "cultural essence," not of one black woman but of black *women*. If this claim is to be taken seriously then cornrows cannot be the cultural essence of only those black women who choose to wear them—they must be the cultural essence of *all* black women. And in this case *all* black women have a stake in the rights claim and the message about them that it will necessarily send—not only those who support the political and cultural statement conveyed by cornrows, but also by those who oppose that statement.

We'd need a fairly detailed account of the cultural and political stakes of cornrows to have a real sense of the political dimensions of this legal conflict. Does the wearing of cornrows track social class (are most cornrow wearers working class "authentics" or bourgeois trendies?) or ideological splits (nationalist v. integtrationist?) within the black community? Do cornrows reflect a sophisticated racial politics in which the essentialist message is subordinate, ambiguous or even ironic or is a crude essentialism a central or indispensable part of the politics of cornrows? Is the symbolism of cornrows widely shared and well understood at least within some subset of American society or is it ambiguous?

It bears noting that we'd also need a definition of "cornrows" or a list of protected hairstyles in order evaluate the implications of Rogers's claim. There are a lot of different all-braided hairstyles: the true "cornrow" style, so named because of the wide parts between each braid, the "style, distinguished only by the presence of tiny braids in lieu of single strands of hair"[2] that law professor Paulette Caldwell defends in her article focusing on the *Rogers* case, the style in which each braid corkscrews in a difference direction, popularized by rap artists such as Busta Rhymes and the dreadlock style (technically not braided, but I suspect most people would include it in a right-to-cornrows) first associated with Jamaican Rastafarians. One might think some but not all of these styles are appropriate for certain workplaces: the style Caldwell describes for instance, is clearly the most conservative while the dreadlock style (especially if divorced from its religious origins) or the Busta Rhymes style might be more analogous to a punk rocker's Mohawk or "liberty spikes."

What's clear is that the assertion that cornrows are the cultural essence of black women cannot be taken as conclusive evidence that a "right-to-cornrows" is an unadulterated good thing for black women. Even if we take it on faith that cornrows represent black nationalist pride as against the integrationist and assimilationist coiffure of chemically straightened hair, it's clear that a right to cornrows would be an intervention in a long-standing debate *among* African-Americans about empowerment strategies and norms of identity and identification. More generally, it is by no means clear that an argument that presumes that blacks or black women have a cultural *essence as blacks* or *as black women* is a vehicle of racial empowerment. A right to group difference may be experienced as meddlesome at best and oppressive at worst even by some members of the groups that the rights regime ostensibly benefits. For the black woman who dislikes cornrows and wishes that no one—most of all black women—would wear them, the right not only hinders her and deprives her of allies, but it also adds insult to injury by proclaiming that cornrows are *her* cultural essence as a black woman.

There are also implications for people who aren't members of the "protected" group, but who want access to the cultural styles or artifacts that the rights regime would link to a particular group. In shorthand, the *Rogers* case implicates that increasingly common fixture of American college campuses and urban centers: the dreadlocked blonde. Most obviously, Rogers's theory of the case implied that a black woman who wished to adopt Cicely Tyson's hairstyle would have a right to do so, while a white woman who wished to emulate Bo Derek's hairstyle (or Cicely Tyson's hairstyle or Bob Marley's hair-style) would not. One might conclude that the Bo Dereks of the world would be no *worse* off after a Rogers's victory—they would have the same limited op-portunity to wear braids as before. But this is not *quite* so. If an all-braided style is the cultural essence of black women *by law*, mightn't this imply that Ms. Derek and her emulators are black-coiffed (if not black-faced) minstrels or "white Negro" wanna-bes? It's likely that a right premised on the immutable link between blacks and braids will discourage white and Asian women from wearing braids by sending the message that the hairstyle "belongs" to another social group. Although a right to cornrows might seem only to enhance the freedom of potential cornrow wearers, it is arguably better understood as a policy of segregation through which a set of grooming styles are reserved for a particular group.

We might expand the "dreadlocked blonde" category to include anyone who believes that society is enriched by cultural cross-pollination. Rogers's favored rights outcome would have two likely consequences. It would almost certainly increase the number of black women wearing cornrows, both because em-ployers would no longer be able to forbid them for black women and because the judicial embrace of Rogers's theory of the case would encourage black women to identify cornrows as their cultural essence and thereby popularize the style. It would also likely reduce the number of non-black women wearing the style as those women would also internalize the legally disseminated mes-sage that the hairstyle was the cultural property of black women and conclude that their adoption of the style would be inauthentic or even a type of cultural trespass. The result would be an increased racial divergence in women's grooming. The stereotypical assimilationist would of course find this result distressing, but so should the type of multiculturalist who believes that groups of differing racial, social and cultural backgrounds should freely mix and freely exchange ideas and aesthetic conventions.

Even for the black women who affiliate with the cornrow hairstyle, legal enforcement comes with hidden costs. The legal discourse underlying such a right-to-difference can easily take on a life of its own and have unintended side effects. In large part this is because the claim that braids are uniquely impor-tant to black women conceals a host of distinct and often contradictory descrip-tive claims and normative rationales. Even in the years that I have spent developing this critique, I have heard a number of distinct arguments for why Rene Rogers should have prevailed. Some people have insisted that cornrows are of particular importance to black women because they are a part of African heritage dating back long before the European encounter. But are we then to limit this right to those who can trace their ancestry to the regions of the continent where braids were worn and limit the protected styles to those worn by the defendants' ancestors (if this seems a fanciful suggestion, notice that courts employ precisely this type of analysis in cases dealing with Native-American cultural claims[3])? Others have argued that braids are one of a few hairstyles that allow many black women to obtain the long, flowing hairstyles favored for women in contemporary society without chemical straightening. On this rationale, should the right to braids be limited to those black women for whom this is true? (Black women with fine-textured hair who wish to wear braids in order to signal racial affiliation would lack standing under this interpretation of the claim?) Doesn't this rationale raise the disquieting implication that black women should be free of ostensibly Eurocentric grooming norms only to conform better to patriarchal ones? In fact, isn't the desire for long, flowing hairstyles actually a symptom of the Eurocentric grooming norms that right is supposed to resist? And doesn't this rationale undercut the "heritage" rationale by locating the impetus for braids in the aesthetic sensibilities of contemporary *Western* culture rather than in ancient African tradition?

Most disquieting is the possibility that the cultural rationale could set precedent that might apply in other cases. If braids are the immutable cultural essence of black women, what else is? There are a great many possible answers to this question—some disturbing—that many people will find as intuitively plausible Rogers's assertion regarding braids. Consider another case in which an employer's policy implicates a theory of racial difference:

> TPG [The Parker Group] is a telephone marketing corporation, often hired to perform work for political candidates. The conduct at issue in this case involves TPG's work making "get-out-the-vote" calls for various political candidates. . . . Approximately 10% of such calling is race-matched, such that black voters are called by black TPG employees who use the "black" script, while white voters are called by white TPG employees who use a different "white" script. . . . TPG employees doing the race matched calling in 1994 were assigned separate calling areas and separate scripts according to race. . . . TPG also physically segregated employees who worked at race matched calling. Black callers were segregated into one room and white callers segregated into another.[4]

Is TPG's policy, as the court held, racially discriminatory because it is "based on a racial stereotype that blacks would respond to blacks and that . . . race was directly related to . . . ability to do the job"? Or is the policy the natural outgrowth of the recognition of cultural differences between the races and therefore justifiable, perhaps even laudable? If Rogers's cultural essence as a black woman gives her an intrinsic relationship to a hairstyle, mightn't even a good faith employer conclude that her cultural essence would also enable her to better persuade other blacks and disable her from connecting with whites?

I hope it's clear up front is that these objections do not necessarily go to the substantive outcome of the dispute, but instead pertain to the rationale employed in an effort to reach a given outcome. My sympathies lie with Rene Rogers; I think she should have been allowed to wear her braids. If I were in charge of the grooming policy I would have rewritten it to exclude the prohibition against braids. If I were a member of Congress I would consider legislation to prohibit employers from adopting rigid grooming policies generally as a matter of federal labor law (although such a legal rule presents a complicated case, as I will argue below.) It is also possible that the regulation as applied to Rogers was a part of a pattern of harassment and should have been construed as actionable racial harassment or as constructive termination. But I think that the argument that Rogers and her attorneys actually made was a bad one and that the court was right to reject it. Similarly, there are countless arguments made with good motivations toward ends I generally support that I will critique in this book.

. . . . .

The logic and assumptions underlying both Rogers's claim and TPG's policy are strikingly similar: both assume that an ascriptive social identity—in these cases race—corresponds to a vague but intrinsic characteristic: culture. Both insist that this correspondence should have consequences for the organization of the workplace. Both Rogers's rights claim and TPG's policy are determined by a thick account of the sociocultural entailments of group identity, an account that is central to what I have called "difference discourse."

Below I'll sketch a portrait of what I will call "difference discourse." I'll use some fairly broad strokes to begin this portrait, filling in the details later in the book.

One broad stroke is the idea of a discourse. My ambition is to describe a set of beliefs, conversations and practices that the reader will recognize as interconnected, mutually reinforcing and socially pervasive. Difference discourse describes social identities such as race as a manifestation of underlying differences—a racial culture—while at the same time generating those very differences: for instance, Rogers's claim describes cornrows as the essence of black womanhood and in so doing encourages black women to wear cornrows while making them off-limits or at least peculiar for non-blacks.

Discourse analysis is inevitably unfair to its objects. It does not, and does not attempt to, do justice to the wealth of subjective sentiment behind a statement or motivations driving an act; it gives short shrift to "authorial intent"; it is indifferent to biography; it is unsentimental, impersonal, cold. The analysis of a social discourse treats individuals, not as autonomous agents, but as agents of a field of social power; human action is symptomatic of ways of thinking and doing, of constellations of habits, of institutional tendencies. So in my discussion of *Rogers* my goal is not to criticize Rene Rogers; instead it is to offer up the social clash in which she participated, the case caption that bears her name, as an object of analysis, as an example of a larger trend to which it contributes and from which it was produced.

Although many of my examples will concern racial identity, difference discourse is not limited to racial identity. Strikingly similar claims, undergirded by parallel conceptions of identity, have been made in the context of gender, ethnicity, national origin and sexual orientation/preference. We are also witnessing the birth of a host of less familiar "identities" with their own difference claims such as the obese and in my hometown San Francisco, dog owners and bicyclists. My approach in this regard is not to advance an elaborate justification for the suggestion that these claims are genetically related, but rather to describe the proposals and arguments and let the reader judge their family resemblance.

A (Abridged) History of Difference

> But at the same time that the universalist ideologues were preaching the merits of Westernization or "assimilation," they were also (or others were also) preaching the eternal existence and virtue of difference. Thus a universalist message of cultural multiplicity could serve as a justification of educating various groups in their separate "cultures" and hence preparing them for different tasks in the single economy. The extreme version of this . . . is apartheid. But lesser versions . . . have been widespread. . . . Furthermore, we can enlist the dominated groups in their own oppression. Insofar as they cultivate their separateness as "cultural" groups[,] . . . they socialize their members into cultural expressions which distinguish them . . . [and valorize] some at least of the values attributed to them by racist and sexist theories. And they do this, in a seeming paradox, on the grounds of the universal principle of the equal validity of all cultural expressions.[5]

Academic literature, legal advocacy and social activism have increasingly focused on a specific approach to racial justice: the assertion of racial *difference*. It is a fantasy of many multiculturalists that the American mainstream is hell-bent on destroying cultural difference, that the new face of racial hegemony speaks the false gospel of assimilation. Consider the following excerpt from an article by law professor Dorothy Roberts:

> In the past whites in the United States used the law brutally to suppress other peoples' cultures. . . . Most of the time, however, the law promotes the dominant culture in much more subtle ways. . . . [W]hites, as a result of their dominant political position, have been able to incorporate their own cultural perspective into legal principles; they have labeled these legal principles as universal despite their one-sided pedigree; then judges claim to be impartial when they impose these principles without regard to . . . people from minority cultures.[6]

Alex Johnson's discussion of the role of the card games Bid Whist and Tonk in African-American culture provides another articulate expression of this view:

> Bid Whist and Tonk, like many other African-American institutions, are maintained because they are ours: they provide us with a *safe harbor* for the preservation of the idiopathic rules, customs, and norms that developed in our community while we were kept separate from whites by law. This safe harbor also allows those who choose not to fully embrace the norms of white society to retain a place in an African-American *community in which confrontation between African-American norms and conflicting white norms never takes place.* Moreover, this safe harbor protects African-American culture, because when the assimilationist version of integration occurs *African-American culture is typically not merged into majoritarian culture but obliterated by it*—leaving no trace of what was once a unique cultural vehicle.[7] (Emphasis is mine.)

In these accounts, certain social practices belong to minority groups and provide safety from a hostile majority with inconsistent practices that threaten to obliterate the practices of the minority group. In fact, more than inconsistent *practices* are at stake according to the account: here a "culture" includes not only practices but distinctive norms, ideologies, cognitive maps, and epistemologies (at one point, Johnson describes the African-American culture as a distinct "nomos" following the work of legal theorist Robert Cover).[8]

The conflict between the norms of minorities and the inconsistent norms of mainstream or white society is assumed to lead, almost inevitably, to the obliteration of the minority group's norms and culture. For instance, Roberts insists that "The assimilationist ideal . . . has only operated in one way. . . . While whites have demanded that nonwhites assimilate to an Anglo-American way of life, the possibility that whites should assimilate to nonwhite cultures seems downright un American"[9] and Johnson argues that "a white cultural perspective or norm . . . has the effect of stifling or *eradicating the consciousness* of African-American[s]"[10]

Here assimilation is comprehensive and inescapable, an imperative and a legal injunction that gives no quarter and brooks no compromise. This reading is both devastating and perversely attractive: The enemy is monolithic and implacable, the multiculturalists can fancy themselves a heroic *resistance*, keeping the flame of liberty alive against all odds as they wait for the reinforcements from the Allies (or the courts).

These claims are impossible to evaluate in the absence of a definition of minority and white culture respectively, a thorough examination of assimilationist policies and a study of at least some instances in which cultural conflict has occurred. Yet the claims are so familiar and so accepted that otherwise thoughtful scholars simply advance them without support. Below I will argue that this narrative is flawed as both a descriptive and a normative matter. For now, however, it is sufficient to dislodge it from its position as a background presumption and to identify it as a subject of legitimate debate.

The difference approach is not the only approach, and, as I will argue, it is not the best approach, to racial justice. The focus on difference diverts attention from racism—a social institution based on a formal status hierarchy and a set of ideologies that justify that status hierarchy—and instead misleadingly suggests that racial injustice is primarily the result of objective and intrinsic difference among natural racial groups. "Difference" invites imprecise analogy: if the problem of the color line is the failure to appreciate and accommodate difference, then any unpopular out-of-the-ordinary social group can claim to be victims of similar prejudice. The resulting set of absolutist rights claims are a bad way of dealing with the conflicts that arise because of real cultural and social difference—conflicts that involve objective social costs, which must be allocated pragmatically. Worst of all, by insisting that socially imposed statuses are defined by real differences in cultural characteristics, the difference focus encourages members of minority groups to define themselves in terms of group stereotypes.

How did we get here? How did the idea that racism is primarily a consequence of cultural difference, and the corollary notion that any and all conflicts arising from cultural difference are analogous to racism, get started? I will suggest that law—particularly civil rights law and the political struggle surrounding its passage and implementation—played a critical role in the development of this approach.

Historian Harold Cruse asserts: "American Negro history is basically a history of the conflict between integrationist and nationalist forces."[11] The "difference approach" to racial justice was a reaction to a mainstream civil rights discourse, which, over time, came to be preoccupied with racial integration, formal colorblindness and assimilation. Over time the American mainstream has come to consider integration and assimilation to be effective strategies for racial justice, considered in terms of economic and political empowerment, as well as laudable ends in and of themselves. As law professor Gary Peller notes, "[t]he embrace of integrationism as the dominant ethos of race discourse is the symbolic face of the new cultural center. . . . Relative to this center, black "militants" and white "rednecks" were defined together as extremists."[12] The utopian aspiration of racial integration and assimilation was captured in the figure of the colorblind society, a society in which race has no normative significance, in which it is scarcely noticeable at all. Indeed, some imagine that racial difference will literally be eliminated through intermarriage and miscegenation: Ward Connerly, former regent of the University of California and key sponsor of the ballot initiative that eliminated affirmative action in California believes that "[a]s our population blends and the lines of race become blurred, eventually the racial categories that many consider 'fixed' will collapse of their own weight."[13] Similarly, the painter Ed Ruscha opined, "I think everybody is gradually mixing here. . . . A hundred years from now there will be some gorgeous mono-ethnic race living here."[14]

It is important to emphasize that colorblindness was not simply an ideal that a white mainstream forced on people of color; instead it was one pole of a long running tension within black liberationist thought. Some of the most passionate advocates of colorblindness, strong racial integration and even assimilation were people of color who truly believed in the moral justice and pragmatic necessity of these goals. In the 1960s and early 1970 colorblindness was a truly radical idea. Programmatic racial desegregation of schools had only recently begun in earnest. Many workplaces and public accommodations had formally excluded people of color a few years earlier. Mixed-race marriages were not legally recognized in some states until 1967: the Supreme Court decision in *Loving v. Virginia* changed the blackletter law but not black-baiting public attitudes. In this context integration and even assimilation—born of a universalist humanism—were the ideas of a courageous avant garde. Historian Clayborne Carson chronicles the emergence of this radical integrationism in the context of the Student Nonviolent Coordinating Committee's (SNCC) organizing efforts in the deep American south during the 1960s:

> [SNCC project director Charles Sherrod] concluded that [it] . . . was necessary to "strike at the very root of segregation. . . . [T]he idea that white is superior. That idea has eaten into the minds of the people, black and

white. We have to break this image. We can only do this if they see white and black working together, side by side, the white man no more and no less than his black brother, but human beings together."[15]

Opposition to integration in the name of tradition and racial difference, while a competing position of the "nationalist" left, was also and most notably the position of the racist right. Indeed, black separatism had its roots in earlier positions that sought to improve black welfare while accommodating white racism. The almost perennial "back to Africa" movements such as Martin Delany's plan in the antebellum period to colonize part of West Africa for the settlement of American blacks and most famously Marcus Garvey's Universal Negro Improvement Association and plans for the "repatriation" of American blacks, arguably had for their prototype the American Colonization Society (ACS). Founded by whites and animated by an explicitly white supremacist ideology in the early nineteenth century for the purpose of resettling free blacks in Africa, the ACS achieved the only successful back-to-Africa movement culminating in the establishment in 1847 of the African nation of Liberia. Garvey's nationalist back-to-Africa movement in the 1920s had the open support of the Ku Klux Klan and other white racists who hoped "it was likely to attract Negroes who might otherwise be resentful of their subordinate caste position in the United States."[16] Booker T. Washington's self-help ideology was likewise met with favor by white supremacists who preferred racial separatism and self-help to demands for civil rights and access to mainstream institutions.

On the other hand, contemporary popular consciousness notwithstanding, the "integrationist" Martin Luther King's vision of racial equality was as radical in its critique of existing social norms and institutions and in its prescriptions as Malcolm X's nationalism. Radical integrationism's ecumenical vision of a society where black and white would join in a humanist kinship did not entail formal colorblindness, but instead a transcendence of social status through a sober and arduous reworking of the social practices that underwrite bigotry and subordination. Those inspired by this vision would not be satisfied with today's status quo of formal equality under the law leavened with de facto racial stratification and tokenism within mainstream institutions. Radical integrationism—the true legacy of Martin Luther King Jr., as his growing focus on issues of economic equity in his later years demonstrates—entailed a fundamental critique of political, social and economic institutions.

Integration (especially colorblindness and assimilation) became the ideals of the mainstream in the late 1960s and 1970s. To a real extent this must be considered a decisive victory for the radicals. But the rhetoric of integration was also deployed for more conservative ends: colorblindness was used against affirmative action, integration was used to undermine any form of racial solidarity, the norm of assimilation became a bludgeon to crush any practice that made the milquetoast mainstream uncomfortable. This story is familiar. But this was not the inevitable result of an integrationist ideology; instead it is the story of the domestication of a potentially radical integrationism.

The tug of war between integration and separatism (and between colorblindness and race consciousness; assimilation and recognition of difference) reflected real substantive disagreements and a pervasive ambivalence about the terms (both conditions and language) of racial justice even among those unequivocally committed to it. Despite the incorporation of integrationism into mainstream civil rights, nationalism and separatism survived as a "loyal opposition" to integrationist civil rights. Some people accepted integration only as a means to an end—"green follows white"—while others embraced it as a goal. Some thought integration should naturally lead to assimilation and a colorblind utopia, others thought it would lead to W.E.B. Du Bois's ideal of separate nations living together.[17] These conflicts became more pronounced when the initial battles for formal equality were won (and the victories proved inadequate): the question "What now?" was as much a philosophical question as a strategic one.

The civil rights movement never resolved the conflict *within the black community* between integration and separatism. Nor could it have. The tug of war arguably reflects not only conflict between committed ideological combatants, but ambivalence as well. Rather than distinctive and coherent options between which one could choose, integrationism (colorblindness and assimilation) and separatism (race consciousness and cultural nationalism) are symbolic and rhetorical oppositions, which one must constantly negotiate and juggle. Even the most extreme forms of separatism contained elements of integration and assimilation: back-to-Africa movements actively courted white support and were self-consciously "colonialist," envisioning American blacks' occupying a position in Africa analogous to that of Europeans in the new world (a position that they, tragically, in fact occupied in Liberia where, in 1930 a League of Nations report accused the Liberian government of sanctioning "forced labor . . . hardly distinguishable from slavery."[18]) Self-reliance movements always envisioned trade with white society and therefore focused on the development of skills and production of goods that would be marketable to whites: in this sense black communities were envisioned as adjunctive to white society.

Conversely, integration assumes racial distinctiveness—or else there would be no reason to care about integration and indeed no meaningful races to integrate. Integration requires intense race consciousness: we need the collection and tabulation of racial data to know whether or not integrationist policies have succeeded. In its accommodationist mode, integration promises to present racial difference in a mild and palatable form for the edification of whites. In its more confrontational form, integrationist movements have long promoted racial solidarity for political purposes and have embraced a pragmatic understanding that colorblindness is a long-term goal of a political struggle that today, takes place in a racially charged, if not polarized, society.

So, contra Harold Cruse, the history of antiracist thought has been, not the history of conflict between integrationist and nationalist *forces*, but rather the history of a wide array of agendas, policy proposals, benevolent enterprises, self-sacrificing struggles and opportunistic schemes, fought out in terms of a finite array of rhetorical resources. The true "stakes" of the conflicts may vary widely, depending on historical, economic, social and institutional context, but the language used to describe them has been remarkably constant: when racial merger is desired, it is "integration"; when resisted, it is "assimilation." Difference is a celebrated as "pride," "authenticity" and "culture" when "assimilation" is under attack; it is condemned as "segregation" and "stereotype" when "integration" is the goal.

All these positions cohabitate in the current rhetoric of "difference." Take higher education as an example: merger is advanced as integration in the university admissions process even as it is resisted as assimilation in the context of ethnically identified fraternities, sororities, clubs and theme houses; difference is celebrated as authentic culture and group pride in the admissions and racial fraternity/club/ethnic theme house contexts, but condemned as stereotyping and segregation almost anywhere else.

To be clear, the charge is ambivalence, not hypocrisy. And in a sense, this ambivalence is an inevitable feature of the terms of racial conflict. Racism's characteristic catch-22 insists on racial difference and then punishes it as deviance. Integration/assimilation is a reaction against the insistence on racial difference, but in its more uncompromising manifestations it underwrites the punishment of any group solidarity as a form of deviance. Difference discourse does precisely the opposite: in reacting against the punishment of difference, it reinforces the insistence that racial differences are intrinsic and real. Ambivalence is perhaps the only intelligent response to this catch-22.

Although the "politics of difference," which has more recently emerged as the dominant discourse of progressive antiracists, was a necessary corrective to the earlier dominance of integrationist colorblindness, it was also a partial victory of one approach or set of approaches to antiracism over another. For those who wished to save the ideals of radical integrationism from their neoconservative hijackers, the rise of the politics of difference is a hard blow.

For example, the historian John Hope Franklin, author of what is still today the definitive history of African-Americans, *From Slavery to Freedom: A History of African-Americans*, insists that "I don't believe you can have a peaceful, multiracial society when people are parceled or separated out, ghettoized, Balkanized or however you want to say it." In an interview with the *New York Times*, Franklin was

> appalled by the degree to which some whites and blacks, frustrated with integration, talk of resurrecting and finally delivering on the South's old empty promise of separate but equal education. "Let's say you've got pristine schools, racially divided, white schools, black schools," he [Franklin] says. "Say they've both got everything and then they graduate. Where do they go now? Where are the whites going to learn about blacks? Where are the blacks going to learn about whites? You're just postponing the conflict until they get grown, and it's much harder to learn anything then." In that vein, he criticizes the media's infatuation with what he sees as the false promise of Louis Farrakhan's black nationalism.[19]

The difference agenda seems to some like a natural extension of civil rights, but resistance to it may reflect not retrenchment but honest disagreement about what racial justice entails and legitimate concern that the difference agenda will lead to a dead end or an ambush.

The Production of Group Difference as Common Knowledge

The politics of difference can be understood as a reaction to the hegemony of integrationism and assimilation, and to their cynical redeployment as limits on racial justice. But what if the politics of difference threatens to become another hegemony, no less totalizing, no less obsessive, no less myopic than the assimilationist ideal that preceded it? Although Rogers lost in court, the theory of racial identity and cultural membership entailed by her Title VII claim is widely accepted, not only among left/liberals and communities of color, but by mainstream American society. The idea that our familiar group identities are defined by *objective characteristics* that are shared by members of the group—a racial culture, for example—is so widespread and accepted that it is taken for granted. Group difference is a matter of common knowledge.

The "Repressive Hypothesis"

It's a familiar story. Ever since the limited but decisive victory of the American civil rights movement, racism—daunted, but not defeated—has sought a new front from which to attack. Meanwhile, the same principles that successfully made the bigots of the 1950s eat Jim Crow have been deployed against analogous prejudices—sexism, homophobia, ageism, the dominance of the able bodied over the differently abled, the tyranny of the thin over the portly. And so too, these bigotries have retreated only to regroup and fight another day, on another battlefield, with new and as yet undiscovered weapons of mass discrimination.

We have it on good authority that one of the most potent of these new weapons is a covert form of discrimination that functions by misdirection. Bigotry will target not natural groups but their distinctive practices. The law will not countenance discrimination against blacks, but we can stigmatize Ebonics; one wouldn't dare discriminate against women, but we can repress feminine styles of social interaction. The result is a new bigotry—not of types of people but of ways of being. To be clear, the goal of the new bigotry is subtly different than that of the old bigotry. The goal is not to exclude the previously stigmatized people through the use of proxies; the idea is not, for instance, to screen out blacks by punishing their speech patterns. Instead, the goal is to transform the previously stigmatized groups, to remake them in the image of the *übermench*. The ultimate goal is arguably more vicious, more comprehensive, than simple exclusion. It is a bloodless extermination—a cultural genocide.

This story is familiar, not only because it has been told so often, but also because it a type of story that has an archetype. The story of the new bigotry is a story of repression; it is a reiteration of what Michel Foucault in the *History of Sexuality, Vol. 1,* called a "repressive hypothesis." The repressive hypothesis that Foucault attacked began with the Victorians and involves dark powers of sexuality, while ours begins with the American bourgeoisie and involves the sexy cultures of the dark skinned. But the parallels are striking.

Foucault argued against the familiar story in which the institutions of bourgeois society from the Victorian era to the present have operated to repress the natural and authentic sexuality of individuals (the "repressive hypothesis"). Instead, Foucault argued, the Victorians were (as we, their legatees, are still today) obsessed with sexuality: they saw it everywhere, they constantly discussed it, insisted on its relevance and deployed it as a description of many forms of human behavior. They *produced* sexuality by defining human behavior in terms of sexuality, defining individuals as sexed in various ways and cataloguing and constructing sexual typologies. Far from repression, this *production* of sexuality is, according to Foucault, what defines the modern attitude toward sex. The production, (rather than or at least in addition to the repression) of sexuality was a means of control. It was (and is) a technology that defined the self according to its sexuality, and thereby kept individuals under a type of sexual surveillance. Further, if anything repressed authentic eroticism (a term whose ontological status is, for Foucault, questionable at best), it was the incessant production of sexuality that limited the possibilities of erotic expression by imposing upon individual eroticism a narrow universe of sexual types.

Finally, *the idea that sexuality is repressed* demands interrogation in its own right.

> The question I would like to pose is not, Why are we repressed? but rather, Why do we say, with so much passion and so much resentment against our most recent past, against our present, and against ourselves, that we are repressed? . . . What led us to show, ostentatiously, that sex is something we hide . . . and . . . do all this by formulating the matter in the most explicit terms, by trying to reveal it in its most naked reality . . . ? [W]e must also ask why we burden ourselves today with so much guilt for having made sex a sin. . . . How to account for the displacement which, while claiming to free us from the sinful nature of sex, taxes us with a great historical wrong which consists precisely in imagining that nature to be blameworthy?[20]

Now let's turn to culture. The implicit presumption underlying the "repressive hypothesis" that I described a few pages ago is that group cultural differences are natural and authentic and that failure to respect these differences is a form of tyranny. Here, as in Foucault's "repressive hypothesis" power is exercised through censorship and repression; justice entails nothing more than the absence of repression; a willingness to let human nature take its course and embrace the mysterious and beautiful forces that already surround and comprise us.

But suppose, with respect to this repressive hypothesis, that something like what Foucault argued for in the context of sexuality is also true of group cultural difference. Suppose our era is defined, not (or at least not only) by the *repression* of group difference, but by its *production*? Suppose further that the repressive hypothesis is one of the mechanisms by which this production of group difference is achieved.

There is evidence to support the proposition. We live in a society in which human beings are sorted (and sort themselves) with remarkable comprehensiveness, precision and efficiency into a number of almost canonical social groups. You know what they are (and more importantly, you know who *you* are.) Think about the neighborhood magazine kiosk, where the grandfather of identity niche marketing *Ebony* magazine competes for space with *Essence* (for black women) *Latina, Yolk* (Asian-Americans, get it?) and *Out* (gay and lesbian) magazines. Consider cable television, where Black Entertainment Television shares the dial with a growing number of identity-oriented lineups, featuring ethnically targeted advertising and ethnic variations on that stale staple of prime time: the family sit-com (as if barbecue sauce, salsa or kimchi could make that week old Wonder bread go down easier) and where bold programming entails a gay character who never has a romantic partner or liason but consistently exhibits stereotypically "gay" mannerisms. Notice the student organizations in colleges (and many high schools), an "alphabet soup" of race, ethnicity and sexual orientation (in law school we have Black Law Students Association (BLSA), joined by South American and Latino Students Organization (SALSA), Asian and Pacific Students Organization (APALSA), and winning the award for both cleverness and for bucking the trend of initials, OUTLAW ("out" gay and lesbian law students)). And consider the new, check-every-box-that-applies U.S. Census, where racial data simultaneously acquires the aura of objective science and the patina of subjective self-affirmation. If there is a plot to repress group differences, it has numerous and powerful enemies in the media, industry, politics and higher education.

This is more than the recognition of group identification born as a collective response to social prejudice. It is the production of identity as a lifestyle, a way of being. In the popular anthropology of group difference there are types of food, music, hairstyles, sports, clothing, television and radio programming, magazines, and intoxicating liquors (or lack of them) appropriate to the various canonical identity groups. These group specific lifestyles offer an easy solidarity, a V.I.P. pass to belonging. For socially isolated individuals, social identities offer companionship, distinction, a sense of purpose, a link to history. Like an arranged marriage, the prefab camaraderie is seductive because it demands acquiescence rather than deliberation and decision. Social identity promises to be the backdrop of all other social relationships, something you can rely on and take for granted because it is the precondition of entry into the social, the sine qua non.

The necessary correlative to this unearned solidarity is an unwarranted presumption about the entailments of group membership. There is a peculiar variant of political correctness: it regulates not what can be said about a minority group by outsiders, but instead the behavior of group members. This political correctness requires and duly produces opprobrium for people who miss their cue: we encounter "Oreos"—blacks on the outside who don't "act black" and therefore presumably aren't black "on the inside"—and, quickly enough, other racial groups acquire similar figures (for some odd reason all refer to food): Asian "bananas", Latino "coconuts," Native-American "apples." These figures of scorn imply that there is a particular type of behavior that is appropriate to a given race, and thereby censure deviation from it. Thus we hear from Henry Louis Gates Jr. that black college students who frequent the library are chastised by other black students with the epithet: "incognegro." Meanwhile their white classmates offer the unwelcome compliment: "I don't even think of you as a black person." Or notice that the complexities of sexuality and gender identification demand an ever-expanding list of homosexual types: butch, femme, queen, dyke, lipstick lesbian. Conformity to these recognizable types is a prerequisite to acceptance in many social circles. These relatively trivial epithets reflect a quite pervasive and potent social discourse, an orthodoxy as powerful and coercive, if not as comprehensive or pervasive, as the social mores of Victorian England.

The fact of intrinsic racial difference is cited (as a story one already knows) in countless and diverse forms: the racist humor of the blackface minstrel, Steppinfetchit, Amos n' Andy, Uncle Remus, Uncle Tom, Sanford and Son, Chico and the Man; but also, in the Moynihan Report on the pathology of black urban culture, the literature detailing the elements of a distinctive "black learning style" and the popular pseudo-science of the metaphysical properties of melanin. In contemporary popular culture, racial difference is the dominant figure in a host of "odd couple/buddy" films (the prototype is the now classic *Silver Streak* starring Richard Pryor and Gene Wilder, perhaps the most popular are *48 Hours* and *Beverly Hills Cop*, both starring Eddie Murphy) in which two protagonists of difference races are forced together by circumstances and overcome treacherous and comic obstacles (at least one of which must involve racial passing or racial displacement—a white guy in the ghetto or a black guy in a redneck bar) and ultimately, *despite their severe cultural differences*, manage to see that people are people after all.

These racial "buddy films" illustrate the Janus-faced nature of contemporary racial ideology. They advance a colorblind ideology while simultaneously reinforcing the idea of distinctive and unassimilable, if not opaque, racial cultures. Issues of racial subordination are generally absent from these films (*Silver Streak* is a notable exception)—racism is reduced to one or two "incidents" that are relatively easily and comically overcome—while cultural difference is portrayed as natural and inevitable: the natural place for Eddie Murphy's character in *Beverly Hills Cop* is Detroit, not Beverly Hills, and after gaining the respect and admiration of the Beverly Hills police force despite his distinctive racial culture, he goes back where he belongs. So the ideal minority is one who retains his distinctive culture, functions effectively in the mainstream despite it, and, because of his culture, both knows his place and wants to stay there.

This orthodoxy sends a pernicious message: The status distinctions that divide society (such as distinctions of race, gender, ethnicity and sexual orientation) are defined (and perhaps justified) by real and profound differences in lifestyle, morality, temperament, norms and aesthetic sensibility. This message not only provides ready justification for continued bigotry and aversion on the part of those outside the group in question; perhaps worse yet, it also encourages group members themselves to emphasize their differences from outsiders, to exaggerate the degree, importance and antiquity of those differences (every trait becomes a cultural practice, every practice a tradition and every tradition hails from the misty domicile of "time immemorial") and even to invent traditions (to borrow Eric Hobsbawm's evocative phrase[21]) that never were. (An apt citation here would be the invention of Kwanzaa by black nationalist Ron Karenga in the late 1960s as an African-American "tradition," as if the heavily Protestant African-American community needed "our own" non-Christian Christmas substitute.)

What passes for an objective description of group difference is all-too-often nothing better than a common stereotype. Moreover, such descriptions of group difference are inevitably exercises of power—attempts to legitimate a particular and controversial account of group culture over the objection of those who would reject or challenge that account. The idea that minorities should hew to "their" cultural traditions is as hegemonic as the idea that they should assimilate to a mythical white-bread mainstream. Therefore, a right-to-cultural-difference will not simply leave people free from repression; instead, it will install a specific set of ideas about what it means to be a member of whichever group the right "protects." The normative component of the repressive hypothesis is in an important sense a self-fulfilling prophesy passing as an empirical observation. (I realize this idea requires a good deal of elaboration; much of this book will be devoted to providing it.)

Like Dr. von Helsing in Bram Stoker's *Dracula*, difference discourse is obsessed with a specific evil: the demand for cultural assimilation. This is an evil that lurks in the dark, unnamed and unknown; it seduces the innocent, attacks the righteous and drains the lifeblood of minority cultures. The counter strategy has been to expose assimilationism to the daylight by naming it and to counteract it with it its opposite: recognition of difference. If public celebrations of difference and condemnation of assimilation are the wolf's bane and holy water of multiculturalism, then a legal right-to-difference is a wooden stake.

But this demon—assimilation—is Janus faced. Assimilation is both compulsory and unavailable. Even as certain formal rules, official proclamations and cultural narratives insist on the moral necessity of assimilation to a common norm and identity, others reinforce the inevitability and natural character of difference. The non-assimilated minority is to blame for her disadvantage, while the assimilated minority is to be apprehended with suspicion—she is a mutant, warped and unnatural like a leopard who changed its spots, but also deceptive, like a werewolf in sheep's attire.

Prescriptively, the repressive hypothesis issues a clear call for a counter attack, or perhaps a preemptive strike: against repression, we need to assert rights to the expression of difference. The more complicated story I have offered suggests no simple prescription. Rights-to-difference might counter unwarranted social repression, but they also might feed popular presumptions about group difference, presumptions that I will argue are forms of regulation and control in their own right. Multiculturalists have been right to argue that pressure to assimilate can be a mechanism of oppression. But they have largely failed to see that the oppressive machinery that produces assimilationism also contains and relies on its opposite—the discourse of cultural difference—and therefore cannot effectively be resisted by simple opposition. The attempt to run from compulsory assimilation toward recognition of difference delivers us all the more firmly into the grasp of a racism that always includes both.

"Diversity": Difference Discourse as Corrupt Détente

> Those who create and re-create race today are not just[,] . . . the people who join the Klan and the White Order. . . . They are [also] the academic "liberals" and "progressives" in whose version of race the neutral shibboleths *difference* and *diversity* replace words like slavery, injustice, oppression and exploitation, diverting attention from the anything-but-neutral history those words denote.[22]

In the 1980s something called multiculturalism made a big splash in the academy and later in political and popular conversation. At first many believed (hoped) that multiculturalism was a fad that would sweep through the ivied halls of higher learning for a time and then fade into obscurity, like designer jeans or mopeds. They were half right: multiculturalism was like designer jeans. The astute reader will note that designer jeans did not exactly fade into obscurity: instead they morphed into designer chinos, designer T-shirts, designer windbreakers, designer polo shirts and even more designer jeans. Similarly, although the heady days of the canon wars and Western Civ skirmishes are behind us, multiculturalism's durability is marked by its new ubiquitous anonymity. Multiculturalism is no longer notable because it is everywhere. As with designer jeans, many who will not admit being fans of multiculturalism still wiggle into it every morning and many more will resort to it when we don't have anything else to wear.

My hypothesis is that despite its popularity today, liberal multiculturalism is best understood as the terms of a sort of Faustian detente that much of the left—especially the race-conscious left—was effectively, if not intentionally, maneuvered into.

Multiculturalism vindicates long-standing and strongly held commitments among many members of socially subordinated groups. For instance, black nationalism's conception of racial difference as the marker of a rift dividing incommensurable norms, epistemologies and social practices offered a sharp, coherent ideological framework and a penetrating political agenda. A nationalist would insist on a significant redistribution of social resources—not onetime cash reparations for isolated historical injuries, but a renegotiation of the background rules through which labor and raw materials are controlled—and on group self-determination, not as a weary trope to support individualist rights assertion but as an ideal to guide institutional reform on the scale necessitated by a thorough, group-focused rethinking of the entailments of democracy itself.[23] To some extent, these powerful ideas are reflected in liberal multiculturalism.

But liberal multiculturalism domesticated these ideas, blunting their sharp critique of specific economic and political institutions and distorting their prescriptions for social transformation. The nationalist belief in a deep epistemological rift between blacks and whites and the radical incommensurability of both groups' goals and values became, in its liberal multiculturalist variant, the idea of a different but epistemologically compatible "perspectives"—a multiracial group of blind men groping at the same elephant—about a unified social field that could be "leveled" by reformist tinkering. The nationalist conception of unsentimental, arms-length negotiations among sharply defined communities with distinct and opaque norms morphed into a liberal multicultural "tolerance" and commitment to "diversity" with its condescending implication of noblesse oblige and its Orwellian hierarchy of equals. The goal of social, economic and cultural autonomy was reduced in its multiculti knockoff to ethnic theme houses and an empty and defensive celebration of isolated and impoverished ghettos under the rubric of "community."

Driven by the imperatives of rights assertion and legalism generally, contemporary legal race consciousness has "split the baby" between the nationalist insistence on incommensurable group difference and the integrationist faith in transcendent humanism. As Solomon's risky bluff would suggest, the infant has been on life support ever since the bisection. Instead of a coherent approach to racial justice we have a contradictory discourse in which difference is deployed as both a mode of regulation and an alibi for continued racial status–consciousness, while the lure of integration undermines durable racial solidarity from within and discredits it from without.

Moreover we have a set of double binds for everyone involved. Minorities are pressured to conform to socially pervasive ideas of their intrinsic culture and are admonished that the continuation of these practices is their birthright and their duty by society in general and by their own communities in particular. But they are also required to assimilate to mainstream social norms—understood to exclude the practices ascribed to minority identities—in order to participate in the institutions that provide esteem and resources in society at large. Meanwhile everyone in society is required to recognize the distinctiveness of various social groups, but we are also chastised for stereotyping when we do.

This now dominant difference discourse was not, I submit, either the inevitable outgrowth of a long-held political consensus among people of color, the left or champions of social justice; nor was it the product of considered and thoughtful strategic or normative analysis. Instead, the development of difference discourse in this peculiar contemporary form was largely reactive and defensive; the commitment to it, the function of a plausible, but I contend misguided, tactical essentialism that has become confused with ultimate ends.

Alan Bakke: Multiculturalist?

One of the most important figures in the development of liberal difference discourse in the United States was neither a lawyer nor a person of color when his ideas so profoundly changed modern civil rights. He was a white male and an aspiring medical student named Alan Bakke. For those few readers not familiar with the notorious case *U.C. Regents v. Bakke*,[24] decided in 1978, a brief summary will suffice. Alan Bakke applied and was denied admission to the University of California at Davis medical school. Bakke discovered that racial minorities with lower grades and test scores than his were admitted under an affirmative action program that essentially established separate admission tracks for different racial groups. Bakke sued the university, asserting that his Fourteenth Amendment rights to equal protection had been violated. Bakke prevailed.

Justice Powell, the author of what is widely considered to be the controlling opinion (the Court splintered 4-1-4 and Powell cast the deciding vote) did not find that all affirmative action was unconstitutional. Instead, he applied strict scrutiny to the university's program, under which in order to be permissible the racial classification would have to serve a compelling governmental interest and be narrowly tailored to the furtherance of that interest.

Powell then found the following: 1) rigid numerical quotas could never be sufficiently narrowly tailored and 2) the governmental purpose of remedying past discrimination was sufficiently compelling only if the university endeavored to rectify and could identify specific instances of institutional discrimination but not to remedy societal discrimination in general.

This was, of course, a bad day for the race-conscious left. But all was not lost. The Powell opinion left one door tantalizingly ajar: a nonquota-based affirmative action plan served a compelling interest (and thereby could overcome strict scrutiny) if it was designed to promote "diversity." Hence, colleges and universities could continue to consider the race of applicants as a factor in admissions provided that their purpose was not to remedy societal discrimination but rather to attain a diverse student body.

Although the opinion was roundly condemned at the time, it didn't take long for race conscious liberals—faced with the alternative of risking the continued viability of affirmative action on the outcome of another round of constitutional litigation—to embrace the *Bakke* diversity rationale like a life preserver. Ever since, a project of race-conscious progressive thought has been to establish that racial minorities have distinctive norms, perspectives, voices and cultural practices. This isn't to say that no one argued for or worked to advance such racial difference projects before *Bakke*. It is to hypothesize that the peculiar idea of racial difference as cultural difference was promoted from one of many ideas about racial salience to a centrality it did not merit because of Powell's *Bakke* opinion.

The diversity rationale embraced in the Powell opinion silently analogized racial diversity to ethnic diversity: both the Powell opinion and the amici curiae brief submitted by Columbia, Harvard, Stanford and the University of Pennsylvania on which Powell relied use the term "racial" and "ethnic" almost interchangably. The Powell opinion silently institutionalized an ethnicity model of race that, by its very nature emphasizes the innocent "fact" of cultural difference over the politically imposed wrongs of status hierarchy. In the ethnicity paradigm, the position of blacks is analogous to that of, say, some Italian-Americans: both have distinctive cultural backgrounds and therefore may contribute a unique perspective to the university environment. What is excluded by this paradigm is any acknowledgement that a very recent history of state-sponsored and institutional subordination distinguishes the two groups. Here the *cultural* identity of racial minority groups is emphasized at the expense of the history of racism.

Before *Bakke*, diversity was one of many reasons selective universities employed affirmative action. For instance, in 1969 a publication of the Stanford Medical School cited the need to remedy and correct for societal discrimination (now a questionable rationale under *Bakke*): "the Medical College Admission Test . . . may be inaccurate in indicating the basic ability and motivation of a minority student who has been subjected to social . . . barriers."[25] The chairman of the medical school's minority search committee reported that the school sought to increase minority enrollment in order to better serve underserved minority communities (also unacceptable under *Bakke*): "The health problems of the ghetto have become serious. We know from past experience that the [typical white] medical student has failed to meet the challenge. . . . [We need minority enrollment] to increase the number of black and brown physicians, not to integrate Stanford with the most qualified minority students in the country."[26]

The diversity rationale is benign when understood as one of many possible reasons a university might care about the racial composition of its student body. But it is dangerous when enshrined as the only or primary reason race is significant. *Bakke*'s codification of the diversity rationale pushed institutions that wished to engage in affirmative action *and* minority groups themselves to *emphasize* cultural difference. Only by highlighting the stark differences in perspectives, norms and experiences marked by race could universities justify affirmative action post-*Bakke*. Despite judicial and university disclaimers, this rationale effectively requires universities to incorporate a substantive theory of racial difference into their admission processes—the post-*Bakke* universities and their minority applicants needed not only to assert that racial minorities would bring distinctive ideas and perspectives to the seminar table, they also needed at least a sketchy working account of the distinctive perspectives that racial minorities would bring. And a more subtle and much more pernicious implication hovered over post-*Bakke* university life: *only* by highlighting their own distinctiveness could minority students justify their presence in the universities that had admitted or might admit them.

Students don't have to read Supreme Court opinions to get the diversity message. For instance, the Kaplan Test's *Graduate School Admission Advisor* nudges the applicant who may not have thought of it herself: "Does your ethnic or cultural perspective give you a different take on the world?"[27] The cover of Kaplan's *Get into Law School: A Strategic Approach* promises "insider advice from top admissions officers" and includes a section entitled "Special Considerations," which is divided into such chapters as: "Older Students;" "Minority Students;" "Women Students;" "Gay and Lesbian Students" and "Students with Disabilities." The chapter directed at "Minority Students" instructs:

[T]he U.S. Supreme Court ruled in *Bakke* that race can be a factor in striving for a diverse student body. Therefore . . . [i]f you participated in a minority students organization, list it in your application. . . . [I]f there is something unique or of special interest as regards your race or ethnicity, whether it relates to your personal or professional development or illustrates how you would add a unique or different perspective to the student body, include it in your personal statement.[28]

These instructions were not lost on applicants to selective universities and professional schools. The number of references to cultural difference in a small sample of personal statements penned by successful applicants to Harvard Law School would make one think she was looking at applications to star in Disneyland's attraction, "It's a Small World," rather than at applications to attend law school:

"My primary motivation for receiving a law degree surfaces from my personal experiences with the struggles of the Latin American immigrant."[29]

"My experience with other cultures give me sensitivity to the voices of today's international America."[30]

"[W]hen I supported funding for the Carolina Gay and Lesbian Association. . ."[31]

"My curiosity about foreign cultures . . . began early."[32]

"As the child of Paraguayan immigrants, I too occupy a borderland."[33]

"I studied American Sign Language and was introduced to Deaf culture."[34]

"By the time I entered college, I had mastered the language of three communities: the Paraguyan Spanish spoken by my mother at home; the profanity-laden slang of our poor, all-black Washington, D.C., neighborhood; and the textbook English enforced in the private schools I attended."[35]

"I am a fourth generation Mexican-American with Cajun ancestry."[36]

"[A]s an expatriate I developed a keen awareness of cultural diversity by actually being a part of different cultures."[37]

"I want to get involved with the law here to preserve a state wealthy with culture and diversity."[38]

"If accepted, I will bring to Harvard Law School a very rich and diverse background."[39]

Anyone who has reviewed admissions applications has read scores of slight variations on these deeply personal accounts of ethnic heritage. No doubt some of these narratives are indeed sincere. But it is equally beyond doubt that some are, to be blunt, crass stratagems designed to improve the applicant's chance of admission to a selective college or university. Many are probably a combination of the two: generations of students are likely to internalize the equation of racial difference with inherited cultural difference and incorporate it into their sincere self-conceptions.

GROUP DIFFERENCE AND STEREOTYPE THREAT

The emphasis on intrinsic group difference may harm the academic performance of minority students in concrete and measurable ways. The internalization of group stereotypes can operate at the subconscious level, often to the severe detriment of individuals burdened with those stereotypes. Consider the research of social psychologist Claude Steele, who has demonstrated that internalized group stereotypes depress the performance of minority race students on standardized tests. In experiments at Stanford University, Steele

> asked black and white Stanford students into our laboratory and gave them, one at a time, a thirty-minute verbal test made up of items from the advanced Graduate Record Examination. . . . When the difficult verbal test was presented as a test of ability, black students performed dramatically less well than white students, even though we had statistically matched the two groups in ability level. . . . We presented the same test as a laboratory task that was used to study how certain problems are generally solved. We stressed that the task did not measure a person's level of intellectual ability . . . and the black students' performance on the test rose to match that of equally qualified whites.[40]

Why? Steele suggests that black students underperform when they feel at risk of confirming stereotypes about their group. He identifies disidentification—a response to the risk of confirming stereotypes:

> [A student] may learn to care less about the situations and activities that bring [the risk of stereotyping] about—to realign his self-regard so that it no longer depends on how he does in the situation. . . . This withdrawal of psychic investment may be supported by other members of the stereotype-threatened group, even to the point of its becoming a group norm. But not caring can mean not being motivated. And this can have real costs . . . [which] African-Americans in all academic areas—may too often pay.

Against this background, pervasive ideas about group difference, especially when connected to academic achievement, may play a significant role in minority disidentification and poor performance. The litigation-driven dominance of diversity rhetoric in almost every university statement concerning race reinforces the already widespread idea that cultural difference is intrinsic to minority race students. Students who are consistently told that they were admitted because of their cultural distinctiveness rather than their academic promise (post-*Bakke* universities can't admit that affirmative action corrects for grades and test scores unfairly depressed due to societal discrimination or stereotype threat) likely will be tempted to embrace all-too-familiar notions of culturally specific learning styles as an excuse for anticipated poor performance. One such siren's song is the theory of Janice E. Hale-Benson in *Black Children: Their Roots, Culture and Learning Styles.* Among the distinctively black cognitive traits identified by Hale-Benson are:

> "Afro-American people tend to respond to things in terms of the whole picture . . . [whereas] the Euro-American tends to believe that anything can be divided and subdivided into pieces."[41]

In other words, blacks are not inclined toward a basic technique of analytic reasoning; if this were so it would not surprise us to find that,

> "Afro-American people tend to prefer inferential reasoning to deductive or inductive reasoning."[42]

So much for the black Sherlock Holmes (not to mention black scientists and philosophers.

> "Afro-American people tend to approximate space, numbers, and time rather than stick to accuracy."

If this were true, it would be a good reason to avoid employing black engineers, doctors, accountants.

> "Afro-American people in general tend not to be "word" dependent. They tend [instead?] to be very proficient in nonverbal communications."

Shocking, given this fact about Afro-Americans, that the literary Harlem Renaissance ever got going.

> "Black people think in terms of approximation of time, rather than punctuality. An "in house" expression is "C.P.T."—meaning "Colored People's Time"! . . . Meetings that begin on C.P. Time usually begin about twenty minutes after the appointed time."

Little wonder, some might think, that blacks have trouble competing in the environment of the industrialized West, in which many enterprises rely on the precision of mechanical time.

Despite her attempt to sugarcoat these tired stereotypes, Hale-Benson's account of black cultural styles reads like an apology for racial hierarchy.

Such unsubstantiated popular hypotheses about racial difference—plausible precisely because they echo familiar racial stereotypes perpetuated for centuries by white racists—can easily become a comfortable rationalization for withdrawing from challenging academic situations. As comfortable as warm quicksand.

Happily, Steele and his colleagues found that minority student underperformance due to stereotype threat could be reduced, if not eliminated. The cure is not racially segregated safe havens or racial diversity cheerleading, but rather racially integrated "living and learning" environments wherein minority students can meet and get to know their fellow students of all races. Steele reports that such environments "greatly reduced underperformance: black students . . . got first-year grades almost as high as those of white students in the general . . . population who entered with comparable test scores."[43] So diversity of a particular sort *is* the answer. But here diversity eschews the separatist path of least resistance and fulfills its promise. Here diversity doesn't involve minority students' exhibiting their distinctiveness for the edification of whites; instead diversity serves minority and white students by allowing them to discover what they share in common. Steele concludes:

> when members of one racial group hear members of another racial group express the same concerns [about academic performance] they have, the concerns seem less racial. Students may also learn that racial and gender stereotypes are either less at play than they might have feared or don't reflect the worst-feared prejudicial intent. Talking at a personal level across group lines can thus build trust in the larger campus community. The racial segregation besetting most college campuses can block this experience, allowing mistrust to build where cross-group communication would discourage it.[44]

This type of experience requires universities to resist racial separatism and insist on integrated environments despite student agitation for comfortable but detrimental segregation. Ethnic theme houses and the other official or quasi-official accommodations of group separatism that exist at most universities typically are considered markers of "diversity," but such policies are inconsistent with the most educationally constructive interpretation of the diversity rationale those universities advance in defense of affirmative action. As Justice Scalia noted in dissent from the majority opinion in *Grutter v. Bollinger*, which reaffirmed *Bakke*'s diversity rationale, one might question

> the bona fides of the institution's expressed commitment to the educational benefits of diversity . . . [in the case of]those universities that talk

the talk of multiculturalism and racial diversity in the courts but walk the walk of tribalism and racial segregation on their campuses—through minority-only student organizations, separate minority housing opportunities, separate minority student centers, even separate, minority only graduation ceremonies.[45]

Diversity *Über Alles:*

Twenty-five years after *Bakke*, the Supreme Court reaffixed its by then faded imprimatur to "diversity" and only "diversity" in *Grutter v. Bollinger*.[46] *Grutter* upheld the University of Michigan Law School's race-conscious admissions policy—a policy that followed the blueprint drawn by Justice Powell in *Bakke*. The law school's admissions policy avoided the use of quotas, but did consider race as one factor among others, for the purpose of achieving "diversity" in its student body.

Writing for the majority, Justice O'Connor endorsed Powell's opinion in *Bakke* and upheld the law school's admissions policy. But *Grutter* does more than simply maintain the post-*Bakke* status quo. It exacerbates the troubling effects of *Bakke*. *Grutter* unambiguously installs diversity as the sole permissible rationale for affirmative action. The majority opinion asserts that "Powell approved the university's use of race to further only one interest: 'the attainment of a diverse student body." And the opinion emphasizes that "Powell rejected an interest in 'increasing the number of physicians who will practice in communities currently underserved.' "[47] And more so than *Bakke*, *Grutter* gives explicit marching orders to applicants as well as selective universities and professional schools: "All applicants have the opportunity to highlight their own potential diversity contributions through the submission of a personal statement, letters of recommendation and an essay describing the ways in which the applicant will contribute to . . . diversity."[48]

The *Grutter* opinion endorses *Bakke*'s rejection of an interest in "reducing the historic deficit of traditionally disfavored minorities" (described as impermissible "racial balancing") and its rejection of an interest in remedying "societal discrimination."[49] Yet, as if the majority were aware that "diversity" alone cannot justify race-conscious affirmative action, the *Grutter* opinion notes in passing that "*By virtue of our Nation's Struggle with racial inequality*, [minority] students are both likely to have experiences of particular importance to the Law School's mission, *and less likely to be admitted in meaningful numbers on criteria that ignore those experiences*."[50] This single sentence all-too-subtly acknowledges a point that the diversity rationale obscures: racial minorities are likely to have suffered from a distinctive type of *discrimination* that often will affect detrimentally their grades and performance on standardized tests. This fact justifies affirmative action as a remedial measure. This remedial rationale, based on a frank acknowledgement of the persistence of racism, need not suggest that minority students must exhibit their racial difference in recognizable forms in order to merit admission. This alternative rationale—less than one sentence buried in thirty-two pages extolling the virtues of diversity and only diversity—suggests a compelling rationale for affirmative action, one which offers a more dignified portal of entry to minority students than diversity alone and one that undoubtedly comes closer to accurately describing the sincere motivations of selective universities and professional schools than does diversity alone. Yet the prospects of anyone openly acknowledging this shadow rationale are dim indeed; because the *Bakke* and *Grutter* courts rejected a remedial rationale in the context of "societal discrimination," to do so would invite a lawsuit.

In order to fully appreciate the costs of *Bakke*'s and *Grutter*'s diversity rationale one need only consider the experiences and performances of racial identity that the opinion excludes. *Bakke* and *Grutter* reject what was one of the most important justifications for affirmative action in professional school admissions before the *Bakke* litigation: the presumption that minority graduates are more likely to serve underserved minority communities. They explicitly exclude the idea that racial identity entails an ongoing and contemporary relationship to patterned and predictable forms of bias and discrimination, which may detrimentally affect the grades and test scores that selective universities rely on to sort applicants for admission. Post-*Bakke* universities want to know all about the unique culture of the ancestors of their minority applicants, but ignore the discrimination suffered by the applicants themselves. "Diversity" allows that the enslavement of a black applicant's great-grandmother over 150 years ago is relevant to her application, but implies that the racism suffered by the applicant herself at the hands of high school teachers and administrators a few years or even months ago is not.

In this light it would appear that a central function of "diversity" is to finesse, if not obscure the salience of contemporary racism. "Diversity" is popular with college administrators and student activists, corporate executives and civil rights lawyers, the Congressional Black Caucus and leaders of the Republican Party because it hints at racism (mollifying the activists) without being so impolitic as to name it (to the relief of the elites). Diversity—an exemplary form of difference discourse—allows all of us to focus on something pleasant, rather than on racism (*so* 1968!); it eschews a blunt assessment of the affects of bigotry in favor of a conversation about culture, a topic fit for social encounters where etiquette demands one avoid controversial subjects such as race, religion or politics. By describing status hierarchy as a problem of intrinsic difference, difference discourse transforms what should be an indictment of social practices of exclusion and subordination into a plea for "tolerance" of a "diversity," the origins of which are left unexamined. As a result, the beneficiaries of status hierarchy are able to misdescribe and misunderstand their position as that of unwitting and repentant cultural hegemonds, too recently converted to the benevolent practice of tolerance rather than as occidental Brahmins who enjoy an inheritance of status privilege. This misunderstanding mangles the historical record, softens the diagnosis of social injustice and as a result prescribes a palatable placebo in place of a badly needed, if bitter, pharmaceutical.

BEND IT, DON'T END IT

To be clear, I do not suggest that the Court's diversity rhetoric is the fruit of a conscious plot to suppress a conversation about racism or to force minority students into a interminable production of "It's a Small World." Much less do I wish to suggest that the lawyers, activists and scholars who worked, in many cases tirelessly, promoting and refining the diversity rationale in order to save affirmative action, deserve criticism for their efforts, as if no good deed should go unpunished. For the most part, I'm certain that the proponents of diversity acted from good motives and on sound principles. First and foremost, diversity is a perfectly respectable justification for affirmative action—my complaint in this respect is that it is not the only justification and, in my opinion, is not even the most compelling. After *Bakke*, diversity was the only rationale that seemed likely to survive judicial review. And diversity, precisely because it soft-pedals—when it does not obscure entirely—the issue of bigotry, is less likely to meet with fear, anxiety and resistance. These are all good reasons to emphasize diversity, whether one is arguing before the Supreme Court or writing for the majority of its members.

And I much prefer the outcome in *Grutter*—diversity and all—to the likely alternative: the invalidation of any and all forms of affirmative action. The *Grutter* and *Bakke* opinions preserved affirmation action, a program that I believe is quite important to the educational mission of selective universities and to social justice and racial harmony in society at large. From a political perspective, diversity represented a pragmatic compromise. The *Grutter* and *Bakke* opinions are "difference splitting" at its liberal best and worst—they limited affirmative action without eliminating it. Or, as law professor Chirstopher Edley noted, "The Supreme Court [in *Grutter*] . . . adopted President Clinton's formulation 'Mend it, Don't End it.' "[51]

It's too early to attribute any substantial effects to the *Grutter* opinion, but, as it amplifies the logic and rhetoric of *Bakke*, it's fair to surmise that it will amplify the effects of *Bakke* as well. And *Bakke*'s difference splitting not only limited the potential *scope* of affirmative action, it also shaped its *character*. With this came an unintended side effect: by altering the character of the institutional treatment of race, it also altered the incentives surrounding the expression and performance of racial identity and ultimately even sincere racial self images, at least among those directly affected by the institutions. Because those so affected were disproportionately wealthy, socially elite and culturally influential (the applicants, students and faculty of selective universities) they in turn profoundly influenced the meaning of racial identity in society as whole. Although a host of factors contributed to the development of racial multiculturalism in its current form, *Bakke* and now *Grutter*, have given the cultural difference conception of race the imprimatur of the Supreme Court and have underwritten it with the force of law. The significance of this intervention should not be underestimated. Hence my hypothesis (which contains an irony that would be funny were it not so tragic): the "conservative victory" in *Bakke* in no small part encouraged the development and popularity of that bête noire of American conservatives: race-conscious multiculturalism.

Difference discourse received a strong "push" from the *Bakke* decision that put diversity at the center of progressive race consciousness in the academy. At the same time *Bakke*'s emphasis on "diversity" hardened into an idea of *cultural* diversity when race-conscious arguments were influenced by a set of arguments developed in Ethnic Studies and the Arts and Humanities faculties that had cultural and symbolic concerns at their very core. These included the emergence of multiculturalism in the academy and later in popular conversation, particularly the "canon debates" in the humanities; the internationalism of cultural studies, which displaced or challenged the more traditional "American Studies" as well as a good piece of traditional sociology and supplemented their focus on America and Western Europe with a study of third world postcolonial struggles; and the growing concerns with semiautonomous cultural and linguistic communities within liberal democratic nation-states.[52] These debates emphasized cultural difference and the challenge that it posed to the dominance of the culture, ideas and values of the United States and Western Europe. They foregrounded the cultural recognition demands of distinct subcultural groups, insisting that liberal societies should accommodate cultural difference and acknowledge the cultural labors and aesthetic artifacts of non-Western peoples. These debates naturally began to focus on the aesthetic and social merit of various social groups.

These debates provided invaluable insights into American race relations. But too often they led to an exclusive focus on culture, a (tactical) exaggeration of cultural difference and denial of commonality, and a subsequent inattention to economic inequality and political oppression. And as multiculturalism further calcified into identity politics, the laudable cosmopolitan quest for multiple perspectives in scholarship and for the expansion of blinkered university curricula yielded place to a provincial obsession with personal identity and in-group solidarity. For student life, the results were less liberation from cultural hegemony than the morphing of one hegemony into another. As sociologist Todd Gitlin notes:

> The newcomer [to the university] . . . finds exclusive identity groups for partying, dancing, listening to music in a familiar style. She finds the Black Sociology Association and the Asian Business Association. . . . . [P]repackaged identities multiply . . . [and] when everyone else seems to have found a group to eat with, party with, hang out with, and date, the newcomer feels the pressure to find one as well. . . . Even students who feel uneasy about the prefabricated categories feel peer pressure to identify with one. . . . The group allays what is already an adolescent anxiety about finding a place. But the spread of identity-group culture heightens that anxiety in the first place.[53]

Of course we can't know what the racial landscape at America's elite universities and in the nation as a whole would look like had Alan Bakke never brought his lawsuit. But it's safe to say it would look different. Without *Bakke* it is likely that affirmative action programs would have continued to consider race as one factor among many in order to serve a number of goals including the promotion of diversity and the remediation of societal discrimination. Free of *Bakke*'s requirement of specific findings of identifiable discrimination, universities may have used (and admitted using) racial preferences as a means of correcting for the societal racial bias that affects the grades and test scores of many individual applicants. The Court could have eliminated "quotas" without limiting universities to the diversity rationale and there is no reason that affirmative action based on a number of racially sensitive rationales should have been any more expansive or severe than that based only on diversity: the effect on applicants who did not benefit from affirmative action would most likely have been the same.

But the effect on racial identity would not have been the same. Without *Bakke*'s requirement that affirmative action be justified in terms of diversity, other approaches to racial inclusion would have been available to universities. A race-conscious policy that focused on the need to undo the legacy of racial subordination and to correct for its contemporary manifestations might have made a greater number of racial "scripts"[54] available and encouraged a richer and more-nuanced understanding of racial identity. Subtle and overt incentives for social integration and at times assimilation might have encouraged a different performance of racial identity had *Bakke* not counterbalanced them by explicitly encouraging the emphasis on cultural difference. The resulting racial identities would not have been less or more authentic than those we have today. But they would have been different, and possibly in ways that both the ideological left and right would have preferred: perhaps more overtly focused on social justice as a political matter and less enraptured with cultural difference and the corresponding production of racial affect.

Bakke-free admission policies would not have focused exclusively on diversity (which later hardened into a quite specific idea of *cultural* diversity) with its implicit requirement that people of color stand out in specific and prescribed ways into order to justify their presence. Instead they might have acknowledged that the history of American racial hierarchy creates a mix of racial identities that are based on a complex relationship to mainstream American culture and institutions—a relationship of cooperation and subversion; of sincere admiration, deep-seated contempt and ironic detachment; of a desire for acceptance and an insistence on distance. Such racial identities are indeed distinctive and do contribute to a vibrant and diverse institution. But such diversity can only be fully appreciated in the light of an acknowledgement of racial status and racial hierarchy. In this respect, racial difference marks the difference in experience and perspective developed because of one's position in a race-conscious society, not necessarily *cultural* difference (and even less so intrinsic or inherited cultural difference) in the sense of different norms, traditions, epistemologies or standards of aesthetic evaluation.

Such an understanding of race may well have pleased people across the ideological spectrum more than has the contemporary racial multiculturalism spawned by diversity discourse. Perhaps fewer people would have associated racial identity and racial justice with a suspension or rejection of mainstream norms. Instead, racial identity might have been more widely understood as fluid and kaleidoscopic, and racial justice as potentially consistent with a range of identities and relationships to the mainstream, including the embrace of majority norms and assimilation to existing institutions. At the same time, racial identity might not have entailed an essentially conservative project of cultural preservation and a fetishism of pedigree and tradition as it increasingly does under the rubric of liberal multiculturalism. Instead, racial identity might have been ripe with the potential eruption of new cultural forms and new ways of being, the liberation of the human spirit and the creativity of the avant garde. Finally, difference discourse might not have seemed a logical extension of antiracism in this alternative reality. Instead it might have seemed to be what it for the most part is—a separate project with different normative stakes, independent factual assumptions and animated by distinct ideological commitments.

It's not too late. We should refine the "diversity" rationale for university affirmative action and admit that the impetus for race consciousness in admissions reflects the common-sense intuition that racial justice and racial harmony require that prestigious selective universities be racially inclusive, and not the questionable (and vulnerable) idea that racial identity necessarily comes bundled with a profoundly distinctive culture. Of course this would require affirmative action proponents to devote the same amount of energy to fighting *Bakke*'s rejection of the societal discrimination rationale that they now devote to securing a stay of execution for the diversity rationale. This strikes me as well worth the effort and the risk. Even the *Grutter* opinion's validation of "diversity" suggests that its days are literally numbered: Justice O'Connor opined that "[w]e expect that 25 years from now, the use of racial preferences will no longer be necessary." Opponents of affirmative action quickly made it clear that when the twenty-five-year reprieve granted by Justice O'Connor has passed, they'll be there to throw the switch. Those of us who believe that race consciousness is necessary might be more effective in presenting the most compelling principles and intuitions underlying our commitment to racial awareness (rooted in a recognition of historical and ongoing subordination based primarily on ascriptive social status—not cultural difference) when freed from the reflexive, exclusive and obligatory mantras of "diversity."

2. Identities as Collective Action

*As a Black lesbian feminist comfortable with the many different
ingredients of my identity[,] . . . I find I am constantly being
asked to pluck out some one aspect of myself and present this as
the meaningful whole, eclipsing or denying the other parts of
myself. But . . . [m]y fullest concentration of energy is available
to me only when I integrate all of the parts of who I am . . .
without the restrictions of externally imposed definition.*[1]

This quotation from Audre Lorde is typical of the sentiments
animating difference discourse. It's easy to see how we'd get
from here to support for a legal right designed to protect
against "externally imposed definition" so that we could all
have our "fullest" concentration of energy available to us.
But is it possible to comprehend, much less embrace or be
"comfortable with," identity categories such as "black," "lesbian" or "feminist," "without the restrictions of externally
imposed definition"? Or are these identity categories (as opposed to their supposed referents: dark skin, female same-
sex eroticism, a commitment to certain practice of gender)
the *product* of those restrictions? These are crucial questions
for the politics of difference.

Note that here status as a member of a social group
("black," "lesbian") becomes an aspect of the self ("one aspect
of myself[,] . . . all the parts of who I am") that can occupy a
position evacuated of social power ("without the restrictions
of externally imposed definition.") Through this prestidigita-
tion, group identities that are the *effects* of externally imposed
social discourses—racism, homophobia—are transformed
into aspects of an autonomous self that can then integrate them "without the restrictions of externally imposed
definition."

In this chapter, I hope to demonstrate that individuals
often are pushed into displays of stereotypical group behavior. Difference discourse, while it claims to free individuals
to express themselves without the restrictions of externally

imposed definition, is a form of externally imposed definition and is helping to push.

Rights-to-difference are premised on a belief that identity has a relatively fixed content that can be protected by rights assertion: Rogers's claim was that cornrows were and had always been the cultural essence of black womanhood; imagine how much less compelling her claim would have been had she argued that cornrows were a passing fancy of some black women right now, but admitted that they were likely to be passé by the time the fall fashion rags hit newsstands. These arguments either simply take it as given and beyond reasonable objection that social groups "own" certain cultural traits, or they argue that the culture of a social group can be determined as a matter of social science.

The simplest claim is that practices that "correlate" with group identity should receive rights protection. For instance law professor Barbara Flagg argues for the protection of "racially *correlated* traits," while law professor Kenji Yoshino argues for an approach to anti-discrimination law that "observe[s] *correlations* between behavior and identity that exist in the world."[2]

At times rights-to-difference proponents adopt an anthropological conception of identity: they argue or assume that identity is a manifestation of underlying cultural practices that are autonomous of the consciousness of individual members of the cultural group—practices that can be observed as a matter of objective social science. Law professor Juan Perea, defending a proposed right to "ethnic traits" seems to vacillate between an assumption that the determination of ethnicity can be ascertained as matter of objective science (he cites sociological literature extensively and writes of discrimination on the basis of "ethnicity" or "ethnic traits" as if these terms were subject to a objective meaning) and a presumption that any trait that an individual decides is "ethnic," should be considered so for legal purposes.[3] This latter presumption reflects a psychological conception of identity: here identity is a matter of a subjective and internal development of a "sense of self" to which certain practices and beliefs become central. Similarly, Barbara Flagg, argues for legal protection for traits that "intersect seamlessly with [the plaintiff's] *self definition*."[4]

Often empirical descriptions are deployed interchangeably with subjective and highly normative conceptions of identity: for instance Yoshino, who at times argues for rights that attach to traits that "correlate" with identity, also writes of traits that "constitute" identity and of "fundamental aspects" of identity.[5] Unlike a claim of correlation, these terms sound in the register of fact but are susceptible to no empirical proof or falsification. They are normative theories disguised as factual observations. Underlying the by and large unsubstantiated empirical claims about correlation is a normative assertion that certain behavior *should be thought of* as inseparable from certain social statuses.

Identity as Social Performance

These conceptions of identity share a crucial conceit: Social identities are things in the world and/or reflections of things that can be taken note of as a matter of fact. The consequence of this conception is that legal and policy arguments can take the following form: "Because black identity *is X*, we should do *Y*." By contrast, the conception of identity that will inform this book is that social identities are processes, possibilities, contingencies or conceptual frameworks that organize thought and action; they are not only contingent on social practices but they themselves *are* social practices such that they are never "formed" but always in a process of formation and reformation that is never complete. On this conception we can never say "black identity *is X*." Instead I'm afraid we're stuck with the more cumbersome statement: "The concept of black identity has, at a certain time and place and under certain circumstances suggested to certain people X commitments or entailments." How such an observation affects our current situation is a matter of prediction and of decision—in others words it is to some extent up to us—not of fact.

I'm sure this strikes some readers as so much needlessly obscure postmodernism, something to ignore and hope I get to the real argument soon, or maybe a reason to toss the book into an active fireplace. I'll try to make the point more concrete. Rene Rogers's claim was that black identity is, as a matter of fact, tied to the cornrow hairstyle. Even if we take her questionable historical account of the relationship of cornrows to racial identity as given, this factual assertion is too hasty. To a real extent, Rogers's lawsuit was part of a struggle over what the relationship of black identity to cornrows would be. A verdict for Rogers would probably have made cornrows more central to the identities of at least some black women. It would have altered the relationship between black women and cornrows by interpolating a judicial opinion into that relationship. And the nature of black identity would continue to be remade and altered each time a black woman wore cornrows, straightened her hair with chemicals or shaved it all off, especially if she and others understood and articulated the "hair question" as a question to be answered by an idea about black identity. Black identity also would have been remade by white and Asian women who chose to wear cornrows (or refused to) and by institutions that established policies that forbade or allowed cornrows, especially if they allowed them for some racial groups and not for others. The point here is that the nature of a social identity is not a simple fact, but instead a collision of ideas and practices with an ongoing and vibrant life. It is always contingent on the next idea and/or practice of identity. And any legal decision or opinion about the identity is itself such a practice and embodies such ideas.

This conception of identity has important stakes: in particular, it puts the nature of social identities on the table as a matter of contestation and potential change. It means we aren't stuck with any aspect of a social identity as a matter of fact, instead we are, as a society, responsible for the social identities we have; to some extent they are matters of policy, even of law. An acerbic critic once remarked that each generation gets the architecture it deserves. Similarly, each generation gets the social identities it produces. This doesn't mean that it is up to the individual to create her own identity but rather that "we" as a society effectively, if not intentionally, collaborate to articulate and act out all of our social identities.

Social critics have called this idea the "performative" conception of identity. It's an evocative term. But it is too easy to leap from the idea that social identities are performances to the figure of an actor on a stage that "performs" a role. On this account, the individual who "has" the identity does all of the work: the only role for society is to demand a particular performance and to punish those who don't perform. If we must use the theatrical metaphor, let's remember that the actors "perform" each other's roles. If an ugly man is playing the role of a beautiful woman in a Shakespearean comedy, the other actors "perform" that role by treating him as we would expect people to treat a beautiful woman. By the same token, when a department store detective looks at me and decides to shadow my every move until I leave the premises, *he* is performing *my* identity. When a well-meaning but misguided white liberal shakes the hand of my white friend in the same way he would shake the hand of a Fortune 500 CEO, but to me holds out an open palm in order to "give me five" or awkwardly tries to give the "soul" handshake, he is performing my identity. By the same token, if another black man gives me the "soul" handshake, he also is performing my identity. This is true even if the soul handshake strikes me as the most natural thing in the world—in fact that is perhaps when it is most true.

We could think of identity as a dance to illustrate this conception of identity formation: the tango, for instance, like, many dances, has evolved to establish quite specific gendered roles for the individual dancers (it is perhaps telling that the tango, that sexiest of dances, was originally performed by two men, mimicking a knife fight). There is a male and a female role, quite assertively marked by costume. The male "leads" and the female "follows." The moves rely on the assumed superior physical strength of the person occupying the male position and the assumed diminutive size and gracefulness of the person occupying the female position. These positions can be seen as simple reflections of a preexisting reality. There is a distinction between men and women based in biological nature; this distinction corresponds to a number of characteristics such as strength, size, assertiveness and gracefulness. The dance just reflects these facts. Men are stronger and more assertive so it's natural that they lead while the weaker and more submissive women follow.

But maybe this way of thinking too easily assumes the relationship of cause and effect. It may be, on the contrary, that hundreds of social practices, of which the tango is one, construct these gendered roles and encourage people to conform to them. A physically strong, tall and assertive woman will not be offered the "male" position, even if she is naturally well suited for it. She will be encouraged by dance instructors, parents, potential partners, and friends to conform to the female role: learn to accept the guidance of the male, develop grace at the expense of strength.

It may become very difficult to distinguish between "coerced" and "voluntary" conformity to the status roles. Our strong and assertive woman will find it easier to conform to the female role than to attack the structure of the dance. If she does not conform, her friends will sanction her by telling her that she could get a date easily if she were a bit "nicer" or "more feminine." Men will silently punish her by refusing to ask her to dance. If she wants to dance, she will conform. Over time conformity will become "second nature." Our now accomplished dancer will remember her assertive past as an "awkward phase" that she grew out of, as a butterfly emerges from a cocoon. At that point the status will have also become her identity.

The dance is a highly stylized context in which gender identity and gendered status is performed or constructed. The tango teaches us that men and women have different statuses because they have different natures. It builds a status and simultaneously justifies that status as a biological or natural fact. It provides its own evidentiary justification: men and women in fact behave differently while dancing; they demonstrate by their own actions that the premises of the gendered dance are accurate.[6]

I would loosely associate this phenomenon with what the philosopher Louis Althusser called "interpellation." Althusser used the example of a policeman who shouts "Hey, you there!" to illustrate the concept. The person in a crowd with a guilty conscience may stop and turn around, thereby "answering" the call. When one recognizes the call as addressing her ("uh, oh, I'm busted") she becomes a subject of an ideology—in this case the ideology of the criminal law. By this we mean that she acknowledges an ideology of criminality and her position in that ideology as a criminal. Similarly, the narrative of group culture shouts "Hey, you there!" to members of the group under examination. And, as the figure of the policeman suggests, we are not free simply to ignore this address and its implications.

Free Time

This account of identity means that much of the "content" or "meaning" of identity is contingent on social practices. It is not only contingent on the practices of businesses such as American Airlines or The Parker Group that might have rules about grooming and other practices arguably linked to identity. It is also contingent on the practices of the private home—what Michel Foucault has called the "little tactics of the habitat"—of friends and family and of noneconomic voluntary associations. Because of the widespread belief that these latter practices are authentic and unforced, in contrast to the acknowledged constraint and "role playing" of public, professional and commercial life, the practices of family, friends and community probably have the greatest influence on identity formation.

We often think of our lives as divided between time at work and "free time." The social performance associated with our free time therefore becomes the model of freedom; if we're pressured to do something different while at work the natural conclusion is that the expectations of work are coercisive and "externally imposed." But a moment of sober reflection is enough to erode this idea. External definition comes from everywhere: our families, friends, spouses and romantic partners have expectations that are as powerful and prescriptive as those of any boss or coworker. This isn't a critique of these free-time relationships, but it is a critique of the idea that they are "free" in any strong sense of the word. Indeed the pleasure and eroticism of our various human relationships derives from the varying expectations each relationship provides. I—and I think most people—often enjoy the movement between varying social roles: serious professional, laid-back drinking buddy, intense intellectual, exuberant bon vivant, intimate friend, devoted son, loving husband, enraptured lover. The reason I enjoy these roles is not because any of them let me express my identity "without the restrictions of externally imposed definition," whatever that would mean. Each of these roles—indeed any position that involves other people—comes with intense and elaborate expectations and the relationships depend entirely on everyone holding up his or her end of the implicit bargain.

So we can't assume that the identity that an individual brings from home is a product of freedom; in fact we can be pretty sure that it isn't. Our self-conceptions and identification develop in a social milieu saturated with power, top to bottom. There is no place from which pure identities, identities forged free of "the restrictions of externally imposed definition," could come.

This doesn't mean that we always experience the free-time identities as oppressive, but sometimes we do. Indeed it is likely that many people experience the institutional rules that rights-to-difference would prohibit as a convenient excuse to avoid social roles that are obligatory at home, or find that unfamiliar institutional norms provide valuable perspective on the norms that prevail in their free time. Some individuals might consciously wish to reconsider their inherited norms, while others might discover over time that customs and norms that were once second nature have gradually yielded to new ideas.

It's easy to tell such a story about gender: we can imagine a woman who is pressured to conform to a Stepford Wifely image by her family and friends silently relishing a "masculine" workplace dress code that requires tailored suits with clean lines, severe hairstyles and low-heeled shoes.

But isn't it true of other groups as well? For each religious conservative who objects to mandatory coed dorms at universities like Yale, there may be countless Yalies from strictly religious backgrounds for whom Yale's coed dorm requirement has saved from an argument with their parents or who were uncomfortable at first but later found coed life liberating. It's likely that many gay men feel social pressure to conform to gay stereotypes—say, wearing "fashion forward" clothing—both because other gay men have internalized and expect the stereotypically gay behavior and because resistance might be taken as a closeting tactic—an attempt to deny or downplay their sexual identity. These men may well conform in order to get along in the social milieu that offers them social support in a homophobic society and the best prospects of getting laid. Work could be an excuse to drop the pose ("the boss makes me wear this boring suit" or "the guys on the construction site wouldn't appreciate Dolce and Gabbana").

I don't want to overstate the case: there's no doubt that many people consistently experience workplace norms and rules as oppressive. But there is a tendency to ignore or explain away the myriad informal norms and expectations associated with free time, while focusing on the requirements of work and other institutions as the exclusive media of power. This tendency finds expression in the idea that some social identities and norms are natural and others artificial and that the former would flourish if we could only protect them from the destructive effects of social power. If we recognize that social identities are a *product* of social power we have to abandon the idea that we could protect a natural or intrinsic identity *from* social power.

It's also plausible that supposedly natural and intrinsic social identities—those commonly associated with "free time"—are at times imposed or amplified by the environment of the workplace. Again, it's easiest to see this in the context of sex difference. In *Price Waterhouse v. Watkins*, the Supreme Court held that an employer's persistent demands that a female employee act out gender stereotypes was evidence of sex discrimination in violation of federal law. The facts in *Watkins* were extreme, but tragically not at all anomalous: partners at Price Waterhouse, who later voted not to extend partnership to Watkins, complained that she was "macho."[7] Her superiors insisted that Watkins "walk more femininely, talk more femininely, dress more femininely, wear make-up, have her hair styled and wear jewelry."[8] One suggested that Watkins enroll in "a course at charm school."[9]

Courts are ambivalent about the extent to which employers may require their female employees to conform to conventional gender roles. Despite *Watkins*, male and female employees can be required to conform to divergent standards of grooming and dress: for instance, it is legal for an employer to require a female television anchor to wear "blouses with 'feminine touches' such as bows and ruffles,"[10] and for an employer to refuse to hire men with long hair,[11] or for a federal judge to require male, but not female attorneys to wear neck ties.[12] My point is not to condemn the Court for inconsistency or an insufficient commitment to sex equity: as law professor Robert Post suggests, it is unrealistic, even undesirable, for anti-discrimination law to seek to eliminate gender norms or attempt to usher in a unisex society. But the persistence of clear rules enforcing gender divergence is evidence that social identities can be an effect of externally imposed definition rather than of nature or free individual choice.

A similar, if more subtle, phenomenon occurs in the context of race. Consider a case that some rights-to-difference proponents cite as an example of compulsory assimilation: *Jurado v. KIIS FM*.[13] Valentine Jurado was a radio DJ who sued KIIS-FM after management required him to stop using Spanish in his radio program. In his affidavit Jurado opined that management's order that he speak only English on the air would "take his character away." Jurado claimed that the English-only order was both discriminatory treatment on the basis of race and would have a statistically discriminatory impact on Latinos.

It's easy to see this case as an example of "forced assimilation." But placed in context, it is more plausibly a story of a seemingly natural and intrinsic social identity that was in fact imposed from outside and only later internalized. Jurado began his career at KIIS-FM speaking only English. Later, *at the request of management* in an attempt to attract Hispanic listeners, Jurado agreed to add some Spanish words and phrases to his broadcast. When ratings among Hispanic listeners failed to improve, management decided to return to an English-only format.

Given these facts, a plausible (but unfortunately for Jurado not actionable) version of events is this: Jurado began his career as an English-speaking DJ working at a radio station with a largely English-speaking target demographic.

Presumably he was comfortable with this position and he worked to build an audience for his radio program. Management then decided to capitalize on Jurado's language skills and race and asked him to emphasize his Latino identity by adding some Spanish phrases to the broadcast. Jurado complied and worked to build a different audience consistent with the new bilingual format of his program. After requiring Jurado to invest time and effort in this new program, management changed its mind and insisted that Jurado go back to an English only format. Jurado balked at the suggestion that he change formats and on-air personae again ("they want to take my character away!") and, of necessity, start from scratch building a following for a show with a different format. Enough was enough.

Notice that in this version of events, Jurado does have cause to complain of racial discrimination: he was made to switch formats and rebuild a viable audience for his program *twice* because he is Latino. *Because of his race*, Jurado became the whipsaw in KIIS FM's fickle demographic marketing tactics. Here however, the action that initiates Jurado's injury is not the order to speak English but instead the order to speak *Spanish*. For all we know Jurado wanted nothing more than to be a successfully assimilated English-speaking DJ on a major radio station (originally his on-the-air name was not Valentine Jurado but the Anglicized Val Valentine). Station management, not an intrinsic identity waiting to be set free, impelled Jurado to adopt a Latino persona and made his future on the air depend on his ethnicity. In short, the *Jurado* case may well involve a compelled performance of racial difference—the antithesis of "forced assimilation."

The ambiguity of the *Jurado* case should caution us against presuming that traits that we stereotypically associate with minority social groups are necessarily intrinsic to members of those groups. It should also suggest that the potential application of anti-discrimination law to such traits involves a difficult set of policy questions. Should Jurado have been able to sue for being pressured to use Spanish or for being forced to stop? Or both? Or neither?

Recognition of Difference as Protective Custody

[E]ven if Big Brother is not everywhere watching you, Language is; media and specialized or expert language that seeks tirelessly to classify and categorize, to transform the individual into the labeled group, and to constrict and expel the last spaces for . . . the unique and the unnameable.[14]

For the sake of argument, let's assume that the image of minority cultures as the helpless victims of thuggery and violence by the mainstream was accurate (as I have argued above, this is at most only part of the story; the important subplot features the less overt but more pernicious production and compelled performance of difference.) Even so, the *best* one can say for rights-to-difference is that they would have the merits of protective custody. Like a person compelled to testify against a mob boss, the identity minority who wishes (or is compelled) to bear witness to her cultural difference fears for her life. The state (interested in securing the testimony) offers a bribe Faust would recognize: a witness protection program, protective custody.

Rights-to-difference are a form of protective custody: the witness gets protection, sure. The aggressor is thwarted in his plot to silence the witness or exact revenge. But the price of protection is incarceration: one's movement is scripted and controlled, the district attorney implements round-the-clock surveillance, a cop sits in one's kitchen or parks across the street. Worst of all, the trial never ends; the watch cannot be lifted; protective custody is a permanent condition, an ongoing public policy. Tempted to take your chances on the outside?

Of course no one is proposing cultural or identity police who tell us what to do. So how are rights-to-difference a form of protective custody? This section makes the case.

Rights as Public Policy

Rights-to-difference are informed by a conception of rights as a limit of social and political power. The proposals envision a legal right that will simply remove a source of repression, freeing the underlying identity to develop without restriction. If the performative conception of identity that I introduced earlier is correct, this idea can't be: There is no underlying identity waiting to be set free. The performative account suggests that a right-to-recognition will be one of the practices that produces the social identities it is directed toward. In this important sense a right-to-difference will be a form of social policy concerning identity formation.

This may seem counter intuitive: mainstream liberal discourse teaches us that rights protect us from governmental regulation, that rights are a limit on state action, not a source of it. But this way of understanding rights is questionable. Legal rights are a form of public policy and therefore of regulation—not a limit on the power of the state.

Some of the most important legal rights enjoyed by Americans—for instance the Civil Rights Acts of 1965 and 1968—were acts of Congress, formally indistinguishable from any other federal policy. Rights may be especially symbolically powerful, especially difficult to change or rescind, and often developed and administered by a different set of institutions than most public policy (courts as opposed to the executive or the legislature) but they are still policy.

As policy, legal entitlements in general and especially rights do not simply protect people from outside interference; they also channel energies and shape perceptions about what is important, necessary and good in life. Rights have a tutelary function; they send a message about what society values.

It may be difficult to see how rights can impose specific (and controversial) substantive norms in this way because we have been taught to believe that rights safeguard freedom in an ideologically neutral fashion. Moreover, the norm-producing process is one that covers its tracks. Because people internalize the norms advanced by the right in question, those norms are experienced as chosen, intuitive and organic rather than as imposed, contrived and to some extent, state–made.

Perhaps an example will illustrate the point. Any first-year law student knows that the First Amendment protects religion and speech from governmental regulation based on content. It forbids government from discriminating against either the content of expression or the teachings of a religion. Therefore, we might conclude, First Amendment rights are ideologically neutral and invariably enhance the freedom of the individual. But this conclusion rests on a questionable framing decision: the rights can be presented as ideologically neutral only by limiting the frame of analysis to the question of distinctions within a sphere (such as speech or religion) and assuming the validity of the ideology that underlies the choice and definition of that sphere. Broaden the frame and we can see that the First Amendment codifies a very specific ideology; one that both asserts that expression is either more important or less dangerous than other forms of activity, and assumes a particular definition of expression and excludes many expressive activities from protection.

The First Amendment generates a practice of "free" expression that is heavily conditioned by the existence of formal rights. One could argue that First Amendment rights serve to channel social activity, protest and unrest in a prescribed way in order to institutionalize particular forms of expression (leafletting, marches, demonstrations and political advertising) at the expense of others (situationist pranks, civil disobedience, transgressive performances, shock art, obscene gestures.) We could say something similar about the religion clauses, pointing out that spirituality is protected to the exclusion of philosophy and politics—Aquinas is protected but not Thoreau—and therefore individuals and groups are encouraged, both by law and by the set of practices that law supports, to join churches and to embrace, experience and present their commitments in a religious form. So even in the context of rights that an individual can assert *against government*, what is at issue is not a *limit* on the authority of "the state" but rather an *exercise of that authority* by one institution of the state as opposed to another.

Describing rights as a form of policy is not in and of itself a critique of rights generally. We can favor legal rights, just as we favor a host of other public policies, while acknowledging that they are, functionally speaking, a form of public policy that controls social relationships. Whether or not such control is good or bad depends on what you think of the practices that are institutionalized as opposed to those that are not. But what's clear is that the rights don't simply give people "more freedom" by providing an option; they also channel activity and energies. They encourage and institutionalize certain practices. Legal rights are a *form* of state action not a limit on state action.

Our analysis of legal rights should then be no different than our analysis of any public policy: we should look to the likely effects of the right in question to determine whether it is good policy or bad.

If rights-to-difference were simply limitations on the power of social institutions to repress preexisting, natural and intrinsic identities, there would be little to need to evaluate them as policy. But if rights-to-difference are better understood as social policies designed to shape and produce social identities in specific forms, to encourage certain social practices and discourage others and to affect the pattern of practices across social groups, then we are entitled, indeed obliged, to ask whether these specific outcomes are desirable.

Rights-to-Difference Require an Official Account of Group Difference

Rights-to-difference claims are presented as a simple matter of freeing individuals and groups from a mainstream cultural hegemony. The conceptual foundation of this claim is that there is a baseline of authentic behavior that members of minority groups would engage in out of unfettered free choice, in the absence of cultural hegemony. But all cultures, including those to be protected by rights-to-difference, are the product of hegemony. What we mean by "a culture" is that certain practices are hegemonic within some group—that's how cultural *norms* become *normal*. So rights will not free us from hegemony, rather rights will *establish* one hegemonic practice as opposed to another.

In many cases what is cast as a battle for recognition waged by a single-minded minority group may be better understood as an *ideological* conflict *within* the group. Such a conflict cannot be evaluated in terms of the repression of difference. It may seem easy to say we support, say, repressed African-American cultural practices as against the cultural hegemony of milquetoast Middle America. But where do we stand on the case-captioned African-American Traditionalists v. The Cultural Avant-Garde (Wynton Marsalis v. Stanley Clarke; Stanely

Crouch v. Gil Scott Heron or Busta Rhymes) or Cultural Nationalists v. Cosmopolitans (Le Roi Jones v. James Baldwin)?

As these examples suggest, group cultures contain a multiplicity of different, competing and at times mutually exclusive projects. Which traits and practices are important or central to the group's culture will be a question subject to debate, change and manipulation. In this important sense rights-to-difference will not protect a culture from outside influence, instead they will take sides in ongoing cultural struggles within a social group. These struggles will be influenced by social pressures and rewards of potentially any source. These influences will include the legal system (indeed, the law may be an especially influential discourse, as I will argue below). The practices and traits that the legal system protects may be elevated in importance, not only because they will be immune from censure or prohibition but also because they will have received the imprimatur of the state.

Unfortunately, rights-to-difference are likely to be quite bad at reflecting the dynamism and complexity of cultural struggle. The legalism of difference discourse encourages, and rights-to-difference require, formal conceptions of social identity that easily can be asserted in courts. Courts and judges will most likely protect cultural styles that can be easily framed in terms of fixed categories, bright-line rules and quasi-scientific evidence. Courts will want to find experts to testify as to the content of the group culture, they will want lists of specific and concrete manifestations of the culture. Judges are likely to want the culture to be fixed and knowable and will want the protected behavior to be reflexive so as to distinguish culture from merely deviant behavior.

The scholarly arguments in favor of rights-to-difference reflect this legalistic need for crude formal criteria and list making. For instance, according to law professor Kenji Yoshino, gay identity is defined by such plausibly characteristic traits and affinities as sodomy, public display of same-sex affection and gay rights activism, but also by more questionably associated traits such as gender atypical behavior and some real head-scratchers such as body building,[15] boxer briefs, goatees, golf and rugby (on these latter definitions, about 75 percent of the male population of the state of California between eighteen and thirty-five years of age is gay). Finally the list includes traits that made me squirm such as sexual promiscuity and affinity with sexual deviants such as polygamists and pedophiles.[16]

Despite some questionable inclusions, for the most part Yoshino's casual list of gay-identified traits is a plausible anthropology of group difference. But in order to generate a list that could be used by courts to distinguish culture from behavior it exaggerates and oversimplifies, often to a dramatic extent. Yoshino's skills as an anthropologist of "gay culture" are not to blame—the list is probably as nuanced as such a list could be. The blame lies with the very project of trying to define group differences with sufficient formality as to produce a list of traits at all. In another context, one would expect angry accusations of stereotyping to follow such a list of group traits. At the very least, one would expect a call for ever greater nuance: gay men as a group are fractured by age, region, neighborhood, race and a host of other subgroup affiliations, each subgroup with its own distinctive subculture.

Similar nuance is called for in the context of racial culture. To be sure most reasonable observers would agree that, in general, blacks are distinguished from non-blacks by some distinctive cultural practices. But those practices vary by region, generation, income, education and host of other factors. Cornrows may sharply distinguish blacks in much of the United States, but in the urban centers of California one is almost as likely to see young white and Asian hipsters in all-braided hairstyles. Much of what is called "soul food" is a variation on the regional cuisine of the American south. A diet of dishes like fried chicken, cornbread and greens distinguishes blacks in many part of the country because blacks migrated from the south in large numbers in successive waves for much of the twentieth century; however, in the south these dishes are not racially distinctive. The sartorial styles associated with hip-hop music (no use trying to describe them because they'll be different by the time this book is in print) are characteristically black, but they are also characteristically youth oriented, urban, to some extent class delimited and associated with style conscious and creative people. These demographic qualifiers mean that not only do most blacks not embrace these black cultural styles but that many non-blacks do embrace them.

Nor can the question be answered by reference to origins. First of all the racial origins of certain practices are notoriously difficult to unearth. Consider the questionable racial pedigree of "Ebonics." Many claim that the nonstandard English speech patterns exhibited by many American blacks are directly traceable to certain West African languages and therefore part of the heritage of all those of the corresponding African decent. An example of such a speech pattern that is particular grating to the Anglophone's ear is the "intransitive be": for example, "we be going to the store." Some have argued that because the intransitive "be" is also found in Yorbu and other African languages, its appearance in African-American speech patterns is traceable to an African root. It's a plausible hypothesis, but linguist John McWhorter points out that Scottish dialects and protomodern English also used the intransitive "be," as in the Bard of Avon's "what fools we mortals be" or that ubiquitous caption of premodern cartography: "beyond here there be dragons." Because the *English* spoken by many of the people African slaves would have come into contract with (crews on slave ships, slavers and plantation owners) included an intransitive "be," another plausible hypothesis is that Africans learned the intransitive "be" from Europeans.[17] The intransitive "be" stuck with blacks and not with white immigrants because black segregation denied blacks access to the discipline of education through which whites learned a standardized modern "King's English."

Far from simply recognizing objective facts about social groups, difference discourse imposes a forced cohabitation of ascriptive statuses and volitional or cultural traits. Granted, there are few black people who don't exhibit *any* of the traits commonly associated with black culture. But most blacks only exhibit some of them, some of the time and with nuances and subtleties that even the most talented anthropologist could never fully grasp. Difference discourse captures a real experience of group difference, but it standardizes it for easy description and in the process it dumbs it down. Difference discourse treats group cultures as if they were a unified text when they are best understood as genres. Most of us think that literary genres describe *something*, but they are notoriously difficult to define in detail. A genre is most useful when used referentially, to conjure or suggest sensations that ultimately must be experienced; it is most dangerous when deployed prescriptively.

This inevitable oversimplification is a problem because a right-to-difference will give an imprimatur to the legally protected cultural styles. One will have a strong incentive to tailor one's self-presentation to conform to the official account of group difference, both in order to appear "authentic" and legitimate within one's own racial group, and also because the prescribed styles qualify for legal protection. Rather than rights simply mirroring preexisting cultural practices, *the culture may mirror the right.*

Worse yet, rights-to-difference may well promote the most socially dysfunctional traits and styles. For instance, Yoshino's list of gay traits, includes, on his own account, characteristics that are associated with gay identity as a matter of statistical fact, characteristics associated with gay identity by at least some gay people, and characteristics that are associated with gay identity as a matter of social convention and common perception: in other words stereotype. In one sense this is logical: one variant of a right-to-difference (we could call this variant "victim focused") demands that we forbid discrimination against traits that members of the group identify with, while another (a "perpetrator-focused" variant) demands that we forbid bigots from discriminating against traits that *they* associate with the group. But because no attempt is made to distinguish them, difference discourse encourages an embrace of the characteristics that *bigots* associate with group identity.

This suggests that those concerned about maintaining "authentic" cultural practices might serve their cause best by resisting difference discourse and rights-to-difference and the rigid, positivistic conception of group culture they reflect.

Difference Discourse as Social Discipline: Delegitimation and Stereotyping

Given the vast diversity of potential accounts of group difference one can expect that virtually any conceivable definition of a group culture—including many that will horrify us—would eventually make its way to a courtroom under a right-to-difference theory. And individuals pressing group recognition claims, when they are successful, will not decide only for themselves what is fundamental to their identity; they will decide for all members of the group what is to be deemed fundamental to the identity of the group.

There's an example of this phenomenon in a context that does not involve a formal rights claim. At the time of the Congressional hearings to confirm Clarence Thomas's nomination to the Supreme Court, sociologist Orlando Patterson wrote in a newspaper Op-Ed column that Anita Hill's reaction to Thomas's alleged sexual overtures was "unfair and disingenuous" because although the comments were "completely out of the *cultural* frame of his white, upper-middle-class work world,"[18] they were "immediately recognizable to Hill and most women of southern working-class backgrounds, white or black, especially the latter."[19] According to Patterson "Hill perfectly understood the psycho-cultural context in which Thomas allegedly regaled her with his Rabelaisian humor"[20] as "as a way of affirming their common origins."[21]

Here I'm not only concerned about women who might have to endure such "Rabelaisian" bons mots. I'm particularly concerned about blacks, especially black women who are implicated in Patterson's description of black culture (Patterson explicitly implicates "nearly all African-Americans"[22] in his description of black culture). His account of racial culture necessarily discredits not only Anita Hill but also any other black person who objects to or disclaims Thomas's alleged behavior). Not only is Hill told that she must forebear Thomas's behavior because it is *his* culture—she is also told she must embrace it because it is *her* culture as well. Not only is she told that she *should* embrace the raunchy esprit de corps that Thomas allegedly offered, she is told that she *does* in fact embrace it; that she "perfectly understands" it and that her objections to it and disclaimers of it are therefore "disingenuous."

The Patterson editorial demonstrates how easily questionable or even insulting ideas about the culture of social subgroups can circulate. Of course, a newspaper editorial is not the same as a published judicial opinion and a social commentator does not write with the authority of a judge. But the Op-Ed page of a mainstream American newspaper is a fairly good barometer of middlebrow-to-elite public opinion: if Patterson's ideas about black culture got onto the Op-Ed page, they would almost certainly convince at least some judges.

So it's not hard to imagine attorney Patterson's successful litigation on behalf of defendant Thomas in a sex harassment suit. The resulting legal articulation of a race based right-to-difference would not affect only Thomas, it would also have implicated Anita Hill, black women generally, indeed "nearly all African-Americans." We cannot be confident that individual litigants will press only, or even predominantly, positive narratives of identity; yet every time such a claim is pressed, it will be pressed, not only for the individual litigant, but for everyone else in the group to which he or she belongs. Ask not for whom the gavel strikes—it strikes for thee.

The risk of writing stereotypes into law or of regulating and compelling the performance of group difference is not limited to cases where a narrative of group culture is deployed to discredit a member of the group in question. Consider law professor Regina Austin's account of the dispute in *Chambers v. Omaha Girls Club*.[23] This case involved a young black woman, Crystal Chambers employed by a charitable club for disadvantaged girls that served a 90 percent black clientele. Chambers was dismissed when she became pregnant outside of wedlock, a violation of the club's "negative role model" rule. Chambers sued, claiming that the club's "rule would have a disparate impact on black women due to their significantly higher fertility rates."[24] Chambers lost.

Austin argues against the club's rationale for the role model rule—that "to permit single pregnant staff members to work with the girls would convey the impression that the Girls Club condoned pregnancy for the girls . . . it serves"—and against the club's aspiration that "its members could be influenced by committed counselors who, by example, would prove that life offers more attractive alternatives than early pregnancy." She argues that single motherhood is unattractive, in part because employers—like the Girls Club itself—condemn single mothers and deny them respect and the opportunity to earn a livelihood: "The club managed to replicate the very economic hardships and social biases that . . . made the role model rule necessary in the first place."[25]

Fair points. But in order to defend Chambers and condemn the court's verdict for the Girls Club, Austin embraces Chambers's generalization about black women's fertility rates. She not only accepts the generalization as a statistical matter but also embraces it as a normative matter, as a potentially important element of black female identity. Austin complains that "[i]mplicit in the *Chambers* decision is an assumption that the *actual cultural practices* and articulated moral positions of the black females who know the struggles of early and single motherhood firsthand are both misguided and destructive. . . . Yet for some of us, their portrayal in the *Chambers* opinion is more flattering than the authors intended."[26] So, according to Austin, single motherhood is the byproduct of the *cultural practices* of black females.

At the same time Austin wishes to condemn the stereotype of the over sexed, pregnant and single black female. She condemns the image of Jezebel, "the wanton, libidinous black woman who was free of the social constraints that surrounded the sexuality of white women"[27] and insists that "black women who attempt to express their sexuality and control their reproduction should not have to travel through a minefield of stereotypes, clichés and material hardships."[28]

The double bind gets tighter still. On Austin's own account Chambers finds herself unemployed, not because her employer was unwilling to acknowledge her distinctive racial culture, but because the Girls Club *did* acknowledge it: she argues that the Girls Club believed that Chambers would function "as an icon, a reminder of the powerful culture from which the club members had to be rescued."[29] Of course, for Austin, the club did not see Chambers's real culture but instead a distorted stereotype: the Jezebel. However, it is not only the Girls Club but also Austin herself who finds this distinction hard to make. For instance, Austin decries the Court's distain for the "actual cultural practices" (not mistaken stereotypes) of black women like Crystal. And even in her condemnation of unquestionably demeaning stereotypes, Austin equivocates, saying that the Jezebel image is "not totally divorced from reality."[30]

In defense of Crystal Chambers Austin celebrates an ethic that, as she describes it, "declares wily, audacious, and good *all* conduct that offends the white, male, and middle-class establishments." This leads her to embrace precisely those negative stereotypes that racists deploy in order to delegitimate people of color. Do people of color who behave as racist stereotypes would depict them, in any meaningful sense, "attempt to break out of the rigid economic, social, and political categories that a racist, sexist, and class stratified society would impose upon them" as Austin suggests?[31] Are we to assume that the goal of racists and sexists is to erase social differences between groups and force, for example, women of color into the same social status as white women? Isn't it more likely that a racist and sexist society requires different roles and constraints for different groups?

Austin anticipates the widespread inclination to lament, if not condemn, Chambers's pregnancy as the consequence of poor decisions and a confirmation of a destructive racial stereotype; in preemptive response she defaults to liberal individualism: "Some of the black women who are not married yet have babies may be young and wise; others may be poor and brave; and yet a third group may be rich and selfish. Whether they confirm or confound the stereotypes, all of them deserve a measure of freedom with regard to their sexuality that the dominant culture withholds."[32]

But even if we were to accept Austin's rhetorical vehicle of individual freedom as a general matter, this seems a particularly awkward place for it to come to rest. *Chambers* (especially on Austin's account of the case) is not a simple employment discrimination case; it is also about the acculturation of minors who, regardless of race, class or gender, our society does not feel are competent to exercise their own unassisted judgment in matters of reproduction. And if Austin is right (as I think she is) to imply that *Chambers* involves a struggle to influence the meaning of racial and gender identity, then it's simply no good to evoke individual "freedom" as if the meaning of that term were not contingent on the meaning of the social identities that are at the center of the controversy.

Austin's account of Crystal Chambers as a rebellious heroine exercising authentic free will is only one of many interpretations of her story. It relies on a host of unstated assumptions about the nature of racism, of mainstream institutions and of black culture. Most strikingly, Austin assumes that Chambers's out-of-wedlock pregnancy is the reflection of an autonomous choice, the manifestation of a deep-seated culture that is her birthright. The stereotype becomes an authentic persona, a youthful indiscretion is elevated to a "moral position" and a "cultural practice."

Philosopher Charles Taylor's discussion of the politics of recognition suggests another account of *Chambers*,

> The demand for recognition . . . is given urgency by the supposed links between recognition and identity, where this latter term designates something like a person's understanding of who they are, of their fundamental defining characteristics as a human being. The thesis is that our identity is partly shaped by recognition or its absence. . . . Nonrecognition or misrecognition can inflict harm, can be a form of oppression, imprisoning someone in a false, distorted, and reduced mode of being. Thus some feminists have argued that women . . . have been induced to adopt a depreciatory image of themselves. They have internalized a picture of their own inferiority, so that even when some of the objective obstacles to their advancement fall away, they may be incapable of taking advantage of the new opportunities. . . . An analogous point has been made in relation to blacks: that white society has for generations projected a demeaning image of them, which some of them have been unable to resist adopting. Their self-depreciation has been, on this view, one of the most potent instruments of their own oppression.[33]

Here identity is produced through dialogue and recognition, not by internal and autonomous choices. Austin's argument depends on this idea: How can we understand identification with a culture "that declares as wily, audacious, and good all conduct that offends the white, male, and middle-class establishment" without a dialogical account of identity formation? And if we embrace the dialogical account, then we cannot distinguish between stereotype and authentic identity by reference to the autonomous choice of the individual.

In the absence of the authentic persona = choice, stereotype = coercion equations, Austin's account of Chambers's pregnancy is at best an optimistic postulate. I'm afraid there is another account of *Chambers* in which a young Chambers plays the victim of racism, not by *failing* to conform to what the "racist mainstream" wants of her, but by her absolute complicity with a racist stereotype. Coerced by the imperative to "stay true" to a distorted image of her cultural roots, influenced by the subtle and overt racism of the mainstream media and pressured by those members of her community who had internalized the stereotypes of the racist society of which they are a part (and perhaps those who cynically used the language of solidarity to have their way with her), Chambers looked at a caricature and mistook it for a mirror. In so doing she remade herself to conform to the caricature, her "free choices" verbatim lines in a long-running tragedy.

Two of Charles Taylor's central insights are that identity is dialogical—it depends on a social interaction in which the understanding and esteem of others plays a crucial role—and the related idea that the internalization of negative stereotypes is a significant source of harm with tangible consequences in terms of psychological health, political empowerment and material wealth. In this light, the Patterson Op-Ed piece and Austin's treatment of the *Chambers* case foreshadow a grave risk: legal recognition of difference could underwrite destructive self-images and misguided commitments with the force of law and the intractability of precedent.

Cultural Reservations

Because difference discourse often establishes lists and canonical accounts of group identity, it tends to favor traditional behavior over behavior that is novel or transgressive within the group. It favors cultural styles that are presented in terms of authenticity, depth, integrity and pedigree over those presented in terms of fluidity, multiplicity, ambivalence and hybridity. In this respect, rights-to-difference include proscriptions and mandates, not only for those who would assert them and their contemporaries but also for future generations. Consider for instance Juan Perea's defense of legal protection for "ethnic traits" against the common argument offered by defendants and many courts that such traits are within the control of the individual and therefore do not merit civil rights protection: "[T]he aspects of our identities *with which we are born, or that develop as a result of our families,* do not become less important because we choose to, or must, maintain them. Nor are aspects of our identities less important because we have chosen them, if we have ability to choose."[34]

Perea emphasizes "the aspects of our identities with which we are born, or that develop as a result of our families"[35] implying such inherited practices should serve as the model of protected ethnic behavior. But there is no reason to imagine that inherited social practices are more benign or more valuable than those that are learned and developed later in life.

Perea is not alone in his conception of identity and culture as inherited. As the philosopher Kwame Anthony Appiah argues, such a conception of identity and culture is inherent in the very idea of cultural survival that underlies much of political multiculturalism:

> [T]he desire for survival is not simply the desire that the culture that gives meaning to the lives of currently existing individuals should continue for them, but requires the continued existence of the culture through indefinite future generations. . . . Let me stress first that the indefinite future generations in question should be the descendants of the current population. The desire for the survival of the . . . identity is not the desire that there should always be people somewhere who speak that . . . language and practice those . . . practices. . . . A proposal to [pay] . . . a group of unrelated people to carry on [the] culture on some island in the South Pacific simply would not meet the need. This matters because it seems to me not at all clear that this aim is one that we can acknowledge while respecting the autonomy of future generations.[36]

In this light Perea's emphasis on "the aspects of our identities we are born with or develop as a result of our families" takes on a troubling undertone. While Perea wishes us to focus on the individual who has already developed the aspects of identity that would be reinforced legally, Appiah directs our attention to the "future generations," whose relationship to any cultural trait or identity is entirely contingent on socialization. The policy question at issue is not well understood in terms of the autonomy of the individuals who are pressing cultural difference claims. Instead, it involves the socialization of future generations and the relationship of future generations to existing ones.

Privileging inherited social practices codifies a narrow and questionable norm of the appropriate relationship among family members and among members of racial and ethnic groups. The necessary premise is that identity modeled on familial and blood relationships is more important—more deserving of protection—than identity based on social norms outside the family or identity based on a rejection of inherited norms. To be sure, difference discourse arguably empowers the person who can put her grievance in terms of family and pedigree. But by casting the family as the author of identity such a proposal can also reinforce problematic and oppressive ethnic and family relations. The individual who wishes to escape suffocating conformity and oppressive social norms of her family or ethnic community will be blessed with a "right" to retain them forever.

The federal courts' treatment of Native American affairs under the Indian Civil Rights Act corroborates this hypothesis. In *Martinez v. Santa Clara Pueblo* the plaintiff, a female member of the Santa Clara Pueblo who had married outside the tribe, challenged a tribal ordinance that denied tribal membership to children born of marriages between a female tribal member and a nonmember (but granted tribal membership to children born of a *male* tribal member and a nonmember). In upholding the tribal ordinance the court focused almost exclusively on the question of tradition, looking to alignment with "ancient" or "traditional" tribal practices to determine the validity of the ordinance. In fact, the *Martinez* majority noted that courts generally defer to traditional tribal practices and uphold laws that are consistent with such practices, even when those laws clearly violate established civil rights enjoyed by non-Indians, but will often apply conventional constitutional analysis and strike down practices that impinge on established rights when a tribe departs from tradition. The result: cultural difference is effectively defined to include only practices that have acquired the patina of age; the cultural minority is defined by its premodern infancy and by its distance from the cosmopolitan life that characterizes the sites of political power, material wealth and social dynamism.

One might defend the result in *Martinez* on the grounds of Native-American sovereignty: the tribe should be free to make its own membership rules. But the application of tribal sovereignty is extremely patchy. "Sovereignty" is evoked to defend Indian gaming in contravention of state law, but few would suggest that it would allow a tribe to operate, say, an opium den or a house of prostitution. Native-American property rights often are adjudicated and enforced against outsiders not by tribal governments but instead by the United States government. And, as Justice Marshall notes in *Martinez*, some federally defined civil rights are imposed on the tribe by federal courts (and others are not.)

Many aspects of tribal membership and family law are hard to square with a straightforward sovereignty rationale. Too often, federal law imposes a rigid idea of Native American identity on all Native Americans under the rubric of respect for tribal sovereignty and Native-American culture. The Indian Child Welfare Act (ICWA), for example, gives tribal courts exclusive jurisdiction over an Indian child who resides or is "domiciled" in a tribal reservation (domicile, as we shall see, is something of a legal fiction and is not synonymous with residence or physical presence) and requires that "In any adoptive placement of an Indian child under State law, a preference shall be given . . . to a placement with (1) a member of the child's extended family; (2) other members of the Indian child's tribe; or (3) other Indian families."[37] This statute was passed in order to prevent what many considered to be a widespread problem: the unwarranted removal of children from Native-American communities by state child welfare officials. But from its inception, the Indian Child Welfare Act confused the real problem of anti–Native-American bias with an independent policy aspiration of cultural preservation.

It bears noting that there would seem to be room for legitimate debate as to the extent of anti-Indian bias in the child welfare system. Law professor Randall Kennedy points out that although

> ICWA's architects stressed the disparity between the numbers of non-Indian versus Indian children who were removed from the care of their biological parents . . . [T]hey did not negate the counterhypothesis that much of the purportedly "racial" disparity was actually attributable not to individual discrimination . . . but to some other cause—perhaps to the disproportionate impact of disease, unemployment, violence and familial dysfunction on Native Americans.[38]

Even if we assume the existence of widespread bias in the child welfare system, that alone cannot justify the ICWA because its reach extends to cases of *voluntary* termination of parental rights and even requires tribal placement over the *objection* of biological parents, cases in which "bias" is not a risk. Consider two cases cited by Kennedy: *In re Bridget R*,[39] in which, four months after signing the adoption papers, at the urging of his mother, a biological father evoked the ICWA to block the adoption he had agreed to and to place his biological daughters with his sister; and *In re Baby Boy Doe*[40] in which a biological father who had no contact with the mother of his child during her pregnancy used the ICWA to prevent adoption of the newborn by the couple the biological mother had chosen. Consider also *In re Santos*,[41] in which the adoption of a "multi-ethnic" child by its foster parents, the only parents the child had ever known, was contested, not by either of the child's biological parents, who declined to contest the placement, but rather by the mother's tribe.

Consider finally *Mississippi Band of Choctaw Indian v. Holyfield*.[42]

> [This dispute involved] the status of twin babies . . . who were born out of wedlock. . . . Their mother . . . and father . . . were both enrolled members of appellant Mississippi Band of Choctaw Indians (Tribe), and were residents and domiciliaries of the Choctaw Reservation in Neshoba County, Mississippi. [The mother] gave birth to the twins in Gulfport, Harrison County, Mississippi, some 200 miles from the reservation.[43]

Here both parents voluntarily placed the twins up for adoption resulting in their adoption by the Holyfields.

> [The] twin's mother went to great lengths to give birth off the reservation so that her children could be adopted by the Holyfields. . . . The mother gave birth to the twins at a hospital 200 miles from the reservation, even though a closer hospital was available. Both parents gave their written advance consent to the adoption and, when the adoption was later challenged by the Tribe, they reaffirmed their desire that the Holyfields adopt the two children . . . [T]he parents went to some efforts to *prevent* the children from being placed on the reservation.[44]

Two months later, the Choctaw tribe moved to vacate the adoption and assert jurisdiction over the twins. The tribe's assertion was based on the ICWA's provision that tribes have jurisdiction over children residing or domiciled on tribal land. But the twins did not and had never resided on tribal land; in fact they had never been physically present on tribal territory. The Supreme Court nevertheless held that the twins were subject to tribal jurisdiction because their *parents* were tribal members.

These applications of the ICWA cannot be explained by reference to a history of biased or over aggressive removal of children from Native-American parents. In Holyfield the parents voluntarily relinquished custody and actively sought to avoid having their children placed on the reservation. In *In re Bridget R* the parents (both of Native-American ancestry) voluntarily terminated parental custody. In *In re Baby Boy Doe* the mother voluntarily terminated parent rights and the father was absent. And in *In re Santos* the parents acquiesced in the termination of parental rights, a process that began because the prematurely born child screened positive for cocaine and continued because the parents' domicile was unfit for human habitation.[45]

Nor can these cases be explained by reference to tribal sovereignty. None of the children in these cases was born on tribal territory. In some cases, as the ICWA provides, the legal standing of the intervening tribe was based, not on the chosen affiliation or formal enrollment of the parents, but rather on their biological ancestry. This is a policy wholly unrelated to combatting bias or to the conventions of sovereignty. By way of illustration, imagine a "Germanic Child Welfare Act," authorizing Germany to intervene in adoptions of children born to American citizens on American soil who are of distant Germanic ancestry and to exercise jurisdiction over the custody of such children in German courts for the purpose of ensuring they were placed with German families living in Germany.

The ICWA is not a incident of sovereignty or a corrective for anti–Native-American bias. Instead, it is a public policy of race matching in adoptions. It is essentially the same policy promoted by the National Association of Black Social Workers (NABSW) since 1972 and widely employed in American adoptions generally until Congress discouraged racial discrimination in adoption and foster care placement (except in cases of Native-American adoptions covered by the ICWA) with the passage of the Multiethnic Placement Act (MEPA) in 1994 and flatly prohibited it with MEPA's amendment in 1996. The presumptions underlying race-matching policies are sharply articulated in a 1972 NABSW resolution, which read in part, "Black children belong physically, and psychologically and culturally in black families in order that they receive the total sense of themselves and develop a sound projection of their future. . . . black children in white homes are cut off from the healthy development of themselves as black people."[46]

Its ironic that black activists pressed for race-matching in the 1970s because race matching in adoption had been the norm for much of the nation's history due to formal segregationist policies and widespread racism. As law professor Elizabeth Bartholet notes:

> During the segregation era, laws and policies systematically prevented placing children for adoption across racial lines. The civil rights movement brought changes in the law and in attitudes in the 1960s . . . [F]or the first time, significant numbers of transracial adoptions took place in the United States. . . . [But after the NABSW resolution] [t]he establishment forces readily conceded . . . that Black and Native American children truly "belonged" with their groups of origin. . . . Latino groups joined the fray, demanding that "their" children stay within their own ethnic community groups.[47]

After the NABSW statement, adoption agencies nationwide began (or resumed) race matching. The results have not been in the best interests of children, as Bartholet notes:

> the numbers and percentage of minority race children in foster care grew dramatically as these children poured into the system, and social workers, given the limited number of available same-race adoptive homes, felt constrained to keep them there. . . . Children of color could be designated as hard to place in significant part because same race-matching policies made them hard to place . . . [although] Black adults were adopting at roughly the same rates as whites, . . . the problem was that there [sic] so many black children in foster care, and waiting for adoption, that blacks would have to adopt at many times the rate of whites to provide homes for all of the waiting children.[48]

The separatism underlying race matching finds its true roots, not in Native-American or African traditions, but in the tradition of German romanticism (a tradition that most Germans today have, thankfully, declined to preserve). As Brian Barry observes:

> "the gist [of German romantic nationalism] . . . was that different people developed their own unique ways of life. . . . Culture was identified with the *volksgeist*, or the spirit of the people, meaning their total way of life." Germans, for example, should sternly resist cultural imports which can only contaminate the purity of their ancestral culture. French ideas are good for the French, and German ideas are good for the Germans, but neither will prosper if they borrow from the other. But why should the mere biological fact of German ancestry somehow make a human being incapable of living well except as a participant in German culture? The obvious answer is that Germans are a biologically distinct people, and that German culture is inherently suited to inborn German traits.[49]

Some arguments against transracial adoptions (and for race matching) do not rely explicitly on a notion of a biological predisposition to group culture, but these arguments are hard to credit if one rejects the racial culture presuppositions. For instance, opponents of transracial adoption argue that the children so adopted will suffer some psychological trauma or deficit as a result. Empirical studies have not demonstrated any difference in self-esteem or intelligence between children adopted trans-racially and those adopted intraracially.[50] Adults who were adopted transracially as children have offered anecdotes, some of which corroborate and some of which refute the presumption that transracial adoptions are harmful. Some recall isolation and loneliness experienced in predominantly white environments and identity crises borne of a mismatch between their ascribed racial identity and their self-conception. Some complain that their white adoptive parents failed to prepare them to function as a person of color in a racist world. Some reported that their own experiences were positive but nevertheless believed that white adoptive parents were inherently less able to impart racial "coping skills." But others cited the benefits of transracial adoption and did not believe that they were disadvantaged as a result.

Another popular argument for race matching, the contention that white parents will fail to impart racial "coping skills," relies on the salience of race and racism rather than of cultural difference. This argument, often confused with cultural preservation rationales, suggests that white parents are unlikely to be successful parents of children who are visibly non-white because the parents will be naive about or unfamiliar with the distinctive racial issues that the child will confront and therefore will fail to pass on important "coping skills" that minority parents would pass on.[51] This is at least a conceptually coherent argument that race matching would further the best interest of adopted children of color. It stands or falls on its empirical presumptions. Is it true that white adoptive parents are less likely to pass on racial coping skills? Even if it is true, how crucial are such coping skills? Are they so important as to override other considerations that militate in favor of the transracial adoptions (paramount among them the fact that many children would face significant delays in permanent placement while agencies wait for same race placements).

There is precious little rigorous empirical study of these issues.[52] Instead, the advocates of race matching have, by and large, relied on the narrative plausibility of their "coping skills" argument. It is plausible. But there are plausible counter-narratives. Suppose we concede, at least for the sake of argument, that white parents *generally* are less likely to possess and therefore less able to pass on racial coping skills. Still, it's quite plausible that the subset of white parents who choose to adopt non-white children are much more likely to possess or work to develop such skills than the general white population. In fact its possible that white adoptive parents who choose to adopt non-white children would be especially sensitive to their child's need for racially specific socialization, perhaps even more so than many minority parents who would take their parenting skills in this area for granted.

Given the absence of empirical evidence and given the availability of plausible counter hypotheses, the resiliency of the coping skills argument is surprising. Perhaps the conviction that whites cannot impart racial-coping skills is underwritten by a conception of racial difference that requires no evidence. Again, we find such a conception in the toxic intellectual mire of romantic nationalism. As historian Eugene Genovese observed, two years before the NABSW public opposition to transracial adoptions: "the insistence that only blacks can understand the black experience . . . is nothing new: it forms the latest version of the battle cry of every reactionary nationalism and has clear antecedents, for example, in the nineteenth-century German romantic movement."[53]

Such presumptions about racial difference serve the larger project of cultural preservation. Opposition to transracial adoption has always collapsed the interest of adopted children with an independent ideological commitment to the preservation of group cultural difference. The supporting language of the NABSW resolution, for example, cited "the necessity of self-determination from birth to death of all Black people," and condemned transracial adoption as "genocide," presumably because it threatened to promote the socialization of black children in the norms of "white culture." Opponents of transracial adoption insist that "*inherent* cultural differences . . . exist between Black and White populations"[54] and cite African and African-American cultural practices interchangeably as evidence of cultural distinctiveness,[55] betraying a racial and almost biological conception of cultural difference, something that one carries in the blood.

Likewise, many of the advocates of the ICWA argue that the policies serve the best interests of the adopted children because they ensure that the children are placed with parents equipped to foster an appropriate sense of identity and to impart the cultural sensibilities and values appropriate to the child's ancestry. Here the interests of child become confused with the interests of the "community" a convenient abstraction through which an ideology of group difference is disguised as an empirical observation. (On its face, this would be a good argument for our hypothetical Germanic Child Welfare Act as well: only if raised by the German *volk*, in the fatherland itself, under the shadow of the Reichstag, strains of Wagner inspiring a patriotic parade, can a Germanic child be aware of her cultural heritage.)

For example, a representative of the Native American Child Protection Council insisted that "the Indian home nurtures the traditions and the way of life for the Indian world. This environment would allow the Indian child to *remain* aware of his cultural heritage."[56] The use of the word "remain" here is telling. It's fair to say that infants are born quite innocent of social constructs such as "cultural heritage." If a child is aware of his cultural heritage, it has been *made* aware of it by someone—usually, although not always, the child's parents. The Indian child, like any other then would not, properly speaking, "remain" aware of "his" cultural heritage; rather he would be socialized to embrace a particular cultural heritage. The idea that a child is born with a "cultural heritage," and indeed born aware of it, is necessary to the culturally based contention that transracial adoption disserves the *child*, as opposed to the tribe or racial community. Ideally, adopted children are placed very early in life so that their adoptive parents are the only parents they ever know. It would seem to follow that the culture of their adoptive parents would be the only culture they would ever know. In most cases then, the adopted child should be as comfortable with the culture of its adoptive parents as the adoptive parents are. Unless one accepts the noxious tenets of romantic nationalism, the problem is not that the child will not "remain aware" of some part of "*its* cultural heritage" but that he will adopt, so to speak, a different cultural heritage than that of one of his biological parents (or in some cases people even more removed from him: in many of the contested adoption cases neither parent had a significant, ongoing relationship with an Indian tribe or tribal practices.) Here the interest of the child in effect becomes a proxy for the interests of adults in the community in question. It is not the *child* (whose relationship to a cultural tradition is contingent on its subsequent socialization), but rather adults who will suffer if the cultural traditions of the group are not passed on to him.

Echoing the romantic nationalist conception of culture biologically connected to a *volk*, opponents of transracial adoptions hypothesize that children raised outside their racial culture are especially vulnerable to personality disorders. As I mentioned in Chapter 1, every racial group (with the telling exception of whites) has a derogatory term for people who fail to exhibit their assigned racial culture: there are African-American "Oreos," Latino "Coconuts," Asian-American "Bananas" and Native-Americans (you guessed it) "Apples."[57] Children of color adopted in white homes are burdened with these bizarre titles, not only by mean kids at school but, remarkably, by adult advocates of race matching, practicing what Randall Kennedy aptly names "junk social science," who equate the Oreo/Coconut/Banana/Apple identity in children of color with a "confused racial identity" and a failure to grasp the role that racism will play in their lives.[58]

Despite unsubstantiated assertions that children who don't internalize the cultural practices and norms of their ascribed race are vulnerable to pathology, there is no reliable evidence to support the claim.[59] Of course, children of color who are unprepared to confront the evil of racism will suffer as a result (this is the "coping skills" argument), but there is no reason to assume that a realistic assessment of racism and racial "coping skills" are exclusively associated with stereotypical minority group cultural practices. The supposed mismatch between the child's ascribed racial identity and his cultural upbringing is not a problem for the child (unless other people make it his problem); rather it is a problem for those people who believe that culture must attach, and attach in a very specific way, to biological ancestry. (And of course, the very notion of such a "mismatch" depends on the presumption that there are cultural practices that naturally belong to racial identities, a presumption which at this point in the book, I hope looks somewhat worse for wear.)

Transracial adoptions may well complicate the nexus between race and culture. A proliferation of "mismatched" personalities would make less plausible the claim that cultural differences naturally accompany ascribed racial statuses. They would also make it harder to collapse atavistic racism (encountered by the entire snack basket of assimilated minorities—Oreos, Coconuts, Bananas and Apples—as much as by minorities with typical or stereotypical minority socialization) with cultural conflict (on which the snack-basket minorities may not find themselves allied with the cultural difference preservation agenda).

If opponents of transracial adoptions want to argue that this is a bad thing, let them be honest about why they think it is bad. It *would* be very bad for people who wish to keep racial identity and cultural difference tightly bound together. But this is not a desire that antiracists, much less child welfare policy, need support. As Randall Kennedy suggests in connection with the ICWA (the suggestion is just as valid in the context of trans-racial adoptions generally) "It would be one thing . . . to justify ICWA simply in terms of enlarging the jurisdiction of Indian tribes and encouraging pan-Indian solidarity (regardless of the consequences to affected children). It is another (and worse!) thing . . . to support ICWA largely in terms of serving the best interest of the children involved . . . [when] the statute . . . fails . . . to fulfill that aim."[60]

Race matching is not, or at least has not been shown to be, in the best interests of children and the real justification for the policy—cultural solidarity—is at best a controversial goal. Unfortunately, the ICWA is still good law and despite the passage of the Multi Ethnic Child Placement Act, race matching appears to continue in violation of the law: Bartholet reports that "Those in charge of enforcement and compliance, including lower level workers throughout the system, are for the most part believers in the tradition of race-matching . . . [After MEPA was passed] [i]n leading child welfare journals articles appeared with titles such as "Achieving Same-Race Placements for African-American Children," telling readers how to accomplish race matching despite MEPA."[61]

Copyrights-to-Difference: Culture as Property

Just as difference discourse justifies group claims of ownership over future generations, so too it justifies group monopolies on forms of art and expression. Here the right-to-difference metastasizes, from a claim that group members should *always* be free to engage in group-specific forms of expression, to a claim that *only* group members should *ever* be free to do so.

The Indian Arts and Crafts Acts (IACA) prohibits "counterfeit" Native-American goods, threatening time in jail and fines of up to 5 million dollars. The IACA is styled as an attempt to prohibit the unscrupulous from "palming off" mass-produced trinkets as authentic Indian handicrafts. In this respect it contains elements of conventional unfair competition and trademark law, which recognizes that "palming off" is unfair to consumers and legitimate producers: consumers don't get what they paid for and legitimate producers lose business and suffer tarnished reputations.

The palming-off rationale underlying conventional trademark protection and unfair competition laws, however, is a poor fit for the IACA. The IACA gives governmentally certified "Indians" as a group ownership of the designation "Indian." By contrast, trademark law seeks to protect discrete producers of goods who have used a distinctive brand name or symbol in commerce. It protects, say, Yves Saint Laurent, a French fashion house, from another manufacturer who would market their clothing with the name "Yves Saint Laurent." It does not protect French clothiers generally from anyone not of French ancestry who would market shirts with "French cuffs."

Because the IACA uses tribal membership or tribal certification as a criterion, it reifies a Native-American identity that was imposed by the federal government, in many cases over the fierce objection of Native-Americans. Historically, many Native-Americans, in acts of resistance, refused to be enrolled in tribes organized under the laws of the United States government. Today, many Native-Americans have chosen not to seek tribal certification. In their minds, their identity as Native-Americans arguably depends on their *independence* from formally recognized tribes. The IACA enforces the tribal scheme of the United States government by depriving these Native Americans of the use of name "Indian" and implying that they and the art that they create is inauthentic.

A year after the IACA was passed, San Francisco's American Indian Contemporary Arts Gallery cancelled a show by unenrolled Cherokee sculptor Jimmie Durham, widely considered one of the most talented living Indian artists. Durham insisted that he didn't need to prove his heritage to anyone, but the gallery's management, fearing the provisions of the IACA, disagreed. According to the curator of the gallery, "Since Jimmie didn't have the documentation, our board of trustees decided to cancel the show. . . . [T]o be on the safe side, the board decided not to present work that couldn't be documented."[62] Meanwhile the *Wall Street Journal* reported the plight of Bert Seabourn of Cherokee descent.

> His work hangs in the Vatican. Like many Cherokees in eastern Oklahoma . . . his forebears didn't register with the Dawes Commission at the

turn of the century. With family memories of the Trail of Tears still fresh, many weren't eager to sign the white man's roll. Now Mr. Seabourn can't call himself an Indian artist because his ancestors aren't on the list.[63]

Unsurprisingly many Native-American artists would rather forgo the "protection" the IACA offers; unfortunately for them, protective custody is not optional. One Native-American artist compared the IACA to "blacklisting of the McCarthy era, with its implied threat that you . . . may not be able to continue your work."[64] Another noted poignantly, "No one else has to prove anything. Black artists don't have to prove they're black. . . . [T]he government still feels we're possessions, that we're part of the National Park System, standing at the cabin door."[65]

In this chapter, I have argued that difference discourse produces group difference by generating stories and accounts of group difference and by providing social incentives for group members to conform to their assigned group-specific modes of behavior and self-presentation. I have insisted that rights-to-difference would be an exemplary manifestation of this process, at best a type of protective custody which would confine and restrict behavior, expression and identity to precisely the degree to which it protects them.

In fact, difference discourse confines and regulates *everyone*, not only members of the groups it stereotypes. The ideology and practice of racial difference not only hinders many black students from excelling in academic pursuits; it also discourages whites from playing jazz. The mythology of a distinctive woman's voice keeps women from becoming aggressive advocates and negotiators even as it also confines men to cool and distant relationships with their children. The idea of "gay culture" ironically reinforces gender stereotypes, associating male same sex eroticism with "feminine" interests such as fashion, homemaking and cuisine and simultaneously punishing and "explaining away" men who resist stereotypical masculinity.

Identity Consciousness: Less Is More

Blacks are indeed loosely bound together by a common cultural heritage; they are tightly bound together by a common set of grievances.[66]

My critique of difference discourse does not entail an outright rejection of identity consciousness. Law and policy must acknowledge the harm done by formal and informal status hierarchies and implement targeted and effective solutions. Further, it is both counterproductive and unrealistic to insist that the people mistreated because of the ideology of group difference not identify as members of groups in order to resist the group-based mistreatment.

But the critique does suggest that social identities be put on a diet: for purposes of legal recognition, it suggests limiting identity consciousness to the recognition of pervasive practices of group subordination and refraining from a questionable sociology of group cultural difference. The legal significance of this position is that civil rights should focus on eliminating status hierarchies, while generally leaving questions of cultural difference to the more fluid institutions of popular politics and the market.

Can we distinguish the two? I believe so. The following three subsections will make the following three points. One: we can endorse a fairly robust form of group consciousness that does not entail a romantic narrative of cultural difference. Two: we can distinguish between discrimination based on group culture and discrimination based on ascribed group status. And three: consistent with these distinctions, we can develop a coherent and effective anti-discrimination doctrine that avoids the pitfalls of difference discourse.

Group Consciousness without Cultural Romanticism

Let's take race as our example. At minimum, a defense of race consciousness entails the recognition that the historical belief in racial categories has produced socially and normatively meaningful social groups defined according to those categories. Racial categories, in this sense, created races by producing the conditions that make racial identity a salient feature of daily life.

Consistent with this idea of race consciousness, a host of nuances are possible. One could believe that racial identity reflects only a minimal solidarity based on a shared political interest in overcoming racial hierarchy. On the other end of the spectrum, one could believe that racial identity reflects an enduring, rich and pedigreed heritage of distinctive norms, modes of artistic creativity and expression, social tropes and ways of knowing, that are not only exclusive to members of the race in question but also are universally shared among them.

To clarify the distinction between these two positions, let's consider the bumper sticker slogan of strong race consciousness: "It's a black thing; you wouldn't understand." This may seem to be the ultimate expression of strong racial difference, a statement that insists that racial culture is so distinctive and so thoroughly structures our perceptions that certain beliefs and norms are simply beyond the comprehension of those outside the group. But the statement has two meanings, one consistent with a thick cultural understanding of racial difference as real and intrinsic and one consistent with a political understanding of racial identity as the effect of racial discourses.

Meaning number one   Suppose in an argument with a white friend about the not-guilty verdict in the O. J. Simpson murder trial, I insist that, given the history of racially motivated arrests and prosecutions in the United States, and especially the revelation of widespread racism in the Los Angeles Police Department, it was understandable and perhaps appropriate for a jury to greet the evidence against Simpson with suspicion. My white friend replies that the evidence was overwhelming, it's paranoid to imagine that the police would fabricate evidence and she can't imagine how any reasonable person could have voted to acquit. I, in frustration say "well, it's a black thing, *you* wouldn't understand." My statement here indicates the salience of race as matter of experiences and political solidarity: I empathize with the black jurors because I, like them, keep track of police racism and internalize the threat it presents as a personal threat, while my white friend doesn't pay attention when police racism is revealed and therefore underestimates it. My retort may be uncharitable and undiplomatic, but it is, I believe, more or less on the mark. Nothing in my quip suggests that my white friend is incapable of transcending her racial perspective and understanding the "black thing." But that doesn't make her present perspective (or mine) less raced.

Meaning number two   Suppose another friend and I are listening to John Coltrane's "My Favorite Things" and she remarks that she prefers the version by Julie Andrews. Quite naturally I am horrified and proceed to lecture her on the history of jazz improvisation and the high place that Coltrane generally and this song in particular hold in the pantheon of jazz masterpieces. She says it sounds like Coltrane just can't remember how the song goes and that he's often off-key: "How," she concludes, "can anyone listen to this noise?" I respond icily, "It's a black thing, *you* wouldn't understand." Here, despite my justifiable outrage at her substantive assertions, the retort is misplaced. It reflects a belief that the artistic achievements of blacks are only fully intelligible to other blacks, and our culture is mysterious and opaque to the outsider.

The statement "It's a black thing, you wouldn't understand" has at least two meanings; one focuses on the salience of racial categories; the other, on the existence of distinctive racial cultures. The assumptions animating the former meaning are necessary components of a practical commitment to antiracism. One need not believe that any objective differences separate the races in order to support race consciousness of this kind. Moreover, even if one believes that the races are distinguished by cultural differences, one needn't advance an inevitably oversimplified account of such distinctive racial cultures: we can acknowledge the salience of race in order to resist racial status without a substantive cultural account of group difference.

Culture Distinguished from Status

Similarly, opposition to discrimination based on status does not imply opposition to discrimination based on culture. There is no normative inconsistency in a position that staunchly rejects hierarchies of status while adopting a stance of diffidence, ambivalence or indifference as to culture.

Consider the following two examples.

Case 1 Suppose two social groups are identical in every respect except that one group has some striking physical feature—say, a star-shaped birthmark on the abdomen—and the other does not. Further suppose that the star-bellied group of individuals begin (for a host of socially and historically contingent reasons that need not concern us here) to believe that they are superior to those without the star-shaped birthmark. Further suppose that the star-endowed individuals, again by means that need not concern us, succeed in perpetuating the ideology of star-bellied superiority to such an extent that the entire society in which they live is organized around the principle of star-bellied superiority and privilege. Yet in every other respect, the two groups are indistinguishable. In such a scenario, we have status without cultural (indeed without any morally relevant) difference.

Case 2 Imagine two groups of German immigrants who settle in northern Wisconsin: one group from northern Germany and one from southern Germany. In many respects we would expect these two groups to exhibit cultural difference: some would recall with fondness the streets of Hamburg; others, the metropolis of Munich. Some would consider lederhosen a national costume; others would consider it foreign. One group would be largely Lutheran Protestants; the other Roman Catholics. One group would eat pickled herring, the other sauerbraten and spatzle. The two groups would speak with strikingly different accents—indeed they might speak what linguists would consider different dialects of the German tongue.

Let's also suppose that immigrants from northern Germany outnumber those from southern Germany and that the northerners control most of the resources in the region in which both groups reside. To the non-German, their cultural differences would be invisible; their identity and ethnic status would be defined in terms of national origin. Nevertheless, both groups retain their distinctive cultural differences, and, in overt and subtle ways, the northern Germans impose their ways on the less-powerful southern Germans (workplaces are organized around northern German norms of precision, formality and rule adherence as opposed to the more relaxed, almost Gallic tendencies familiar to southern Germans; northern German accents are a mark of status—the northern German dialect is favored while that of southern Germany is frowned upon; the canteens at many businesses serve northern German but not southern German specialties.) But, aside from the occasional comment about regional practices the two groups quickly come to think of each other as "fellow Germans" in a milieu populated by Anglos and Swedes; southern Germans who assimilate to northern German customs (now thought of as simply "German" customs) succeed as easily as northern Germans born with such customs. In this case our two groups of German-Americans would be, in terms of status and *identity*, just that: Germans and not northern Germans and southern Germans. But the cultural differences between the northern and southern German immigrants might, for several generations, remain as significant as those dividing Germans generally from the Dutch or the French.

It is reasonable to think of the status distinction between the star-bellied and plain-bellied Sneeches[67] in entirely different terms than the cultural distinction between the northern and southern Germans. While a just Sneech society might believe it necessary to pass legislation outlawing discrimination on the basis of plain-belliedness, it does not follow from that commitment that we would be compelled to prohibit discrimination on the basis of any of the cultural characteristics (let's put the potential issue of religion aside for purely doctrinal reasons) that distinguish immigrants from northern Germany from those from southern Germany.

Discrimination on the basis of star-belliedness is without normative justification and star-belliedness is a characteristic outside the control of the individual (or at least "natural" star-belliedness is: once Mr. McBean turns up with his "star-on machine", all bets are off): star-belliedness is both normatively irrelevant and immutable, moreover, in Sneech society the discrimination was historically pervasive. Star-belliedness is an ideal form of a status distinction.

Discrimination among cultural traits raises much more complicated issues. Unlike pure status differences, cultural differences often *are* normatively relevant; this fact is central to the moral position of those who would protect them with legal rights. But if they are, there may be good reasons to discriminate between various cultural traits. Some cultural traits may be "better suited" to certain tasks or institutions than others, some cultural traits may be less valuable in general than others and some cultural traits may be downright destructive of a society or enterprise. This seemingly harsh conclusion is unavoidable if we think that cultural traits matter.

There's more than the writings of Dr. Seuss to recommend my position (although he is quite a persuasive authority on ethical questions): the shameful and relatively recent history of institutionalized American racism is by and large a story of formal status hierarchy. There is the ongoing racism manifested in police shootings and beatings of innocents, racially segregated cities and metropolitan areas, the odd corporate executive who is bigoted and stupid enough to actually let slip an overt racial slur within earshot of a reporter or the effective range of a recording device (for which we can imagine scores of others smarter or luckier than to get caught with foot in mouth).

There can be little debate as to the fact of historical and contemporary racism. We can identify with precision a number of practices whose unambiguous purpose was to create and enforce a racial hierarchy, and we can identify with only slightly less confidence the contemporary manifestations and consequences of racist practices and racist ideologies. African-Americans were enslaved; after emancipation they were subject to peonage through neofeudal sharecropping arrangements that kept them tied to the land and to landowners just as surely as if they were formally enslaved (and often with even fewer material rewards). Jim Crow denied blacks basic human dignity while discriminatorily applied poll taxes and literacy tests transformed the formal extension of the franchise into a cruel joke. Nor was racism exclusive to the former confederacy. The Jim Crow of the deep south had his cousins throughout the nation (the grim joke about my hometown San Francisco is that its citizens were too refined to embrace Jim Crow; here it was *James* Crow.) Discriminatory practices on the part of employers and labor unions ensured that blacks occupied the least remunerative, least desirable and least secure forms of employment in the industrialized northern cities as they migrated to escape the cruelties of the post reconstruction South. Racism in the forms of overt discrimination and systematic violence forced blacks into segregated and overcrowded ghettos, different in kind from the ethnic slums occupied by white ethnic immigrants in both the comprehensiveness of their segregation and the impoverishment of their conditions.

Such systemic discrimination was not limited to African-Americans. Historian Herbert Ashbury described the racial climate of California in the mid-nineteenth century, as follows:

[s]ystematic and heartless persecution of the Spanish-American . . . remains one of the blackest pages of California history. The miners . . . harassed the poor "greaser" in every conceivable manner, stealing and destroying his goods and mining equipment, driving him from his claims and farms, raping his

women, beating his children, flogging or killing him on little or no provo-cation, and hanging him with elaborate pretensions to justice . . . the miners . . . lynched a young Mexican woman . . . when the mob seized her, there was a great roar of "Give her a fair trail and hang her!" which aptly expressed the sentiment that prevailed throughout California. . . . [A] man who tried to interfere with the lynching was dragged bodily from the platform and literally kicked out of the town. The miners arranged themselves in two lines and buffeted him as he ran the gantlet.[68]

The legal system did not work to cure the evil of racism; instead it served as a incubator and medium of transmission for the disease: "An early Alcalde (an official with the power to try civil and criminal offenses in mid 19th cen-tury San Francisco) knew little law but had a violent antipathy toward Mexi-cans and cigarette smokers. To admit being either or both was tantamount to conviction in his court."[69]

Similarly, anti-Asian racism has long been an ugly fixture of the American scene, aided rather than hindered by the law for a good deal of American history:

[T]he Chinese had survived innumerable campaigns of persecution even more systematic and cruel than those which had been directed against the Spanish-Americans. . . . Scores of laws were enacted for the sole purpose of hampering him in his efforts to earn an honest living. . . . [I]n 1863, the Legislature passed a law prohibiting the giving of testimony by Chinese in any legal action in which a white man was involved, and repealed a statute, passed in 1850 which had thus discriminated against only Negroes, mulat-toes and Indians. . . . [T]he state constitution as ratified by the voters of California in the spring of 1879 . . . forbade the employment of Chinese by all corporations, debarred them from the suffrage, annulled all con-tracts for coolie labor, directed the Legislature to provide for the punish-ment of any company which imported Chinese, and imposed severe restrictions on their residence in the state.[70]

Through a combination of legal victories, political compromises, public demonstrations, compelling speeches, vivid personal sacrifices and one-on-one conversations, American society has reached a fairly durable consensus that such practices are unacceptable. Part of that consensus is the conviction that these practices are joined by something that modern society should con-demn: invidious distinctions of status. Anti-discrimination law and the corre-sponding legal recognition of group identities are appropriate and necessary, not because American society is divided by cultural differences that corre-spond with social identities, but because certain social identities have been the instrument of gross and systematic oppression. Constitutional rights and anti-discrimination law have outlawed, if not eliminated, the most overt types of discrimination, but the legacy of past discrimination is an unwelcome bequest to present generations. Years of segregation and discrimination leave African-American families with less valuable real estate holdings, less accumulated capital and therefore significantly less wealth on average than white families to pass on to future generations. Residential and social segregation, established by state and local law, federal policy and private practices, and reinforced by custom, mutual aversion and distrust, leave blacks without the informal networks that secure many of the most prized jobs and promotions in an increasingly competitive employment market.

Discrimination persists today in part because anti-discrimination law is conceptually inadequate and practically underenforced. Studies continue to find that black applicants for loans, jobs and housing consistently fare poorly when compared to otherwise identical white applicants.[71] Racism, both subtle and overt, in national, state and local politics, the private employment market and interpersonal relations exerts a profound and constant tax on racial minorities.

This is a rough and (tragically) incomplete account of the common set of grievances that bind blacks to each other and to other targets of discriminatory practices. I could write a great deal more about this (and have elsewhere) but suffice it to say that inumerable people have written eloquent, detailed and rigorous accounts of the sorry history and present state of American racism.[72]

Cultural difference is neither a necessary nor a sufficient condition for the emergence of this system of status hierarchy. Many late-nineteenth-century immigrants to the United States from southern and eastern Europe differed as much from the American mainstream *culturally* as did black migrants from the American south in the early twentieth century. Indeed, culturally both groups shared many common characteristics and challenges: acculturation from a rural, agrarian lifestyle to an urban milieu and to the norms of an industrialized economy. As historians D. R. Fusfield and Timothy Bates note, "black migrants . . . exhibited the traits that peasants throughout the centuries have displayed when first exposed to urban existence."[73] What distinguished the successfully integrated and upwardly mobile European immigrant from the segregated and economically trapped black immigrant was the ideology and practices of race—not the "trait or characteristic" of culture.

Against "Racial Characteristics"

Rights-to-difference conceive of anti-discrimination law as an injunction to ignore those individual characteristics that are plausibly, if controversially, described as "elements" of a protected group identity. For instance Juan Perea argues that discrimination against "ethnic traits" should be prohibited as such[74]; similarly Barbara Flagg's proposes to prohibit discrimination against "racially correlated traits," whether or not such discrimination results in a racially segregated or exclusive workplace.[75]

This way of describing the anti-discrimination prohibition follows from the popular norm of "colorblindness." The mandate of "blindness" seamlessly morphs into a right-to-difference: if cultural differences are defined as characteristics of a protected identity, then it follows that employers who are required to act without regard to the identities should act without regard to the cultural differences as well. Ironically, the "blindness" mandate requires us to focus on and define the identity in question in order to make sure we ignore it.

In this formulation anti-discrimination law is a sort of endangered species act for social identities: if we're going to protect spotted owls we need a definition of a spotted owl; if we're going to protect race, we need a definition of race. Driven by the perceived need to define social identities for entry into the endangered species register, difference discourse advances a sophisticated array of positivistic accountings, statistical correlations, philosophical theories and logical syllogisms to establish the nature of the social identity in question. The reader will recall Kenji Yoshino's list of gay traits and practices, a list that includes gender atypical behavior, body building,[76] boxer briefs, goatees, golf, rugby, sexual promiscuity and affinity with sexual deviants such as polygamists and pedophiles. Janice Hale-Benson argues that Afro-American cultural traits include a "keen sense of justice," "altruism," and a tendency to focus on people (do whites *as a group* lack these qualities?) but also, we will recall, a tendency "to approximate space, numbers and time rather than stick to accuracy," and "a preference for inferential over deductive or inductive reasoning."[77] Barbara Flagg writes of traits that "intersect seamlessly with . . . self definition": a subjective, psychological theory of identity. Drucilla Cornell and William Bratton advance an elaborate philosophical argument in service of the connection between Spanish and the meaning of Latino/a identity. Juan Perea and Kenji Yoshino both admonish us to determine what is "fundamental" to certain social identities and suggest empirical methods for making this determination.

These arguments share a central premise: An inquiry into the nature of a social identity will yield, not only an objective answer, but also an inescapable legal conclusion. But, as the diversity of methodologies above suggest, there is no agreement as to what defines any given identity or even on how one would begin to answer the question. The definition of a social identity is not a factual matter but rather a conceptual one, akin to the debates in scholastic theology over the number of angels that can dance on the head of pin, or, more proximately, akin to the analyses of nineteenth-century legal formalists who sought to derive the correct resolution to a labor dispute from a correct understanding of the nature of property. As legal historian Morton Horowitz asserts:

> Late-nineteenth century courts were "conceptualistic" in the sense that they believed that one could derive particular legal rules and doctrines from general concepts such as property. . . . [T]hey . . . believed that one could logically deduce these rules from the nature of property itself. Property then was thought to have an essence or core of meaning, even if there could be legitimate argument about what was . . . at the periphery. Moreover, the orthodox idea of property was that it was a pre-political, Lockean natural right not created by law. . . . [I]t was thus possible to make statements such as "a labor boycott is inconsistent with the right to property." . . . What workers could and could not legitimately do was thought to follow logically from the very definition of their employer's property rights.[78]

This should sound familiar. A parallel conceptualism underlies the rights-to-difference approach to anti-discrimination law: what institutions can and cannot do is thought to follow logically from the definition of their employees' group identity. So, for instance, when Kenji Yoshino suggests that we ask "which are the fundamental aspects of any given identity," he echoes the nineteenth-century jurists who asked what the core elements of property were: he, like they, assumes the such a question is answerable as a matter of positive fact and that the answer will lead us to the correct resolution to a dispute between an employer and employee over the legitimacy of a workplace rule.

But to answer this ultimately conceptual question, Yoshino offers, not objective facts but rather a hypothetical plebiscite: he concludes by assuring us that "communities will be able to reach consensus"[79] on the fundamentals of identity. Here a question about the fact of identity has yielded not a factual answer, but instead a power play. What Yoshino offers us is not an account of the fundamental aspects of an identity, nor a method for determining what they are, but instead a proposal that "communities" (or their putative leaders) should decide what the fundamentals of the identity *should be* and enforce a set of policies that will encourage group members to conform to them.

Stripped of its metaphysical pretensions, the inquiry into the nature of identity that rights-to-difference advances is revealed as an assertion: We should think of our commitment to civil rights and anti-discrimination as an injunction to stabilize, intensify and canonize subgroup difference. These are not social facts that we bound to take account of; they are value judgments that we are free to reject. I think we should reject them.

Status and Immutability

It may seem that *any* type of anti-discrimination protection requires a definition of the protected identities. If we refuse to extend rights protection to traits and cultural attributes—if for instance, we insist on limiting anti-discrimination protection to "immutable characteristics" such as skin color and facial features as current anti-discrimination law does—doesn't this also impose a narrow definition of the identity and give *that* definition the imprimatur of the state? For instance, as Yoshino argues: "If a court holds that (1) race is protected, but (2) language is not protected, then the only logical inference is that (3) language is not race. What is pernicious about these cases is that race is being defined *sub silentio* by statements about what race is not, without any obligation to define precisely what race is."[80] *If* we accept his formulation of anti-discrimination law—"race is protected"—then Yoshino's logic is airtight. If the law requires either strict "blindness" to an identity or comprehensive protection for it, we're stuck with the unenviable task of legislating identity from the bench.

But suppose we could limit legal recognition of group difference to the effects of some form of caste or status consciousness. We might then say that the law prohibits, discrimination based not on racial characteristics, but rather discrimination arising from the belief in races or based on an ascribed racial status. This formulation recognizes that someone can suffer from racial discrimination without exhibiting any racially distinctive characteristics whatsoever: the black person who "passed" as white suffered the full brunt of Jim Crow racism as soon as she was found out. Conversly if someone is discriminated against based on arguably racial characteristics but not based on racial status (as might be the case if an employer forbade a number of unconventional hairstyles, including but not limited to cornrows), this type of discrimination is not actionable as racial discrimination. Indeed, we are entitled to dismiss the idea of "racial characteristics" generally as an element of a pernicious ideology yet still retain a robust anti-discrimination law because here anti-discrimination law does not prohibit discrimination on the basis of so-called racial characteristics, rather it prohibits discrimination on the basis of racial status.

On this account the focus on "racial characteristics" is an over inclusive attempt to identify a proxy for racial status. In order to capture racial discrimination that is not of the explicit, "no blacks allowed" variety (a majority of all cases because, with anti-discrimination laws on the books, to be explicit is to invite a lawsuit) the law must also prohibit discrimination on the basis of indicia or proxies for formal racial status, such as skin color. And in order to capture more subtle cases of discrimination, the law must also prohibit or at least scrutinize discrimination on other bases that might be used as proxies for racial status.

But then aren't racially correlated traits—racial cultures—all potentially proxies for racial status? Yes, and when we have reason to believe they are intentionally used as proxies, discrimination based on them should be illegal. But, because the essence of the employment relationship is that employees are expected to conform their behavior to the demands of their employers, it is reasonable to exclude discrimination based on volitional behavior as a general matter and limit the legal protection to characteristics that are not within the control of the potential employee (please notice that I say only that it is reasonable to do so; I do not say that it is necessary and indeed, I will propose a slightly different application of the immutability limitation when I return to the subject in chapter 4). Hence as one court puts it: "Save for religion, the discriminations on which the Act focuses its laser of prohibition are those that are . . . beyond the victim's power to alter."[81] Our critique of the notion of "racial characteristics" offers a circuitous defense of an established legal doctrine that holds that anti-discrimination law (at least as far as race and sex discrimination are concerned) prohibits only discrimination based on "immutable characteristics."

The "immutability requirement" has, unsurprisingly, been a consistent target of legal rights-to-difference scholarship. As Yoshino notes, "recent academic commentary seems univocal in calling for its retirement even as a factor" in anti-discrimination analysis.[82] Much of this criticism presumes that "immutable" is synonymous with "biologically determined" and on this basis attacks the immutability requires as naive, based on an anachronistic understanding of race as a biological classification.

However, legal anthropologist Donald Braman has demonstrated that courts that have adopted an immutability requirement, have not done so, by and large, based on a biological conception of racial identity. Instead,

> the Court's scrutiny is heightened when a person is unable to alter her status through meritorious action. The immutability of the status is the relevant issue, not the relationship between the status and a biological trait . . . the Court's repeated consideration of and reaction to the varied and contradictory depictions of racial differences demonstrate, not the triumph of a racial standard presumed to be natural, but a pragmatic approach to a

particularly American social formation. The Court, when directly presented with the question of classification and the basis for racial status, has consistently . . . treated and discussed the two as the products of social and political institutions."[83]

Here characteristics are immutable when they are outside the control of the individual for any reason. A characteristic may be immutable because it is biologically determined, but it may also be immutable because it is socially ascribed—the product of a social discourse that an individual is powerless to change—rather than because it is the product of biology or genes.

Characteristics that are immutable in this latter sense—we could call them "socially immutable" characteristics—are entangled with socially ascribed statuses, but not in any straightforward sense. It is often the case that a status is ascribed to people who exhibit the associated characteristics (dark-skinned people are understood to be "black"); but at times the *characteristics* are ascribed to people who have the associated status (black people are seen to have dark skin). A striking account of this latter, perhaps counter-intuitive phenomenon is the reaction of Gregory Howard Williams, former dean of Ohio State University College of Law, to the discovery, made during his childhood, that his father (and therefore he) was African-American: "I saw my father as I never had seen him before. The veil dropped from his face and features. Before my eyes he was transformed from a swarthy Italian to his true self—a high-yellow mulatto. My father was a Negro!"[84]

Of course the father's appearance didn't change; rather features that signaled Italian heritage before the revelation, marked him as black once he revealed that he was black. Once so marked, his status as black was immutable—Williams would from then on see his father's features as evidence of his "true self": "a Negro." But the immutability of his father's racial status is not, properly speaking, biologically determined: he was a swarthy Italian before the revelation; he became a "Negro" not because his biology changed but because Williams's perception changed. Williams did not know his father was black because he had black features; instead he knew his father's features were black features because his father—a black man—had them. Yet as soon as Williams knew his father was black, those features became "evidence" of his race.

This circularity is instructive. Although most racial minorities can't pass as white, something similar nevertheless may be true about racial identity generally. People have to learn to identify racial differences. We must be taught to look out for those telltale features that distinguish the races, whether they are facial features, skin color or cultural traits. Once these features are figured as racial characteristics, anyone who is seen to exhibit them may potentially acquire "their" racial status. If someone is identified as black, he may be discriminated against on that basis even if, objectively speaking, he does not exhibit any characteristics—mutable or immutable—that distinguish him from a Caucasian. Perhaps the most notable citation for this phenomenon is *Plessy v. Ferguson*,[85] the 1896 Supreme Court case that produced the notorious doctrine of "separate but equal" overruled by the Court in 1954 in *Brown v. Board of Education*. The plaintiff in the case, Homer Plessy—an individual who was formally "one-eighth" black but could easily have passed as white—objected to a state law that mandated racially segregated railway cars. The white-in-appearance Plessy was chosen as a plaintiff in a carefully planned test case because of what we might call his white racial characteristics. A central part of Plessy's litigation strategy was to emphasize the arbitrariness of the segregation law; it did not discriminate on the basis of characteristics—if it had, then Plessy, who exhibited none of the characteristics commonly associated with the black race, would have been allowed—indeed *required*—to ride in the white car of the train. Instead the law discriminated on the basis of a socially ascribed racial status. Plessy had been assigned the status black by virtue of his distant black ancestors and that was that. Once a status is ascribed, it is "immutable" in the pragmatic sense that the individual cannot readily alter it. This is the sense in which immutability is relevant to anti-discrimination law.

The mutability *of a racial characteristic* then, is strictly speaking, irrelevant, but not because—as difference discourse would have it—anti-discrimination law should prohibit discrimination based on mutable as well as immutable racial characteristics, but rather because racial characteristics *generally* are irrelevant. And it is quite right to say that anti-discrimination law prohibits discrimination on the basis of "immutable characteristics." But it does not follow that the immutable characteristics in question are characteristics *of race*; instead they are *any* characteristics of potential plaintiffs that may be proxies for racial status.

This cuts against some common locutions: that the law prohibits discrimination against racial groups; that it prohibits discrimination on the basis of racial characteristics; that it protects racial minorities; worst of all that it "protects race." On my formulation it does none of these. Indeed it could not do these things because to do them it would first require a definition of a racial group, racial characteristics and/or race—none of which courts have readily to hand. Instead, law prohibits discrimination on the basis of race—something that it can do without knowing what race is and indeed without accepting that race is something that is knowable. To prohibit discrimination on the basis of race, we need only know that there is a set of ideas about race that many people accept and decide to prohibit them from acting on the basis of these ideas.

Appiah makes this point when he notes that one need not believe in races to believe in and to oppose racism: "[U]nderstanding how people think about race remains important . . . even though there aren't any races. To use an analogy . . . we may need to understand talk of 'witchcraft' to understand how people . . . act in a culture that has a concept of witchcraft, whether or not we think there are, in fact, witches."[86] Suppose in such a culture, many people believe that they can spot a witch by certain telltale signs—warts on the nose, or, conversely, exceptional beauty and a "bewitching" personality, red hair, pointy black hats, casting of spells and possession of cauldrons of "witches brew." To prohibit effectively discrimination on the basis of witchcraft or status as a witch we would need to prohibit not only explicit discrimination but also discrimination on the basis of those telltale signs that people could not easily change—hair color and facial features. We could do this without accepting for a moment that there is any such thing as a witch or witchcraft. Nor would we need to prevent employers from barring pointy black hats, ritualistic incantations or large bubbling cauldrons containing eye-of-newt from the workplace.

Below I will explore the implications of this account of anti-discrimination law in three contexts in which one might question its application: sexual orientation, sex and religion.

SEXUALITY

Sexuality has been one of the areas in which difference advocates have made their most convincing arguments against the immutability doctrine. Homophobic legislation has been justified by reference to the immutability requirement: for instance, consenting adults who engaged in homosexual sodomy faced prosecution because of their mutable *conduct* and not their *status*. The anti-immutability position concludes that because we cannot so easily separate conduct from status, "a commitment against status discrimination might require us to prohibit discrimination against an act constitutive of that status."[87]

But in the two most prominent contexts—antisodomy laws and the military's "Don't Ask, Don't Tell" policy—the idea that volitional acts could be "constitutive" of an ascribed status have underwritten not anti-discrimination protection, but antigay policy. These antigay policies rely not on an application of the status/conduct distinction, but rather on a status/conduct dialectic that, like difference discourse, defines acts as constitutive of status, or as law professor Janet Halley puts it, "ascrib[es] status on the basis of conduct and conduct on the basis of status."[88]

Halley makes the point dramatically in her detailed analysis of the military's "Don't Ask, Don't Tell" regulations regarding homosexuality.[89] Although

"Don't Ask, Don't Tell" may at first glance appear to be a perfect example of a policy that punishes the assertion of difference (don't tell), in fact the policy worked its most oppressive consequences through the interrogation and the production of identities. Halley demonstrates that in practice the policy operated through a little-discussed (but formally codified) regulation that declared that "conduct manifesting a propensity" to engage in homosexual acts was a legitimate reason to suspect or infer a violation of the "Don't Tell" prohibition. The idea underlying the "conduct manifesting a propensity" rule seems to be that such conduct could be a covert signal of homosexuality, a coded message legible only to others in a homosexual underground. To perhaps abuse the double entendre, the regulations suggested that certain conduct was "telling." The regulation offered guidelines based on questionable stereotypes and popular fantasies about homosexuals for identifying conduct that manifested a propensity. Enlisted men and women who had not, and presumably had no interest in, "telling" of their sexual proclivities were then interrogated (colloquially one might say "asked") on the basis of suspicions that arose from their homosexually telling conduct. What is crucial for our purposes is that many of the soldiers who suffered under "Don't Ask, Don't Tell" suffered not because their identities were repressed—not because they "told" and were punished or because they wanted to tell but couldn't—but because their identities were *produced* by the "conduct manifesting a propensity" regulation. The regulations did their dirty work, not by refusing to recognize homosexual identity but by insisting on it, and by ascribing it to individuals who preferred and in some cases pleaded for privacy and anonymity.

Is there a difference between "conduct manifesting a propensity" and the cultural traits and behavior for which rights-to-difference would seek legal recognition? Of course, rights-to-difference would attempt to "protect" rather than punish the conduct, but they share the equation of conduct and intrinsic identity (propensity) with the military's antigay policy. This legal "protection," like the "conduct manifesting a propensity" rule in Don't Ask, Don't Tell, would serve to validate the presupposed link between the status and stereotypes that underlies homophobia.

A similar dialectic is at work in antisodomy statutes. For instance, in *Bowers v. Hardwick*, a case that infamously upheld an antisodomy law, using openly homophobic arguments, the Court considered a statute that on its face applied to heterosexual and homosexual couples alike—a statute that regulated *conduct*—but treated the case as one about *homosexual* sodomy alone, turning it into a case about status. Indeed, practically speaking, the antigay result in *Bowers* depended on producing a distinction between the homosexual litigant and a heterosexual couple who also claimed to be victims of the sodomy statute but whom the Court dismissed from the case for lack of standing. Only by excluding consideration of the heterosexual couple could the *Bowers* Court successfully depict the case as one about the deviant sexuality of a subgroup rather than as one about the autonomy of adults to engage in consensual sex free of state surveillance and intrusion. *Bowers* was famously *not* a case about status neutral conduct—instead the case was from beginning to end an attack on (I should say a production of) homosexual *status*.

The logic of rights-to-difference insists that, if homosexual status and the practice of sodomy are correlated, then in order to protect homosexuals from discrimination, we need to protect the practice of sodomy *as their practice*. This position validates a powerful element of antigay animus: the presumption that we can infer a *status* from conduct and vice versa. Antigay animus needs this presumption to drive its crude circular "logic": homosexuals are deviant people because they engage in a "deviant" act: sodomy. And sodomy is deviant because it is practiced (Only? Predominantly?) by deviants: homosexuals.

This presumption is so powerful that most people use the term "sodomy" as if it were synonymous with "homosexual sex." It isn't and never was: not in its biblical articulation (wherein generic wickedness and perhaps rape appear to have been the characteristic offenses of the ill-fated residents of Sodom and Gommorah) and not in the statutes that make sodomy illegal. The Georgia statute at issue in *Bowers* on its face applied to heterosexual sex and provided that "A person commits the offense of sodomy when he performs or submits to any sexual act involving the sex organs of one person and the mouth or anus of another,"[90] while the Texas statute invalidated seventeen years later in *Lawrence v. Texas*, although it criminalized only "deviate sexual intercourse between people of the same sex," defines "deviate sexual intercourse" as "any contact between any part of the genitals of one person and mouth or anus of another person or . . . the penetration of the genitals or the anus of another person with an object."[91]

So let's get this straight (oops!): the offending conduct includes, not just anal sex but also oral sex ("getting to third base" in the lingo of American high school students) and the use of most sex toys. I must confess that, in the course of what has been for the most part a fairly conventional heterosexual sex life, I have regularly committed sodomy as defined by the Georgia statute, and regularly enjoyed "deviate sexual intercourse" as defined by the Texas statute (though never, to the best of my recollection, in the states of Georgia or Texas).

As an actively practicing heterosexual sodomite, I feel duty-bound to refute the presumption that sodomy is the exclusive domain of homosexuals. Because it is not, it can't be the case that sodomy is constitutive of homosexual identity. Of course, the homosexual difference agenda could struggle to hang onto the idea of identity-constitutive conduct by defining it as "homosexual sodomy" but this is a transparent tautology: the constitutive conduct could just as easily be "homosexual hand-holding," "homosexual love poetry" or "homosexual bank robbery" at this point since the qualifier "homosexual" makes any conduct *by definition* exclusive to homosexuals. Sure, a law that criminalizes homosexual sodomy, like the Texas law invalidated in *Lawrence*, discriminates against a class of people: homosexual *sodomites*, just as a law that criminalizes sodomy generally, like the Georgia law upheld in *Bowers*, discriminates against the class of sodomites generally. But, as Justice Scalia points out in his angry dissent to *Lawrence*, "the same could be said of any law. A law against public nudity targets 'the conduct that is closely correlated with being a nudist' and hence . . . is directed toward nudists as a class.' "[92]

None of this is to say we cannot or should not prohibit discrimination on the basis of sexual orientation; it is only to say that such a prohibition must not be confused with the protection of traits or behavior. The dynamics of anti-homosexual animus provide a prime example of why the criterion of social immutability is appropriate to anti-discrimination law. Antigay legislation makes homosexual status socially immutable by ascribing "deviant" conduct to individuals based on their deviant status while simultaneously defining the conduct as deviant because of its presumed association with deviant individuals. Once entangled in this structure, the status of homosexual is immutable: it doesn't matter whether one has engaged in sodomy or any "homosexual act" or not because homosexuality is not defined by homosexual conduct, rather it is defined by a metaphysical *propensity* to engage in such conduct. As Halley points out in reference to the military's "Don't Ask, Don't Tell" policy, almost anything can "manifest a propensity" to engage in sodomy or homosexual acts: stereotypically gay traits, but also the total absence of such traits (what's he trying to hide?); effeminate behavior for a man (femme), but also hypermasculine behavior (butch) or a bland, preppy asexuality (log cabin republican). Civil rights law should prohibit this tautological ascription and it can do so consistent with the immutability criterion. In fact the idea of discrimination on the basis of a socially immutable status offers a more illuminating description of this dynamic than does the idea of discrimination against group-correlated traits. As Halley notes, this structure is not well described as discrimination *against a group* because "no one belongs in any extrinsic way to an advantaged or disadvantaged group; heterosexuality, not the group "heterosexuals," is the chief beneficiary."[93]

Of course, such a formulation of anti-discrimination law would leave the state free to criminalize sodomy. This is as it should be because a convincing argument against anti-sodomy laws must begin with a convincing defense of *sodomy*. Those of us who think antisodomy laws are wrong think so because we think sodomy harms no one and should concern no one other than those engaged in it. Because we approve of, are indifferent to or at least don't strongly disapprove of the practice of sodomy, we believe that people who engage in the practice should not be mistreated because of it. It may well be that homosexuals are by and large more likely to engage in sodomy than the rest of the population (much to the chagrin of many *hetero*sexuals). But we would oppose antisodomy laws even if the practice were not statistically correlated with any social group.

Sodomy got its day in court and won on its own terms when *Bowers* suffered its overdue demise seventeen years later in *Lawrence v. Texas*. Notably, *Lawrence* did not invalidate Texas's anti-sodomy statute as illicit discrimination against homosexuals, instead it invalidated it as an unconstitutional intrusion on sexual privacy, following earlier decisions that invalidated state laws that restricted the distribution of contraceptives. *Lawrence* demonstrates that reversing *Bowers* did not require a rejection of the immutability criterion and legal recognition of homosexual difference; instead it required recognition of a universally applicable privacy right that protects consensual sexual activity between adults from state regulation; as the Court insisted "[antisodomy statutes] seek to control a personal relationship that, whether or not entitled to formal recognition in the law, is within the liberty of person to choose without being punished."[94]

Conversely, even if we were certain that sodomy was inextricably bound to homosexuality, if we thought it was, in Justice Scalia's terms, "the conduct that defines the class,"[95] a general commitment to eliminate status-based subordination would not relieve us of the need to evaluate the practice of sodomy independently. A fundamentalist Christian who believes sodomy is a sin against God and nature and who also happens to be a political liberal (meaning she believes, among other things, that government must refrain from disparate treatment of individuals on the basis of status distinctions) would surely not be persuaded to support the repeal of antisodomy laws if we could convince her that sodomy was inextricably tied to homosexuality. Instead her convictions would lead her to condemn homosexuals as children of the devil or insist that they resist their sinful urges. ("We all have our crosses to bear; think of the temptations of Christ.") Her liberal-Christian motto would be "love the sinner; hate the sin" (or, rights for the sinner but to jail for the sin.)

It's somewhat puzzling that anyone would think otherwise until one considers the influence of constitutional doctrine—specifically the *Bowers* decision, which upheld a state law criminalizing sodomy against a privacy-based, substantive due-process challenge. Perhaps the reaction of gay rights activists to *Bowers* is parallel to the reaction of affirmative action proponents to *Bakke*: in both cases the activists eventually accepted a ill-considered and poorly reasoned opinion and tried to work with or around it—post-*Bakke*, by stuffing all of our eggs in the diversity cornucopia; post-*Bowers*, by developing a circuitous identity politics end run around the opinion's decisive validation of antisodomy laws—when the best and most direct path to our goal was to reject and seek to overturn the offending precedent.

The privacy rationale adopted in *Lawrence* has at least three advantages over a right-to-difference based protection of sodomy. One: it addresses what ultimately must be addressed, the *practice* of sodomy, and defends it as worthy of extraordinary legal protection on its own merits. Two: it emphasizes the universal concerns of the conflict. The idea that sodomy is "deviant" can only survive in a vacuum of knowledge about the pervasiveness of the practice. Defining sodomy as constitutive of homosexuality creates this vacuum by suggesting that only or primarily homosexuals engage in sodomy. This is almost certainly not true: it may be that most or all homosexuals are also sodomites but from this it does not follow that most or all sodomites are homosexual. And sodomy aside, the need for privacy in sexual relations is something almost everyone understands: we all do things in bed (or elsewhere) that we'd rather not put to a vote. Finally, the privacy rationale doesn't reify the status of homosexual by defining it in terms of deviant sexual conduct (precisely the equation that the homophobe urges).

Far from neglecting the problem of antigay animus, a law prohibiting discrimination based on socially immutable status (status that is socially ascribed rather than based on traits or "propensities" intrinsic to a person), combined with the right to sexual privacy, which is articulated in *Lawrence*, would provide a better defense against antigay animus than a right-to-difference, which would reify a formal status and formalize sexual conduct. By sharply distinguishing between status and conduct we short-circuit the logic that stigmatizes both: homosexuals are no longer plausibly condemned as deviant because of their suspected intrinsic propensities and sodomy is no longer plausibly described as deviant because of its association with a deviant subgroup. Instead individuals are more likely to be evaluated based on their actual conduct and not their ascribed propensities, and that conduct is more likely to be apprehended without prejudice. By putting social identities on a diet, we also starve social animus of the ideological resources it requires.

Sex/Gender

Sex/gender is another social classification that may seem to make the immutability principle unworkable. Like race, sex is a legally prohibited basis of discrimination. Courts regularly make analogies between race and sex discrimination, applying doctrine developed in one context to the other: for instance, sex harassment doctrine was developed by analogy to an established legal prohibition of racial harassment.

Feminist theory echoes many of the themes of group difference I discuss: most famously, psychologist Carol Gilligan in *In a Different Voice* proposes that women communicate in a distinctively gendered "feminine voice" that male-dominated institutions unjustly dismiss or undervalue. Later "difference feminists" expanded on Gilligan's work, developing a theory of distinctively feminine virtues (nurturing, emotional sensitivity, relationship orientation). Some theorists suggested that these distinctively feminine characteristics were the natural predispositions of female caregivers. Although as a nominal descriptive claim (in fairness to Gilligan, this is the only type of claim she made in her famous study) the different voice theory is almost certainly accurate, the causal and normative claims are more questionable. Other feminists pointed out that a gendered voice is as likely a troubling reaction to gender oppression as it is a natural outgrowth of biological sex difference or natural sex roles: "I'll know what my voice sounds like when your foot is off my throat."

The sex/gender problematic has no obvious parallel in race or sexuality. A facile parallel is tempting: Sex and race are biological substrates that determine gender and racial culture respectively. But this strikes me as misleading. First of all it is not obvious that sex and gender are well understood in terms of a biological substrate and a social facade; our understanding of sex difference is profoundly shaped by gender ideology so it may be as accurate to suggest that gender ideology determines sex difference. Moreover, the social practices we might identify as a racial culture are much less well developed than the practices of gender. Sex and gender are mutually implicated—each seems to refer to the other—in a way that race and culture are not: it is at least unconventional to think of gender without reference to sex, whereas it is commonplace to think of culture without reference to race. To say this is not to advance any particular account of the relationship between sex and gender, rather it is to suggest that, whatever the relationship between sex and gender, it is not sufficiently analogous to the relationship between race and culture to serve as a steady companion in my discussion. In fact, one might say that a concern that underlies this book is that racial cultures, aided and abetted by difference discourse, might become as entrenched and seemingly natural as the practices of gender are today.

Still, I believe my analysis is at least suggestive in the context of sex/gender. One example, discussed earlier in the book, is *Chambers v. Omaha Girls Club*, wherein a black woman is fired when she becomes pregnant out of wedlock. Her race discrimination claim—based on an account of black culture—was properly rejected by the courts. But one might argue that Chambers should have prevailed on a theory of sex discrimination. In fact, the federal Pregnancy Discrimination Act (PDA) defines discrimination on the basis of pregnancy as a form of sex discrimination.

Is pregnancy an immutable characteristic? We can begin by noting that pregnancy, similar to many attributes of culture, straddles the line between status and conduct. I trust a digression into the activities of birds and bees is unnecessary: pregnancy is the direct result of conduct. All women do not become pregnant, there are numerous ways to avoid the condition and a constitutionally protected right to change it should it develop. The mainstream of American public opinion firmly supports liberal availability of birth control and finds little or nothing objectionable about its use. But once a pregnancy occurs, everything changes. The psychological costs and moral implications of terminating a viable pregnancy are profound; the suggestion that abortion is a simple "option" that one could be expected to choose as a condition of employment would strike almost everyone as callous and many as monstrous.

Is pregnancy a characteristic of female sex? Of course it is true that only women become pregnant. But although all pregnant people are women, all women are not pregnant; nor do all women have the capacity or the desire to become pregnant. Pregnancy discrimination may reflect an underlying bias against women or an insensitivity toward women that is difficult to distinguish from sex bias as a practical matter. But discrimination against pregnancy is not necessarily a proxy for sex discrimination: it is possible that an employer who is happy to hire women would object, for nonsexist reasons, to hiring pregnant women (the defendant in the *Chambers* case, an organization that was devoted to, among other things, decreasing the incidence of out-of-wedlock pregnancy among its young and impressionable clients, was such an employer).

So is discrimination on the basis of pregnancy not discrimination on the basis of sex? This was the position of the Supreme Court (much criticized by "difference feminists") in two opinions that spurred Congress to pass the PDA. In *Geduldig v. Aiello* and *General Electric v. Gilbert* the Court held that otherwise comprehensive employee disability insurance plans that excluded pregnancy from coverage did not discriminate on the basis of sex for purposes of the Equal Protection Clause and Title VII.

A decision to exclude pregnancy from disability insurance coverage *may* reflect an underlying insensitivity or even animus toward working women. If a plaintiff can demonstrate the underlying animus, circumstantially or directly, a sex discrimination action should lie. But the statistical correlation between sex and pregnancy should be relevant only as evidence of bias. If an employer excluded several types of disabilities—whether pregnancy or some others—exclusively or most often experienced by women, but included similarly costly conditions suffered disproportionately by men, one might properly infer the underlying animus. But in *Gilbert* the Court found that the expected value of the insurance coverage was greater for women than for men even given the pregnancy exclusion; while not conclusive evidence this is at least suggestive that the exclusion of pregnancy was not sex discrimination in the conventional sense of the term.

Congress responded to the *Gilbert* and *Geduldig* decisions with the aptly named Pregnancy Discrimination Act. In one sense the title of the act suggests precisely the type of conduct specific analysis I have argued for. Although the act defines discrimination on the basis of pregnancy as sex discrimination I would insist that a substantive commitment to pregnancy is an indispensable part of the act. A legal requirement that an employer cover pregnancy in an insurance policy must reflect more than a commitment to avoid sex discrimination; it must also reflect a desire to promote or at least an extraordinary solicitude for pregnancy and procreation. If society were indifferent to pregnancy—if we thought of procreation as a leisure pastime akin to skydiving or rock climbing—then the decision of an employer to exclude it from insurance coverage would be as unremarkable as a decision to exclude any type of coverage that would substantially raise insurance premiums if included.

Similarly, if for instance, Congress believed that we suffered from a crisis of overpopulation it would be quite consistent with antisexist commitments for Congress to encourage employers to provide *disincentives* for pregnancy, for instance encouraging employers to exclude pregnancy from health insurance coverage after a couple's first child (this is not to say that it would be good policy, only that it would not be sex discrimination.)

It is telling that the act covers pregnancy-related benefits but explicitly declines to cover abortion-related benefits, reflecting a predictable substantive preference for the decision to carry a child to term over the decision to abort a pregnancy. The decision to cover pregnancy but not abortion reflects a substantive commitment that is distinct from that underlying sex discrimination law: Congress determined that *pregnancy* and procreation were so important as to merit extraordinary protection from possible disadvantageous outcomes in the market and collective bargaining.

To be clear: I think we should have a policy that prohibits discrimination on the basis of pregnancy in most circumstances. There are very good reasons for Congress's substantive solicitude toward pregnancy. For many people, giving birth to and raising children is one of the most important and rewarding experiences life has to offer. And needless to say the future of any civilization quite literally depends on it.

Conflating pregnancy discrimination with sex discrimination however is not only conceptually flawed; as an ideological matter it reinforces sexism. It can't be that pregnancy—a condition indispensable to the propagation of the human species—is attributable to only women simply because they get stuck with the heavy lifting. The Pregnancy Discrimination Act does not protect women as a group; it does not even protect the reproductive choices of women (it does nothing for women who choose to terminate a pregnancy). Instead, it protects *the practice of pregnancy* and indirectly serves to promote it. This is a legitimate policy objective, but we should be clear about who and what benefits. The class of people who benefit from the Pregnancy Discrimination Act is not "women" but rather anyone who wants a woman or women generally to be able to both work and get pregnant. This category of beneficiaries includes a great many men who hope both to enjoy biological offspring and to share in their female partner's incomes. A cynic might suggest that the decision to define the Pregnancy Discrimination Act—a policy which in fact and by design benefits *men* as well as women—as protection *for women* serves a devious ideological function: it wrongly suggests that the costs of pregnancy are costs associated with "women" rather than costs associated with, alternatively, sexual intercourse, antiabortion moralism or the promotion of families.

RELIGION

Many arguments in favor of applying anti-discrimination protection to volitional behavior proceed by way of analogy to religion. For instance, philosopher David A. J. Richards argues that religious freedom provides a model for homosexual rights as rights of individual conscience,[96] law professor Juan Perea argues for legal protection of "ethnic traits" by comparing them to religious practices and law professor Neil Gotanda argues:

> The Free Exercise and Establishment Clause decisions [which concern religion] provide a model for constitutional adjudication in the area of race. . . . Culture-race, with its wide range of social and cultural references, makes possible a form of free exercise of the positive aspects of race, recognizing Black and white cultures. . . . Also protected will be the culture, community, and consciousness of American racial minorities.[97]

But religion, unlike race and sexuality, is not primarily an ascribed identity; rather, it is a chosen affiliation. Whereas race and sexuality correspond only ambiguously with distinctive beliefs, practices, mores and customs, and, in any event, have ample social meaning without such a correspondence, religion is nothing other than distinctive beliefs, practices, mores and customs.

Moreover, while the content of a racial culture will always be subject to a debate for which there can be no legitimately authoritative referee, religions are generally formally organized, based on sacred and canonical texts and entail strictly defined rituals and agreed upon articles of faith. Although religions are split by inter-denominational divisions and doctrinal disputes, there is still a relatively consistent core set of beliefs and practices that we can identify as characteristic—indeed defining—of the world's major religions and indeed most denominations and sects. Christians may disagree about the literal truth of the Immaculate Conception, the transubstantiation of the sacraments or the fitness of women or homosexuals for the clergy. They do not disagree that Christ is the Son of God: those who do, whatever else they may believe, are, by definition, not Christians. Protestants may disagree about the doctrine of pre-destination to salvation or the literal truth of the miracle of loaves and fish; but they are united in protest against the authority of the Roman Catholic pope and the worship of icons: those who are not so united are not Protestants.

Because religions are literally defined by belief and custom, it follows necessarily that any legal protection for religious liberty must include protection for the practices associated with religion. It would be nonsensical to decree, for instance, that no one may discriminate in hiring or promotion on the basis of religion, but to allow employers to make a recitation of the apostle's creed or a renunciation of the authority of the pope a condition of employment. We could of course decide that religion doesn't merit legal protection. But, having decided otherwise, there is no way to avoid protecting beliefs, practices and customs because these, in sum, *are* religion.

The complexities entailed by legal protection for practices and beliefs have necessitated doctrine that would be questionable if applied to race. Most obviously, while the Constitution provides for the free exercise of religion—a provision that multiculturalists would like to extend or analogize to racial cultures—it also provides that the state may not "establish" religion or become entangled in it. Historically, the Establishment Clause has been interpreted quite robustly, to prohibit many references to religion in state institutions; at one time it prohibited even student organized religious groups from using public school facilities.

In the context of private employment, employers have greater leeway to discriminate on the basis of religion than the proponents of a culture-religion analogy may believe; in fact in many respects, more so than in the context of race. Most obviously, religious organizations may discriminate on the basis of religion; by contrast there are, thankfully, no "racial organizations" with parallel

exemptions. Because of the reasonable concern that employees may mix the sacred and the profane, offering religious justifications for what are in fact secular
desires (for example, exemptions from union dues or from weekend or evening
shifts) employers and unions need accommodate religious practices only if the
burden to the business or union is *de minimis*.[98] And many courts have refused
to require accommodation when the sincerity of the employee's beliefs are in
question—in practice this can require *courts* to determine what a given religion
requires of its adherents, raising legitimate concerns about the entanglement of
the courts in the practice of religion.[99]

Religious freedom under the First Amendment of the Constitution and
under anti-discrimination statutes is characterized by a struggle over how to
protect religious liberty without getting "entangled" in the affairs of religion.
The legal doctrine is notoriously vexed. For instance, because religious liberty
should not depend on the popularity of the religion, the form the belief takes, or
its content, the courts insist that a religious belief or practice need not be widely
shared or confirmed by an organized church or clerical authority in order to be
protected. But, understandably, courts are far more comfortable when they can
rely on established and uncontroversial religious doctrine, rather than having to
wade into the mire of religious interpretation themselves to determine whether
a practice is or is not religious in nature. Not surprisingly then, in practice, formally organized religion defined by canons, sacred texts and established clergy
has become the paradigm with the consequence that the further away from the
paradigm a belief system lies, the more likely it is to be deemed a personal philosophy or code of conscience (hence legally unprotected) rather than a religion.
As Yoshino asserts, "to the extent religions do not fit into mainstream conceptions of religion, they are likely to remain unprotected."[100]

Perhaps group cultures could, over time, develop the institutional appara-
tuses, authoritative leadership and formal content of organized religion. But
they do not have it now. The various proposals to treat culture like religion for
legal purposes could be understood as in effect proposals to use the law to
make at least certain group cultures more like religion: to make them more
formal, more canonical and more *sacred*—outside the domain of ordinary
conversation and debate. Given this reading, the proposals do not misunderstand the nature of legal treatment of religion or attempt to force the square
peg of culture into the smooth round hole of religious accommodation;
rather, they seek to initiate a profound change, not only in the legal treatment
of certain sub group affiliations, but in the nature of those affiliations.

This proposal is neither incoherent nor necessarily quixotic. But it is a
very bad idea. The possibility that races and other ascriptive social identities
might become like religions—formally and hierarchically organized, defined

by canonical texts and authoritative leaders, characterized by commitments that sound in a register audible only to the converted and demanding and fostering loyalty that is as fierce as it is blind—is perhaps the greatest threat that difference discourse poses.

Intimacy and Identity

"Priest quits, doesn't think Jesus Son of God" reads a headline on CNN's web site. Yes, I suppose *that is* a problem. Few would suggest that a church should not expel or discipline members who reject established religious doctrine and practice. An important reason that even extreme religious doctrine and practice is socially acceptable is that anyone, even a priest, *can quit*. The availability of exit justifies a thick, substantive conception of religion: if you don't love it, you can always leave it.

Ascriptive identities are different because you can't leave or at the very least exit is difficult and uncertain. As Appiah writes: "To ignore one's race and one's gender in thinking about the ethical project of composing a life for one self requires, in many minds, a kind of ignoring of social reality which amounts to attempting to fool oneself . . . a certain inauthenticity."[101]

To the extent an ascriptive identity is thought to entail a worldview, a set of social norms and practices, tastes and habits—to the extent it is thought to entail a Culture—the charge of inauthenticity extends, not only to those who ignore their identity, but also to those who, for whatever reason, fail to exhibit the traits and embrace the norms of the culture. The derisive epithets for people of color who fail to exhibit the expected cultural traits—Oreo, Banana, Coconut, Apple meaning, respectively, (racially) black, yellow, brown or red on the outside but (culturally) white on the inside—figure racial identity as a superficial gloss on an underlying white self, but the implication is of course exactly the opposite: culturally assimilated minorities are covering or denying their authentic selves. Their pathetic apologies—they grew up in the suburbs, they went to predominantly white schools, most of their friends were white, they were adopted and raised by white parents, their parents were divorced and the custodial parent married a white person when they were three years old—are all seen as the flimsiest of alibis. Who do they think they're fooling? We can all *see* what they really are!

By contrast, if our erstwhile priest was born into a Catholic family but, after deciding that Christ was not the Son of God, decided to discard all his rosaries, stop attending mass, refuse the sacrament, cease praying and reciting catechism and renounce the authority of the pope, he would not be accused of "denying" his Catholicism or trying to "act secular." He would no longer *be* Catholic: he would have left the Church. Race and other *ascriptive* identities aren't like religious affiliations because membership is not chosen by the member or conferred or withheld by the group—it is imposed by society at large. The Congressional Black Caucus can't kick Clarence Thomas or Ward Connerly out of the black club and they can't quit.

But people do try to quit. A working hypothesis: a good deal of the support for color blindness (and related ideas vis-à-vis other social identities)—especially the small but significant amount of support among members of the groups themselves—is a reaction to the discipline of cultural difference discourse. Colorblindness offers the (false) hope of exit. By the same token, I wonder how many race-conscious young men and women gave up sustained engagement with racial politics when faced with demands to conform to rigid norms of "correct" behavior and thought. I wonder how many black conservatives, antifeminist women and "log cabin republicans" were *pushed*, rather than pulled to their ideological positions by the inhospitable environments on offer for progressive racial minorities, women, gay men and lesbians who don't toe the party line or exhibit the traits prescribed for their group. Ironically, difference discourse can undercut rather than bolster group-based political solidarity.

Similarly, much of the movement to recognize biracial and multiracial identity may be motivated by the understandable desire to escape compulsory performance of prewritten racial scripts. I suspect that a significant number of the people who push for biracial categories do so because they find stereotypical accounts of racial difference inconsistent with their own experiences and self-conceptions. Consistent with the politics of recognition, biracial individuals insist on a category that reflects their true and intrinsic selves. When Tiger Woods describes his race as "Caublinasian"—an amalgamation of Caucasian, Black, Indian and Asian[102]—he doesn't deny the existence of races (this works in the academy but it doesn't play to the national television audience of the PGA) or even the existence of distinctive racial cultures. Instead, he claims multiple citizenships. Woods thinks of himself as the product of a number of cultural communities. And the idea of race-as-culture is part of the reason that his complex mix of identifications and affiliations strike him and so many others as inconsistent with the racial identity "black."

When this understandable impulse to complicate racial identity becomes a form of identity politics of its own, it is misguided for the same reasons that difference discourse generally is misguided: there is no necessary correspondence between the ascribed identity of race and one's culture or personal sense of self. In this respect it's telling that biracialism and multiracialism have morphed into a string of multiple identity amalgams that increasingly tend toward autobiography. Anyone who has attended a cultural or ethnic studies conference has heard a statement prefaced with something like this: "As an African-American (not Afrocentric but enraptured with black cultural modernism—Louis Armstrong, Zora Neale Hurston, Miles Davis, James Baldwin, Public Enemy) heterosexual, married, able-bodied northern Californian, male law professor, postmodern urbanist (but with an affinity for modernism, high and low—Baron Hausmann and Jane Jacobs, Le Corbusier and Norman Bel Geddes, the international style and dime-store art deco, the nouveau roman and Marvel Comics), transplant from New York but almost a California native, pop culture Anglophile (the Sex Pistols, Paul Smith and the BBC but not the royals, except maybe Diana) I'd like to say." If I can only catalogue *all* of my "identities," I could make you recognize me as I really am! But somehow I never seem to finish the list. Maybe it would be easier if I just had you over for cocktails. For a year or two.

The autobiographical reflex is symptomatic of a characteristic tension of difference discourse. A social identity reflects what *other people* believe about an individual. This may not correspond with what an individual thinks makes her unique. These divergent "identities" can produce a tension between practical political imperatives (based on an ascribed social identity) and the expressive desire to tell a story that makes sense of one's life and to be recognized for whom one really is. Because, measured by the criterion of personal expression, the canonical accounts of cultural identity ultimately satisfy no one— they are much too crude for that—the attempt to make the two cohabitate produces an endless string of autobiographical qualifiers dressed up as additional "identities" (I'm black *but* I'm also a northern Californian, bohemian postmodernist with affinities for high modernism). And when people lose sight of the political goals, the desire for autobiographical recognition can produce reforms that are politically counter productive.

For example: respondents to the 2000 federal census could, for the first time, identify themselves as members of more than one racial group. Previously, the federal census required that individuals and families choose one of a list of racial categories. The reformed census allows individuals to check as many boxes as they deem necessary to reflect their racial identity as they personally conceive of it. This reform was adopted in response to agitation by individuals of mixed racial backgrounds and their parents who complained that the old census did not recognize or allow those of mixed racial parentage to express their full identity. As the organization Project RACE (Reclassify All Children Equally) complains:

> Being forced to choose only one race forces us [biracial and multiracial people] to deny one of our parents. It also requires us to do something

illegal, since we are defining ourselves as something we are not. Multiracial people should have the option of recognizing *all* of their heritage. "Multiracial" is important so that children have an identity, a correct terminology for who they are."[103]

Another multiracialism advocate opines even more forcefully:

Forcing a Multiracial child to define herself only as Black perpetuates the myth that Multiracial people do not exist. . . . Since it is not acceptable to acknowledge one's Multiracial status, the Multiracial person suffers in silence. . . . [A]lthough society has told Multiracial people to choose, in actuality, society makes the choice for them. The rich diversity literally embodied by Multiracial people remains hidden from view, hidden from discourse, hidden from recognition and thus, invisible.[104]

Taking as given the popular belief in the biological races, these complaints are valid. It's fair to say that the reformed, check-every-box-you-like census more accurately reflects the subjectively identified "races" of the responders. For many, that's an improvement over the old census that instructed respondents to identify as one and only one race.

But must we take the popular belief in biological races as given? There's an argument that the old census didn't. Instead, perhaps it meant, not to catalogue the intrinsic characteristics or biological heritage of citizens, but to catalogue their socially ascribed identities. On this account, the ultimate goal was to know the society, not by knowing its individuals in their intrinsic individuality, but to know it by mapping its social practices, its collective identifications, its popular hierarchies. Its racial categories were necessarily crude, mainly because they reflected the crude social categorization that racial ideologies have produced. They did not, and did not attempt to, reflect either biological essence or the nuanced and complex ways in which individuals think of and describe themselves. Instead, the racial portion of the census was designed to produce a necessarily stylized set of statistical data in order to further a specific set of governmental objectives, such as monitoring racial discrimination. As William Spriggs, Research and Policy Director of the Urban League asserts: "The data . . . is not used in some biological sense, and it's not used in some sort of touchy-feely sense of who are your parents and who do you want to recognize. It's related to the persistence of gaps born of legal segregation."[105] Given its objectives, the old census appropriately asked individuals to check the one box that "best described" their race, relying on common sense identifications to generate the "correct" response most of the time. To be sure, the old census was understood by many to record race as a natural fact rather than as a social practice. But the actual use of census data for such governmental purposes as equal opportunity monitoring reflected a conception of race-as-social-practice.

By allowing individuals to mark multiple boxes, the census may now *less* accurately reflect the socially understood racial identity of the responders: the type of racial identity that governmental policies such as affirmative action, electoral reapportionment, and equal opportunity monitoring need to consider. This is why a host of civil rights and racial advocacy groups, including the NAACP, the National Council of La Raza, the National Congress of American Indians and the National Asian Pacific American Legal Consortium opposed the reform.[106] In California, civil rights organizations mounted a public education campaign, urging respondents who might be tempted to tick-off multiple races to "check the black box" and only the black box in order ensure that African-American political influence was not diluted.[107] The NAACP and Asian Pacific Legal Consortium mounted similar, nationwide campaigns.[108]

In the end, the 2000 census, for all of the rhetoric about individual choice, gives government the final say in racial assignment. A prudent response to the need for equal opportunity monitoring and enforcement, the White House Office of Management and Budget issued guidelines to reduce the sixty three possible racial categories and combinations of the census to a manageable and familiar group. To do so, the guidelines allocate responses that combine any one minority race and white race to the minority race and allocate responses that include two or more minority races to one of the selected races.[109] For most governmental purposes, "Caublinasians" are still just black.

To many, this was a betrayal. But what was the point of the reform anyway? Is the ultimate goal some kind of verisimilitude, achieved simultaneously on a collective and personal level, some aspiration that the census should, as the Op-Ed pages of the *San Francisco Chronicle* opined, "reflect the changing face of America and . . . answer statistical queries that go the heart of the question, 'Who am I?'"[110] Here, the ostensible goal of the reform is to reflect racial identity accurately, implying that racial identity is an objective attribute of a person and the census simply had too few categories to capture all of its nuances; that it is a question of using the "correct terminology" in the words of Project RACE. But what exactly should the census measure; what should it be correct about? Should it treat race as an objective fact—a matter of biology or an artifact of ancestry? Or should race be a matter of subjective identification and choice?

The census racial categorization elides this question. Race-as-ancestry smacks of biological essentialism and echoes the insidious "blood quantum" racial categorization that defined the "mulattoes," "quadroons" and "octoroons" of nineteenth-century Mississippi. Race-as-subjective identification would appear to avoid this unfortunate resonance, allowing each individual to decide her race for herself. But racial self-identification in the census allows only for a very limited range of choices. The clear intention of the census bureau is that people will self-report based on their belief in some generally accepted folk ideas of racial ancestry; for example, in response to the suggestion that a person with two African-American parents might identify as multiracial because "Practically all African Americans—practically the whole planet—have multiracial backgrounds," Roderick Harrison, former head of the Census Bureau Department of Racial Statistics chided, "This isn't an academic exercise. The question was intended for those who have serious commitments to multiracial identity."[111]

What is a "serious commitment" to multiracial—indeed any racial—identity? Project RACE believes that the census and similar forms can offer our children "correct terminology for who they are." That's serious commitment. The Op-Ed page of the *San Francisco Chronicle* declares, the census should "go to the heart of the question 'Who am I?'" That's serious commitment. The census, if we take it seriously, is to do no less than capture the truth of our identities in the terse geometry of its racially identifying boxes and return it to us with a government stamp of approval. The new and improved 2000 census, with its uneasy combination of subjective and objective conceptions of racial identity, encourages respondents to internalize the folklore of objective, biological race. The racial categorization of the census is one of the most obvious examples of state power in the service of the idea of intrinsic racial difference.

The older census, with its relatively crude racial categorization, was vastly preferable in this respect, precisely because the categories failed so miserably to capture the complexities of ancestry or the nuances of self-perception and identification. It was preferable precisely because its categories did not even try to offer "correct terminology." The older census was unobtrusive. One could check the race box on the old census without having a serious commitment to it; it was a cheap date, a one-night stand, a marriage of convenience at most. The new census, with its sincerity and its politically "correct terminology," wants intimacy. It wants to know you for who you really are. It wants to meet your parents and leave a toothbrush in your bathroom.

The census bureau's newfound sensitivity to the nuances of ancestry is an improvement over the old, pick-one-box census, only if one assumes that the reported racial identities to which we should have a "serious commitment" are somehow uncorrupted by oppressive racial power. But as I have argued at some length, such identities are necessarily a product of racial power. The subject of the new census—the individual's "sincere" or intrinsic racial identity— is an *effect* of the racial discourse the older census arguably sought to map and understand. In effect, the reformed census replaces an admittedly crude but pragmatic science designed to monitor racial practices and their social consequences with a more subtle and more insidious science that endeavors to record the subjective identification of individuals that results from those racial practices.

The effort to make the census' racial categories more "accurate" in positivistic terms serves to reinforce the belief in racial identity as an attribute of the self that could be accurately recognized and measured. To the difference advocate concerned with the recognition of identities, the reformed census may look empowering. But if I have convinced you to understand racial discourses as modes of power that *produce* rather than record their objects, the new census may look like a seductive bit of interactive propaganda—a stroke to the ego as foreplay to a mind fuck.

Of course, many people were seriously committed to the old census race categories as well—but the categories didn't return the favor. This unrequited commitment has led people to push for a more "accurate" census. But wouldn't it be better if we were all just honest about the potential of the relationship from the start? Werner Sollars offers a prescription for a census that knows when to get dressed and call a taxi. It would ask about only five races and would come with the following disclaimer:

> The Attorney General has determined that the United States government had discriminated against people based on what were once believed to be black, red, yellow, and brown "races." Though there is no scientific basis for this belief, it is important to collect information about the following five categories in order to protect citizens' rights and to enforce antidiscrimination legislation today. These data are used only for these specific purposes and do not reflect the belief of the U.S. government or the Census Bureau that such races actually exist. Which of the following "races" might have been used to describe you?[112]

This proposal, informed by a conviction that we should give unto Caesar that which is Caesar's but save our intimate inner truths for more sacred entities, has the merit of facilitating anti-discrimination law without reifying racial difference. It retains racial categories, but insists on their extrinsic, ascribed character. It puts racial difference on a diet.

This leaner racial categorization doesn't allow for the nuance that subjective self-identification would suggest. That's appropriate because the only reason government should inquire about race at all is to counteract the effects of its involuntary ascription. Any other type of racial identification should be a private matter. Government can't and shouldn't try to stop people from identifying racially, but it shouldn't help either: outside the limited domains in which official recognition of race is necessary, racial identity should be left to individuals and the various collectivities and institutions of civil society.

When it comes to race and other status identities, we should adopt the credo of architectural modernism: "less is more." This does not suggest that the law must be "blind" to all group differences. (Indeed, the popularity of formal ideologies like color blindness is a predictable reaction to the crude and prescriptive accounts of the entailments of identity produced by difference discourse.) But anti-discrimination law should be refined so as to recognize only those differences attributable to the production of formal status hierarchy, for the purpose of eliminating or reducing the ill effects of such hierarchies. Difference discourse, by metastasizing status into a thick social identity, distracts from and confuses the vital task of correcting status hierarchy. Legal decision makers need to be aware of status differences and castelike social practices in order to correct the injustice that they do. But we should resist the temptation to write a speculative sociology of group difference into law or to enlist the state in a psychotherapeutic quest to validated "repressed" identities.

3. "Cultural Discrimination"

My argument against rights-to-difference in the last two chapters contains three major assertions. One, group difference is not intrinsic to members of social groups but rather contingent of the social practices surrounding group identification. Two, anti-discrimination law need not "protect group traits" in order to prohibit discrimination on the basis of group statuses. Finally, any decision about whether or not to protect a mutable group correlated trait or practice involves two decisions: one, about the merits or demerits of the trait or practice and another, about the merits or demerits of encouraging the association of the trait or practice with a ascribed social identity or status.

I do not insist on what must follow from this analysis, although I've certainly suggested what I think should follow from it. One could believe that it's a great idea to make racial cultures and other group cultures more formal, more dogmatic, and more a matter of common knowledge than they are already. If one so concluded, she might, based on this commitment conclude that anti-discrimination law should protect group-correlated traits. I can't dismiss such normative judgments as matters of logic or reason—they aren't somehow inconsistent with the logic of anti-discrimination law or ruled out by human nature—but I think they are very bad judgments, for reasons I have already suggested and for reasons I am about to suggest. I do insist that rights-to-difference are not a logically necessary extension of our existing liberal commitments to eliminate hierarchies of status; instead, an honest argument for rights-to-difference requires one to endorse these, at best questionable, judgments.

One reason the normative and policy judgments underlying rights-to-difference are bad ideas is that they reflect an oversimplified conception of cultural pluralism. Rights-to-difference promote a peculiar type of cultural pluralism by requiring social institutions to accommodate cultural practices commonly associated with what I have called "canonical" social groups: racial and ethnic groups and other groups with socially ascribed identities (such as "homosexuals" or "the disabled"). This is not the only approach to cultural pluralism; I will argue that it is not the best approach. Viewed as cultural policy, rights-to-difference do more than seek to promote cultural difference; they seek to codify the idea that legitimate cultural difference resides first and foremost, if not exclusively, in the canonical social group. Rights-to-difference should be understood as a policy decision to assign the power to make certain decisions—labeled "cultural"—to specific institutional locations; for instance, to families and the informal representatives of the canonical groups and ultimately to the federal courts—as opposed to others—business associations, limited liability partnerships, universities, local governments. As I will argue below, this assignment is questionable.

The privileging of groups with socially ascribed identities is somewhat odd in a society that generally prefers voluntary association and individual liberty to formal legacies, pedigreed titles and inherited statuses. Moreover, much of what we are pleased to call cultural difference is developed and fostered in the type of voluntary associations that rights-to-difference would deprive of the authority to shape culture (at least whenever the preferences of the association conflict with those of a canonical group). Rights-to-difference begin with the (often quite reasonable) presumption that the group differences for which rights protection is sought are often highly relevant, at least to the group that seeks the protection. This suggests a delicate parsing: the practice or trait for which protection is sought should be quite important to the individual or group (as Brian Barry suggests, if it "were merely a personal preference, it is doubtful that it would be appropriate to bring to bear the ponderous machinery of the law in order to enforce a right to . . . it"[1]) but quite unimportant to the business or institution charged with the corresponding duty to accommodate it. This is true much less often than the rights-to-difference literature would suggest. When it is not true, rights-to-difference would impose a real cost on the institutions they would govern and on society generally, a cost that may well outweigh any benefits they would offer.

Further, cultural production is often and perhaps at its best a synthesis of ethnic traditions, institutional imperatives, marketing ploys and political expressions. The rough and tumble of culture on the street, despite its Darwinian violence and incivility, offers a better model for multiculturalism than the fantasy of preformed ethnicities passing their static and uncontroversial cultures around the room for show and tell. A better approach to cultural difference would acknowledge the inevitability of conflicts between various potential sites of cultural production and the difficulty of distinguishing as a matter of judicial analysis, legitimate and illegitimate attempts to "make culture."

Why "Cultural Bias" Is Like Death and Taxes

Many policies that government or other social institutions regularly adopt will influence the formation of group identity and culture: some policies that intentionally and explicitly attempt to influence group cultural practices or group-identified traits and some that have an unintentional or incidental effect. Short of hermetic segregation there is no way of avoiding such influence, no way of inhabiting our identity as Audre Lorde suggests, "without the restrictions of externally imposed definition." This is a central point of this chapter and this book.

In this sense we can't prohibit cultural discrimination; other people's decisions will influence our own, including those related to our cultures. This leaves us with some tough decisions: we have to *decide what to do* about cultural differences and a pluralism of social identities. There is no possibility of an effectively laissez faire approach (although a formally laissez faire approach is possible and probably desirable, as I will argue). The advocates of cultural rights are correct to insist that the absence of explicit regulation of culture and identity do not leave them unaffected by law and formal regulation. But rights also will regulate the practices and identities of social groups as I have taken pains to point out.

Background Rules as Cultural Discrimination

Without explicit cultural protections, the regulation of culture and identity nevertheless will take place in the form of "background" norms and rules. Of course, it is certainly possible for a liberal state to be evenhanded in a strictly formal sense: it can insist that all religions receive state funding or that none do; it can insist that all cultures receive an official imprimatur or that none do. But the goal of evenhandedness is harder to grasp if we want, not simply formal evenhandedness, but effective neutrality. By effectively neutrality, I do not mean equality of result: for instance I do not insist that in order to be neutral the state must guarantee equal resources or equal numbers of adherents, or even the survival of cultural traditions despite contrary preferences of the individuals who make up the society in question. If so few people want to speak Esperanto in the United States that the few who do want to speak it cannot sustain it as a living language, this is not evidence of bias on the part of the state.

But even a formally neutral state is not effectively neutral because it enforces a set of "background rules"—for instance, legal rules establishing the meaning of private property and the terms of legitimate contractual exchange—that operate in the "background" of overt social conflict and are taken for granted but which structure social interaction generally and can make formally neutral policies effectively partial and biased. This idea—that the very terms of social and economic relations are the product of potentially controversial legal rules—has been a foundation of pragmatic and critical legal thought since its articulation in the 1920s by legal theorist Robert Hale. As legal historian Morton Horowtiz explains: "Since all market transactions are affected by the prior distribution of property and [legal] entitlements, Hale argued, the market was in fact an organized form of coercion of the weak by the strong. . . . Hale's basic goal was to attack the prevailing vision of the market as a system of free and voluntary exchange."[2]

Let's suppose a Native-American tribe's traditional way of life, which involves hunting big game on very large tracts of undeveloped land, is dying out. Assume the state is formally neutral as to its way of life: there are no laws against hunting the game they traditionally hunt in the way they traditionally hunt it and the tribe could sustain its way of life if it had the resources to purchase hunting rights on the land on which the game in question could flourish. But the tribe has few resources with which to purchase the land or the rights. Their use of land, unlike cultivation and farming, does not produce marketable goods and unlike improvement for residential use, does not support gainful employment. And this creates a vicious cycle: as the traditional ways become harder and harder to sustain, the conventions and customs that bind the tribe together weaken and more and more members drift away, depriving the remaining members of even the meager resources that they once enjoyed. We could run a similar analysis involving almost any cultural practice that requires a critical mass of people and resources to maintain: African-American churches are threatened by neighborhood decline or, if not that, then by gentrification and spiraling expenses. Immigrant communities face powerful economic incentives to learn English in order to compete in the market economy, achieving and maintaining language proficiency is time consuming; therefore future generations may well find the languages of their parents an expensive luxury they cannot afford to maintain.

How is this the business of the state? From a narrow perspective it isn't: the market economy and the choices of individuals—not the state—have conspired to make some ways of life hard to maintain. But from another perspective—a pragmatic perspective developed by American legal realism—the market economy and to some extent even individual choices are the children of the state. "Property" is not a natural given, instead it refers to an elaborate array of legal rules and policies backed by the coercive power of government: if our Native-American tribe hunts on public land or private property, they will be subject to arrest as trespassers. It is the *law* that makes them trespassers and it is government that will prevent them from trespassing and punish them for so doing. If immigrants who focus on their native tongue and neglect English find themselves unemployed, the laws of property and contract decree that for the most part, employers are free not to hire them and the law of contract and property will throw them onto the streets when they fail to make their rent payments.

These background rules of contract and property generally work to favor individuals (and groups) who have the lion's share of resources in society. Now, if the initial distribution of resources was just and the subsequent terms of exchange were just we might think the present distribution also just by extension (although this would be at best a questionable conclusion given the existence of inherited wealth). But of course an "initial distribution" of resources is a philosopher's conceit, the stuff of hypothetical shipwrecked crews and deserted islands. And the real world distribution of resources reflects a string of thefts, swindles, enslavements and illegitimate hierarchies as far back in time as anyone can perceive. The background rules reinforce these injustices (some of which were quite recent); injustices with patterned, group specific biases. Worse yet, even if the distribution of material resources were just, the background rules still favor some lifestyles over others: the market, and private property are biased in favor of improvement and cultivation of land and against subsistence use. Given this, the state cannot be neutral, in the sense of effectively even-handed, now or in any practically conceivable future.

But if it is true that state neutrality in the stronger, effective sense, is impossible, the failure to be neutral cannot be an indictment. Even in the best of all possible liberal states, the state would not be culturally neutral. It could try to correct for certain identifiable injustices, but there is no way of correcting for the pervasive and systemic bias of background rules that structure the relations of a society, that determine the very nature of the society. Our goal then, must not be neutrality, but rather some identifiable substantive outcome (more big game hunting or more non-English languages). Many advocates of rights-to-difference, after insisting that cultural neutrality is impossible, go on to suggest that we try to "approximate" it by creating special rights for the groups that lose out in the market and democratic politics. This strategy is at best an odd one (why not just redistribute wealth to disadvantaged groups or subsidize certain activities?); more importantly, the "neutrality" justification for it is incoherent. We've established that the state cannot be neutral, not because it "falls short" of neutrality in some measurable sense, but because of the salience of background rules that are indispensable to modern life.

Of course we could change the background rules to favor the practices of groups that they now disfavor. But this would not make the background rules "more neutral." It would make them biased in a different way. For instance, if our long-suffering Native-American tribe were to successfully achieve changes in the law of property and contract so as to make their traditional way of life easier to maintain (suppose it were no longer a trespass to enter and use private property while hunting wild game or in order to establish a base camp from which to hunt.) This change would not make the law more neutral; instead it would benefit hunters at the expense of farmers, ranchers and opponents of game hunting (these groups might well be politically or economically disadvantaged too). Approximating cultural neutrality is as hopeless a project as achieving it. Rights-to-difference cannot make the state perfectly neutral or even "more neutral"; instead they will simply make it biased for and against different interests.

Of course it's possible that rights-to-difference will make the state biased in a better way. But in order to know this we'd need to have some idea of what counts as "better." And the idea in question cannot be that what is better is "more neutral"—we've dispensed with that possibility already. Instead, we need a *substantive* conception of the good, described in terms of culture and in terms of racial and ethnic group relations.

The Inevitability of Discriminatory Laws

The situation is worse than I have painted it because, not only will background rules conspire to discriminate against certain minority cultures, legal rules that are very much in the foreground will also do so. Although "the law" is not a monolith with *a* singular culture—courts, legislatures and the laws they pass undoubtedly reflect a number of different local legal cultures as well as a set of compromises between multiple cultural influences—legal institutions and law are not and cannot be culturally neutral. This of necessity means that law will weigh more heavily on those people whose cultural norms most sharply diverge from those of the laws and institutions under whose authority they must live.

But this is not a critique of law, it is a truism about it. In a sense any legal rule or policy that intervenes in the vast field of social conflict involving ideals, sensibilities and taste (in contrast to raw conflict over social resources) will be "culturally biased." Rights-to-difference are premised on the idea that this cultural bias is a conceptually and practically detachable side effect of the law's legitimate function. But from the perspective of the authors of a given law or regulation it is most crucial to coerce precisely those people that rights-to-difference would exempt: those who do not accept the norms that the regulation wishes to promote.

Many laws are of necessity directed to those people who will object the most if forced to conform to them. One passes a law in order to press a norm upon people who would not otherwise accept it. The speed limit is designed to control lead-footed speed demons, public intoxication laws target barflies, age of consent laws are written with pedophiles in mind. It is not an unfortunate side effect of these laws that they unequally burden these groups—in a sense it is a central objective of the laws.

Since any law or rule will indeed be more burdensome for those people who do not share the norms informing it than for those who do, if a distinctive national, ethnic or social group does not share the norms underlying a law or rule, that group will often experience the law as especially, if not singularly, oppressive to them.

For the most part, the laws and rules that upset cultural rights proponents do not intentionally target a social group—instead they are aimed at a practice and incidentally burden a social group, or certain members of that group. But even in the extreme case where a law or rule intentionally targets the group, that fact *alone* cannot discredit the law or rule. This is true due to precisely the insight that multiculturalism urges upon us: different social groups do in fact have different norms and different practices (some of which may be objectionable).

Suppose social group *X* has a number of distinctive social practices including ritual animal sacrifice that involves slow torture of the animal for several days. This group establishes a presence in an animal-loving, pet-friendly town and begins, among other practices, this ritual. Suppose the town has no general ordinance prohibiting cruelty to animals because, up until now, it has not needed one. The town council (who does not share group *X*'s culture) responds with an ordinance outlawing animal sacrifice. To be sure the ordinance was directed at the group. But it does not necessarily reflect prejudice or bias against the group as a group—instead it reflects disapproval of the practice in which the group engages. The reason for the conflict is cultural difference. But to point this out tells us nothing at all about how the conflict should be resolved.

Cultural difference is often hard to distinguish, in practice and in principle from garden-variety ideological conflict. The unfamiliar cultural practices of foreign nationals or insular groups or subgroups are troubling, in large part because they force us to confront, in embodied form, the type of ideological, theological, aesthetic and normative conflicts that trouble society more generally. Cultural difference is not only a problem of the outsider, it is also a conflict of the self; conflicts *within* "mainstream" or "dominant" society are often fought out in the arena of multiculturalism. For instance, the long-standing conflict between the privacy of the home and the rights of women and children to exit coercive family relations or to enlist outside assistance to alter them is recast as a problem of "culture" when immigrants from non-European countries are involved in domestic violence or participate in arranged marriages. The old feminist debate over arguably oppressive standards of female physical beauty ("Is it okay to want that boob job?") and control of female sexuality ("If men got pregnant, abortion would be a sacrament") is transformed into a question of "cultural sensitivity" when members of "alien cultures" engage in rituals and practices, such as female circumcision, designed to enhance (a culturally specific idea of) female beauty and perpetuate social control over female sexuality.

Cultural diversity arguments that imagine monolithic minority cultures threatened by an equally monolithic mainstream serve to camouflage the ideological conflict and ambivalence *within* Western political culture as to these issues. Should police intervene in violent households when the victims of the violence themselves are ambivalent about the desirability of outside intervention? Should arrest and prosecution be mandatory even when the victims wish for law enforcement to withdraw from the dispute? Is surgical alteration of the body for the purpose of achieving gendered standards of beauty empowering or oppressive to women? Should parents be allowed to endanger the health and welfare of their children in order to conform to religious mandates and prohibitions? These conflicts are not the product of foreign immigration or racial difference, and they would not go away were a program of forced assimilation miraculously to succeed.

The same is true of cultural practices identified with social groups. Questions such as whether employees should be free to dress and wear their hair as they please despite the wishes of their employers, whether they should be free to speak in a dialect, slang, or language of their choice and whether institutions should be allowed to require conformity to common norms and practices as condition of admission are not unique to identity politics and they would be only slightly less vexing were categories such as race, ethnicity, and sexual orientation not salient in American social and political life.

Everyone Can Make a Difference: Difference Discourse as Cultural Zeitgeist

Brian Barry notes that at least one account of the "oppressed groups" in American society includes "women, Blacks, Chicanos, Puerto Ricans and other Spanish speaking Americans, American Indians, Jews, lesbians, gay men, Arabs,

Asians, old people, working class people, and the physically and mentally disabled. This implies that about 90 per cent of Americans are oppressed."[3]

In an important sense, difference discourse is a symptom of a zeitgeist. Difference discourse informs the racial separatism of the Nation of Islam, multiculturalism on college campuses, much of the modern gay pride movement and the push for recognition of the children of racially mixed parentage as a distinct racial category. It animates the anomalous legal treatment of indigenous Americans in contexts as diverse as child welfare, the unique property rules governing tribal lands, the treatment of Native American arts and crafts, exemptions from state antigambling laws and the vexed relationship of government to indigenous people in the state of Hawaii.

It informs the articulation of what might once have been called class politics as movements to protect the "culture" of middle American small farmers with agricultural price supports and to protect the "culture" of lumberjacks in the Pacific Northwest from environmental regulations. "Difference" also justifies the incorporation of the confederate stars and bars in South Carolina's state flag as a symbol of southern heritage.

This is a long and seemingly disparate catalogue of social groups and movements. If they were forced into the same room, as I have forced them onto the same page, one would expect, not a consensus, but a brawl. Nevertheless, all of these movements share a common ideological commitment: the idea that the social validation of a group-based identity and lifestyle is an entitlement that is enforceable against others. This idea is a seductive one but I hope it also strikes you as a bit quixotic: a legal right to a specific lifestyle, to social esteem, to a meaningful life?

Tilting at this windmill has become an American pastime. So it shouldn't surprise us that enterprising business people have turned this joust into a growth industry. The marketing of multiculturalism has been evocatively described by social critic David Rieff:

[T]he multiculturalist mode is what any smart businessman would prefer. . . . For if . . . the point of art is not greatness but the production of works of art that reflect the culture and aspirations of various ethnic, sexual, or racial subgroups within a society, then one is in a position to increase supply almost at will in order to meet increases in demand. Instead of being a rare and costly thing, culture becomes simultaneously a product, like a car—something that can be made new every few years— and an abundant resource, like, well, people . . . The result is that the consumption of culture can increasingly come to resemble the consumption of goods.[4]

Rieff is not the first person to make such an argument about the consumption of culture: as early as the 1960s black radical Robert Allen made a strikingly similar point:

> [B]lack culture has become a badge to be worn rather than an experience to be shared. African robes, dashikis, dress, and sandals have become standard equipment not only for the well dressed Black militant, but even for middle class hipsters who have gone Afro. Business firms advertise hair sprays especially suited for natural styles, and some of the shrewder cultural nationalists have turned a profit peddling African trinkets and clothes to naive young Blacks.[5]

Group difference has been inducted into the consumerist cult of the self; social justice becomes the right to purchase mass produced quirkiness and canned authenticity and the freedom to buy assembly line individuality and niche-marketed group consciousness. That apotheosis of late-twentieth-century African-American culture—hip-hop—exemplifies this contradiction of modern identity politics. We have an art form that has undeniable roots in the raw experience of a particular kind of black cultural life: when Public Enemy brought the noise in the early 1980s, we witnessed a pop cultural moment whose racial authenticity was genuine, compelling *and* a central part of its marketing appeal. On the other hand, we have "keeping it real" morph into mass marketing ("turning rebellion into money" as the British punk band the Clash put it years earlier) and when the sales pitch comes down to Jennifer Lopez, a *Hollywood actress* turned MTV pop star who adopts a hip-hop image and insists, "I'm Real," there's enough irony to satisfy a convention of postmodernists.

There's nothing sinister and certainly nothing new about the influence of the mass media and consumer capitalism on the social identities of young people—James Dean is reborn in the next generation as Brad Pitt; yesterday's girl next door is now Jenny from the block. But the connections between difference discourse, consumer capitalism and the psycho-social obsessions of the postmodern bourgeoisie suggest that the drive for the recognition of particularities may, paradoxically, be a universal one. The need to differentiate ourselves on the basis of group membership may itself be something that transcends group differences, the outgrowth not of distinctive subcultures but of a shared mass culture: the anomie of modern society and the manufactured needs of modern marketing.

The proliferation of "oppressed groups" seeking legal rights raises a thorny question when people turn to litigation to secure what the culture industry fails to deliver. In 2002 the San Francisco Human Rights Commission held that an overweight woman had a legal right, under the city's so-called "fat and short" ordinance, which prohibits discrimination on the basis of weight and height, to a job as an aerobics instructor. Other than her size she fit the profile of an aerobics instructor: "[The] Jazzercise teacher was so impressed by her stamina and ability that she invited Portnick to audition to become a Jazzercise certified instructor. But a company manager said Portnick would have to develop "a more fit appearance."[6]

I must admit that when I think of an aerobics instructor, "thin" is almost the first adjective that comes to mind. But is being thin legitimately job related? Why? Because most customers expect it? Most soda fountain customers in Alabama during the 1960s expected their lunch counter companions to be white. You can see how the argument goes.

Another incident of weight discrimination involved a decision of Southwest Airlines to enforce a long-standing but long-ignored policy requiring especially overweight people to purchase two seats on full flights in order to avoid crowding their neighbors. In a charming display of sensitivity the president of the Air Travelers Association remarked in support of the policy: "If passengers have supersized themselves and are encroaching on the space of others, fairness says you should be paying for the space."[7] Should Southwest's policy be actionable?

Weight, like cultural difference straddles the typical anti discrimination distinction between status and conduct. Both are ambiguously mutable: it may be that most overweight people are overweight because they overeat and don't exercise (although that certainly wasn't true of the Jazzercise applicant) but many biologists believe that obesity is at least partially a biological predisposition. And just as we needn't think that cultural differences are biologically determined to acknowledge that they are often instinctual and difficult to change, once one is obese, however he got there, it can be very hard to lose the weight, as any dieter knows. Finally weight, much like cultural difference, can become a part of a person's self-conception. Adopting the logic of difference discourse, there are political movements of "fat" people such as the National Association to Advance Fat Acceptance whose members are proud to be "fat" and wouldn't change for all the Ultra Slim-Fast in the world. A rally celebrating the verdict against Jazzercize's "fit appearance policy was attended by:

> rotund cheerleaders waving pompons, poetry about poundage and assorted fat activism:
> "Two-four-six-eight, we do not regurgitate. Three-five-seven-nine, love your body, it's just fine."

Amanda Piasecki, 27, a graduate student in Oakland, wore a lavender slip, fishnet stockings and a photo of herself as an anorexic teenager. Shackled by a chain on her ankles were two scales.

"A lot of women are shackled to the scale," says Piasecki, who weighs 225 pounds. "I went on a lot of extreme diets. I ate 800 calories a day for two years. I'm now at my natural body size, and I'm a lot happier."[8]

We can stretch the logic of rights-to-difference further still. On the streets of San Francisco, a once-genteel city is now the site of thousands of daily little wars between motorists, pedestrians and cyclists, each vying to be King of the Concrete Jungle. There's plenty of blame to go around: motorists run bikes and pedestrians off the road and, as SUV's proliferate, the iron law of traffic physics applies—both skill and civility are inversely related to the size of vehicle. Pedestrians are the smallest and therefore the most self-righteous, walking into heavy traffic at night, stealthy as a jewel thief in all black, and screaming in outrage when a startled motorist stops short or a cyclist has to dodge to avoid them. Cyclists disregard traffic laws, sailing through red lights, dodging into on-coming traffic, jumping curbs to utilize sidewalks and regularly forming a mob scene known as "Critical Mass," in which hundreds of cyclists with axes to grind or time to kill ride through the city's major thoroughfares in a parade so dense as to block motorist, pedestrian and chicken alike from crossing the road. These unauthorized events often stretch for miles and tie up traffic for blocks in every direction. The resulting traffic related tensions reached their inevitable conclusion when some cyclists pressed the city to make traffic confrontations between cyclists and motorists actionable as *hate crimes* (of course, only when the motorist wins the fight).

Cyclists, unlike racial minorities and homosexuals, aren't attacked because of widespread prejudice against them; they're attacked (when they aren't on the attack) because of a social conflict over a scarce resource: the city streets. For the most part these conflicts should be resolved in the streets, not the courts (confrontations that come to blows should be settled according to the identity-indifferent rules governing criminal assault).

What goes around, comes around: in San Francisco and Berkeley the idea of a "dog culture" developed around efforts to overturn leash laws and now has spawned its own political rally for off-leash parks entitled: "Critical Mutt." Taken to not illogical extremes, the "dog culture" argument insists that those who care for animals have a unique culture that is undervalued by the mainstream (people who don't like dog shit are, after all, just bigots.)

I imagine most rights-to-difference proponents would agree that we have to draw the anti-discrimination line somewhere well above "cyclists rights." Indeed, many supporters of cultural rights bristle when it is suggested that their logic might extend to prohibit discrimination based on physical attractiveness (studies have shown that "attractive" people get better jobs and higher salaries than similarly talented "ugly" people[9]) or against nonconformists such as gender cross-dressers, punks with purple hair or Mohawk hair cuts or "urban primitives" with multiple body piercings, scarification or bold and visible tattoos.

I suspect that they bristle for two reasons. One is psychological. Difference discourse aspires to more than practical policy reform—it also aspires to political recognition for certain groups, a message of respect and inclusion communicated through the imprimatur of the state. Like cash, the value of that imprimatur is diminished as it is multiplied. It is ennobling to be one of the handful of social groups recognized as especially important and deserving of recognition, but it means little to be one of scores of groups in an everyone-but-the-kitchen sink list. Indeed, at some point the inclusion of ever more marginal groups can be downright insulting to the more established ones. Suppose, for instance, that a state legislature decided to recognize gay marriage. This would arguably be a profound statement of respect for homosexuals. But suppose that when the bill was assured of success, a disgruntled member of the Christian Coalition added a rider to the bill, repealing laws against polygamy or extending recognition of marriage to unions between siblings. We would correctly see this as an attempt to undermine the social value of the gay marriages.

The second reason for bristling is practical. There's a nagging suspicion that beneath its command of formal neutrality, anti-discrimination law involves a subtle shift in social resources. Businesses spend time and money on sensitivity training and outreach in order to counter the possibility of bias against the protected groups. They won't just multiply their efforts by the number of protected groups, as that number continues to grow. There is a limited amount of time that a law firm partner or Fortune 500 CEO will spend in sensitivity workshops. Although in theory adding groups to the list *shouldn't* diminish the protection for more established groups, in our fallen world of limited social resources, it will. If "everyone" gets anti-discrimination protection, in a sense, there's less of it to go around. The gripes of newly minted minority identity groups such as San Francisco's cyclists and dog owners—even if legitimate—justifiably strike many people as trivial in comparison to those of society's long-suffering minority groups. There are minorities and then there are Minorities; some people lose out in the political process and the market because their causes and behavior are simply unpopular. From these "minorities," rights arguments don't sound like justice; they sound like a way to circumvent democracy and free ride on the free enterprise system.

Discrimination on the basis of many personal attributes is inappropriate and unfair. For many purposes, factors such as height, weight, physical beauty, personal grooming and certain cultural practices are irrelevant and therefore unfair bases of discrimination. A job applicant passed over because a potential employer favors taller or more handsome employees (check into a trendy New York hotel and try to find a short, portly, ugly or even average-looking porter, clerk, concierge, bartender or waitress) is arguably the victim of unfair discrimination and is just as unemployed as one passed over because of race or gender. As law professor Mark Kelman notes, "any . . . straight, white, able-bodied male may be the victim of irrational treatment by a partic-ular employer or public accommodations owner. He might, for instance, remind the person with whom he wishes to deal of some loathed stepfather."[10]

But there are good reasons that anti-discrimination law does not prohibit all "unfair" discrimination, reserving what Brain Barry calls "the ponderous machinery of the law" for the most pressing, pervasive and stigmatizing wrongs. Discrimination on the paradigmatic bases of race, color and sex as well as disability and in my view sexual orientation raises distinctive concerns because it participates in the production of socially inferior classes of people, groups of permanently lower social status, inferior castes. Such discrimination is based on tragically widespread social prejudice and folklore about the groups in question. It perpetuates such prejudice by reinforcing the perception that the group in question is unfit for dignified and equal treatment. Because the prejudice is widespread, members of the socially inferior groups can expect to encounter it regularly if not unremittingly. As Kelman notes:

> [Whereas] members of socially advantaged groups are unlikely to face such [discriminatory] treatment persistently, across a wide variety of settings . . . we may reasonably believe that prejudice against African-Americans . . . is widespread among those with social power. Stereotypes about members of socially salient groups are both socially created and social-norms-enforced and are thus repeatedly in play. . . . [B]oth the African-American and the white [who reminds the employer of a hated stepfather] are victims of discrimination[,] . . . but the discrimination against the latter and not the former is likely to be corrected by market competition rather than state action.[11]

Social prejudice directed at a stigmatized group impoverishes and isolates the group as a whole, effectively quarantining its members in limited social roles and adds insult to injury by insisting that their isolation is deserved and justi-fied. By contrast, discrimination on other bases, even when unjust, is usually sporadic, episodic or individualized. Randy Newman's famous parody of bigotry, "Short People" ("don't want no short people round here!") was humorous because there is little risk of systematic bias against short people which might result in a socially inferior "short" caste.

For reasons similar to those that it should not attempt to proscribe unfair discrimination generally, anti-discrimination law should not attempt to prohibit "cultural discrimination" even if it disproportionately affects the canonical social groups. Cultural discrimination may in fact be motivated by things other than animus toward a social group. If for instance, an employer bans cornrow hairstyles along with many other unconventional hairstyles because she wants to communicate a conservative business image, discrimination suffered by the cornrow-preferring African-American is in principle indistinguishable from that suffered by the white person who prefers another prohibited hairstyle. Because such discrimination is likely to fall more equitably across members of many social groups, rather than concentrating its effects only on one or a few, it should be easier to combat through collective bargaining and should not result in the persistent isolation or subordination of any given group. And, such discrimination is likely to be much less pervasive than discrimination based on ascribed social status: some employers will want to promote a conservative business image, but many will not. By contrast simple racial prejudice, for example, is widespread. Finally, when the target of discrimination is mutable behavior, the putative plaintiff can avoid the discrimination; it is reasonable to assume that at least some of the potential victims of discrimination (those individuals predisposed to exhibit the disfavored traits) will in fact avoid it by changing their behavior thereby reducing the isolating effect of the discrimination on the group as a group.

Difference as an Expensive Taste

Rights-to-difference arguments are essentially demands that we accommodate certain preferences of members of the canonical social groups. I've argued above that many groups have analogous preferences and I've suggested that it would be bad policy to require employers and other institutions to accommodate all of them. In societies dominated by markets and majoritarian political institutions, minority preferences often suffer. Minority preferences suffer in markets because of economies of scale: it tends to be relatively cheap to provide goods and services in large quantities and relatively expensive to provide them in small quantities. In the United States broccoli is much cheaper than broccoli rabe. There's nothing inherent in broccoli rabe that makes it expensive—it doesn't require expensive imported soils, it's not unusually susceptible to pests, it's not hard to grow. But there are a lot of broccoli eaters and not many broccoli rabe fans. Farmers produce lots of broccoli and very little broccoli rabe: as a result, at every stage of the production process, broccoli rabe is more expensive per unit to bring to market.

Cyclists suffer a similar problem. If most San Franciscans used bicycles to get around town, traffic patterns would favor small, very maneuverable but relatively slow vehicles over larger, more cumbersome, speedier vehicles. But cyclists are in a minority and this makes their favored means of transportation "expensive" in the sense that things aren't set up to accommodate it. Above the cost of purchasing a bike and helmet, cyclists "pay" for cycling in the form of hassle and risk, while motorists "pay" for it in the form of hassle and delay. These costs aren't inherent to cycling—they are result of the incompatibility of cycling with the use the majority makes of the roads. San Francisco's Critical Mass dramatizes this point on a monthly basis—if there were enough cyclists, they'd be able to force the motorists to accommodate them—or more accurately, it would be the cyclists who would decide whether or not to accommodate the motorists.

We could say something similar about people with unconventional hairstyles. I don't imagine that most of the people who choose dreadlocks, pink hair or a Mohawk think of themselves as indulging an expensive habit (although some of these coifs are achieved in chic hair salons and require regular professional maintenance); nevertheless, in many contexts, they are. If the hairstyle is off-putting to a majority of other people, it is expensive: those who dislike it "pay" for it in terms of subjective emotional discomfort and those who wear it may pay for it in terms of lost job opportunities or social disapproval. Again, there's nothing inherently off-putting about these hairstyles: they are off-putting in a social context in which very few people have them.

The philosopher G. A. Cohen argues that the same can be said of minority cultural practices that require extraordinary legal protection: they are an expensive taste. Cohen's definition of an "expensive taste" is quite specific: he doesn't mean Robin Leach's taste for champagne wishes and caviar dreams. By a taste, he means an involuntary disposition that affects one's ability to experience pleasure or satisfaction:

> A person's tastes are expensive if and only if they are such that it costs more to provide her than to provide others with given levels of satisfaction or fulfillment. A person who insists on expensive cigars and fine wines is not eo ipso possessed of expensive tastes, in the required sense. For she may be insisting on a higher level of satisfaction than the norm.[12]

It's at least hypothetically possible, for instance, that many people experience the same "amount" of pleasure from guzzling a Coors Light beer that I can achieve only by imbibing a very well mixed, ice-cold martini made with premium gin. Compared to the Coors Light drinker, my taste for martinis is expensive; he can enjoy his cocktail hour beverage every bit as much as I enjoy mine, for a fraction of the price.

Cohen argues that, as matter of distributive justice, it is unjust to distribute resources without regard to the fact that some people require more than others *in order to achieve the same level of satisfaction*. Of course, matters are different if *everyone* would enjoy the martini more that the beer (quite plausible) but I am simply unwilling to settle while others are. This is my own affair and justice requires me to pony up and forgo some other luxury. It only counts as an "expensive taste" if I require it to achieve the level of satisfaction that a cheaper alternative would bring others. If the Coors drinker is happy with a $1.50 can of beer whereas I *require* a $10 martini to achieve the same level of satisfaction, it is just (given a distributive justice regime in which we are only concerned about happy hour) for him to receive $1.50 while I receive $10 for the bar tab. By the same token if my editor requires vintage champagne, he should receive $30 to buy a glass of Krug.

At first blush this idea seems perverse: *justice* requires us to subsidize people with expensive tastes? But given Cohen's narrow definition of expensive tastes (remember, for Cohen expensive tastes are a sort of disability—one is cursed with a need for expensive things in order to achieve the same level satisfaction that others receive from cheap things), the idea is not only a plausible implication of distributive justice; it also arguably underlies some existing policy. We could consider a rural lifestyle an expensive taste. Modern utilities are relatively inexpensive to provide in cities due to economies of scale, but they are quite expensive to extend to rural areas. Yet federal telecommunications regulations require telephone companies to service rural areas and spread the cost to urbanites through taxes and regulated rates. Similarly a taste for classic architecture is expensive: older buildings are expensive to maintain and fail to offer many modern amenities unless significantly renovated at great cost. Yet landmark preservation ordinances in many American cities require owners of landmarks to preserve them and require renovations to comply with expensive requirements in order to maintain the integrity of the original design.

Cohen argues that cultural practices that require extraordinary legal protection are an expensive taste. Surprisingly perhaps, he argues from this premise that distributive justice demands that we subsidize them. However, he concludes that, as with many other types of expensive tastes, the practical difficulties of administering the subsidy ultimately doom the idea (how, for example, can we know when someone has truly expensive tastes as opposed to a desire for greater than normal satisfaction?)

I'm less concerned here with the specific demands of abstract distributive justice than with Cohen's conceptualization of cultural difference as a question of distributive justice. I question the practical value of the idea of abstract "levels of satisfaction" that could be "equal." Given individuals with different desires, biographies, self-images and psychological predispositions, the practical meaning of the equivalence of satisfactions may be elusive (the reason the Coors Light drinker likes his brew may be precisely because it is cheap, plebian, and down-to-earth, just as part of the reason I like my martini is because it's refined and urbane—is there any useful sense in which these disparate indulgences could be commensurable?) But I think Cohen is right on the mark in thinking of these profane pleasures as on a continuum with what multiculturalism holds sacred.

This isn't to suggest that if society chooses to subsidize racial cultures, it must also subsidize martinis and cashews. A continuum does imply the ability to make distinctions. I believe that the expensive taste for art moderne style architecture, such as that of San Francisco's Redwood Room Bar (where, until its insensitive remodeling, I took my martinis on a regular basis) is a better candidate for public subsidy in the form of regulation (San Francisco's landmark preservation ordinance ensured that the Redwood Room's remodeling was merely insensitive, rather than catastrophic) than is the expensive taste for martinis served there. Likewise, we may believe that certain cultural traditions or styles that the market would discourage are expensive tastes deserving of subsidy. What is critical to notice here is that the decision requires us to evaluate the social value (and social costs) of the activity in question, the likelihood that it would continue unsubsidized, and the broader distributive justice effects of the subsidy (for instance, subsidizing an expensive taste that is predominantly suffered, however undeservedly, by the rich, is perverse from a broader distributive justice perspective.)

It is likely that some of the behavior that rights-to-difference would protect would merit protection as a matter of distributive justice. But none of it would merit protection merely because of a statistical correlation with a group identity; instead, it would merit protection because the behavior in question is worth protecting and because the group of people who enjoyed the behavior in some sense deserve the redistribution of social resources that such protection would entail.

Institutional Cultures

Difference discourse has an ironic blindness: a blindness to the culture of institutions. Proponents of rights-to-difference regularly complain that existing anti-discrimination law, in its refusal to recognize cultural rights, reifies a public/private split: it requires the putative plaintiff to "leave her culture at home"—in private—in order to participate in the public (in the sense that government, public accommodations and institutions participating in the economy are all "public" in comparison to intimate relations and casual gatherings of friends) world of the economy and other social institutions.

But rights-to-difference arguments, by ignoring or downplaying the culture of institutions adopts an equally problematic public/private dichotomy in a more formal and explicit fashion: because of their "public" status the institutions governed by rights-to-difference would be required to limit themselves to a set of narrowly defined business or technocratic objectives, while the private individual member of a canonical social group would be ensconced as the exclusive locus of cultural identity. Hence advocates of individual rights-to-difference often ignore entirely the effect of their proposals on the cultures of the institutions that will have the corresponding duty to accommodate.

Institutions have cultures just as much as less formally organized social groups and individuals do. These institutional cultures make up much of the cultural diversity in any society. Institutions affect the lives of everyone with whom they come in contact. Their various cultural styles, as much as and perhaps more than those of individuals, are what give most of everyday life its richness and texture. Given its insistence on the salience of groups, it is surprising that difference discourse largely ignores these specific manifestations of group allegiance and culture.

How might an institution promote and maintain a unique culture? An employer may wish to eliminate *any* unconventional styles or practices in order to cultivate an image of conservatism, mainstream tradition and stability. Financial institutions, professional firms, high-status restaurants and hotels and airlines may have such a goal. Or, an institution may wish to present a uniform image or promote an esprit de corps that would be undermined by overt expressions of individual eccentricity or subgroup affiliation. A chorus line and a military platoon are two exemplars of such institutions.[13] For the same reasons that these employers might require uniforms, another might proscribe personal styles likely to draw undue attention.

If an institution is required to accommodate the cultural styles and norms of its employees or enrollees, it is prohibited from making adherence to an institutional style or norm a requirement of membership. This may not seem like much of a loss—especially if the institution is kept conveniently abstract or if unattractive institutions are chosen as examples. Accordingly, the proponents of rights-to-difference cast the putative plaintiff as the owner of a rich and vital cultural life (that he or she is forced to "leave at home" by a callous institution) while describing the opposing institutional culture as "bland," "antiseptic," or "sterile." But in fact many institutional cultures are rich and varied, while often the minority cultures that are advanced in difference discourse make the Stepford Wives seem exciting.

The crucial point is that sometimes rights-to-difference will conflict with the goal of promoting a institutional culture that is arguably quite valuable and praiseworthy. In these circumstances, rights-to-difference will have significant institutional costs that traditional anti discrimination rights, by and large, do not have.

Consider the following case:

> One of the most popular innovations on college campuses across the country a generation ago was the introduction of coeducational dormitories and the elimination of rules that tried to keep young men and women apart. So it may provide an insight into current college life, as classes begin here at Yale this fall, that one of the most-discussed topics is the claim by five Orthodox Jewish students that those unrestricted living arrangements have established a free-for-all that they compare to Sodom and Gomorrah. A war of words between Yale and the Orthodox students has drawn extensive local media coverage and national attention in Jewish newspapers. The Orthodox students have demanded that they be excused from Yale's requirement that all freshmen and sophomores live on campus. They say their religion's rules of modesty, privacy and sexual abstinence until marriage forbid them to live in residences where condoms, alcohol and shared bathrooms are common.
>
> Yale has refused. . . . Experts on higher education say that Yale's dilemma is a common one on campuses in the 1990's, as administrators grapple with demands from interest groups of all types, including increasingly vocal conservative religious groups, for accommodations, food and academic offerings that meet their special needs. . . . Some students and faculty members on campus here say the debate raises fundamental questions about how much universities should channel people into shared experiences and how much they should encourage students to maintain their own group identities.[14]

Let's leave the important doctrinal questions specific to religion to one side and treat the conflict as if it concerned only our pet topic: culture. The "Yale Five" case brings the conflict between group culture and institutional culture into sharp relief because Yale's policy of co educational dormitories is itself the outcome of intense cultural struggle over gender relations and the requirement of campus residency is a policy designed to promote acculturation to a new and unfamiliar environment. Yale has an institutional culture that most of its students, graduates and employees are proud of and wish to promote. Yale undergraduates maintain a connection with their freshmen residential "college" throughout their college years and many alumni still identify with their residential college long after their years at Yale are over.

Yale's residential education program is deliberately designed to prevent the self-segregation that the "Yale Five" insist on.

> Richard H. Brodhead, the dean of Yale College, said in an interview that part of Yale's offering was the chance for students to learn about other outlooks by living in that community. "If you allow all groups based on affiliation or conviction to separate themselves from the whole university community," Dean Brodhead said, "you open the door to all kinds of self-segregation that this place has worked very hard against."[15]

A similar conflict emerged at Cornell University in 1996 over a proposal to bar freshmen from living in ethnic theme houses. Much like Yale's Dean Broadhead, Cornell's president Rawlings defended the policy as providing a common college experience and as foiling self-segregation: "New students arriving at Cornell should have an experience that demonstrates that they are entering an academic community, first and foremost."[16] The Cornell controversy came to a head when the Reverend Al Sharpton equated the university's attempt to provide a common freshmen year experience with racism. Sharpton mocked: "We want more blacks and Latinos on campus; we just want them to merge in with everyone else so we don't know they're here."[17]

Cornell was caught in a double bind that reflected the internal conflicts of contemporary multiculturalism: a year earlier Cornell was accused of discrimination for establishing and maintaining the ethnic theme houses that Sharpton insisted it must not tamper with. We can imagine those opposed to the theme houses mocking Sharpton: "We want more blacks and Latinos on campus; we just want them to keep to themselves so we don't know they're here." Does social justice demand that minorities be segregated in order to accommodate their distinctive cultures and social norms or does it demand that they be integrated into the common institutional arrangements and modes of socialization that account for much of the prestige and social capital attached to an elite university education?

Both the disgruntled Cornell students and the Yale Five complained that integrated dormitories might undermine their group specific identity by exposing them to more seductive alternatives. In a sense this is exactly what the universities intend. Part of the program of liberal education is designed to ensure that university graduates have been exposed to a variety of norms, ideals and lifestyles and thereby have been forced to consider their inherited cultures in the light of multiple alternatives. Yale and Cornell University have adopted a very self-conscious policy designed to promote a specific institutional culture. The university is not and does not claim to be neutral in this regard—its policy is actively to foster socially and culturally integrated living arrangements and to make them a part of the educational program. This objective requires them to forbid culturally segregated living arrangements and opting out of the shared university life.

One might object that Yale and Cornell should confine their educational agenda to the classroom: on this account the point of college is classroom education, not acculturation in residential settings. But this narrow definition of a university's institutional mission is at best questionable; certainly the administrations of most universities do not define their mission so narrowly. Especially in light of the academic benefits that psychologists such as Claude Steele have found may flow from it, an integrationist housing policy is a matter of academic policy, no different in principle than a requirement that students take a prescribed set of courses as prerequisite for graduation, some of which may challenge or offend the cultural norms of some students. If we allow individuals to in effect define a university's mission and academic policy through claims of cultural difference, what is to stop, say, a Christian fundamentalist who objects to learning Darwin's theory of evolution as part of a required curriculum from defining the college's mission as "career preparation" or "prestige credentialing" so as to exclude the offending curriculum?

Admittedly one might fear that this hill has another slippery slope: if antidiscrimination law doesn't prevent universities from making "cultural policy" can it prevent, say, Bob Jones University's prohibition on interracial dating? After all, Bob Jones's response will parallel Yale's and Cornell's: preventing interracial romance and the ultimate evil of miscegenation is part of the university's institutional culture. But there is an important distinction: the interracial dating prohibition has a racist pedigree. Similar prohibitions have been part of explicitly racist policies, informed by discredited ideas of racial purity and motivated by an unambiguous desire to maintain racial hierarchy. This makes it quite unlike Yale's or Cornell's policies, neither of which reasonably can be described as intentionally biased. The implementation of many legal norms requires us to make such context specific evaluations; I'll have more to say about how we should do so in the context of group difference in chapter 4.

Rights-to-difference are a bad approach to cultural pluralism because they are likely to undermine many of the institutional supports for a diversity of cultural practices. Institutional cultures are the cultures of minority groups as well as those of the "mainstream." Consider law professor Alex Johnson's argument in favor of black colleges: "[T]he existence of a separate African-American community and ethnicity, rather than serving as a justification for forced integration, instead mandates the continued operation of predominantly or historically black colleges. These schools transmit those amorphous values unique to the African-American community, its nomos."[18] While I question Johnson's conception of black culture, his main point is valid: cultures thrive in institutional contexts. I doubt that the integration of historically black colleges with historically white ones will destroy black culture, but a legal requirement that black colleges cater to the cultural differences of their non-black enrollees might destroy, if not "black culture" generally, at least the specific culture of those institutions. Should Morehouse be required to accept practices inconsistent with its historical mission in order to accommodate white, Latino or Asian students? Must a Chinese bar and social club allow dominoes on its Mah Jong night in order to be inclusive? Must a Latino bar that signals its identity by playing salsa allow its African-American employees to play hip-hop or jazz? Should the insistence of such institutions that their norms and social practices—their culture—remain distinctive be actionable as invidious discrimination?

It is not helpful to say that only cultural minorities, but not the hegemonic majority, should enjoy rights-to-difference. As these examples suggest, some conflicts will be between minority groups. Even if the institution in question is "mainstream" (like Yale and Cornell universities) its institutional *culture* may be the embattled and fragile result of a considered experiment or of an ongoing struggle involving the terms of social interaction. A university's insistence on mandatory residence in sex-integrated and racially integrated dorms is itself a profound and potentially fragile cultural intervention; should the law weigh in against the university's norm and favor that of its separatist students? And even if the institutional culture in question is durable and hegemonic, this may be because it is better suited to a given environment or set of legitimate institutional goals.

Rights-to-difference also may stifle cultural pluralism in another way. Although in some instances cultural rights might force institutions to become more interesting, more vibrant and more inclusive by requiring them to incorporate the cultural styles of their employees and patrons, it is likely that in many cases cultural rights will have the opposite effect: by requiring "cultural neutrality," cultural rights will encourage institutions to adopt the most bland, antiseptic and predictable styles possible.

Anti-discrimination law typically prohibits discrimination directly by outlawing explicit and intentional discrimination, and indirectly by scrutinizing policies that have a *disparate impact* on the groups that the statute protects from discrimination. The disparate impact doctrine can be seen as a means of rooting out well-hidden, unconscious or institutionalized discrimination: a policy with a statistically disparate impact on a minority group makes us suspicious of a hidden motive or systematic bias. The institution can overcome this suspicion by demonstrating that the policy is necessary to the legitimate goals of the institution.

Presently, the bases of prohibited discrimination are limited both in number and in scope. Although we may not have a precise and comprehensive definition of, say, "racial discrimination"—we constantly work out the meaning in the context of specific factual disputes—the term has a widely accepted core meaning ("color prejudice") that implies certain common-sensical limits. We know for instance, that institutions generally are free to regulate the *behavior* of their members without fear of violating the rule against racial discrimination because anti-discrimination law does not extend to policies that regulate behavior. In this context, institutions are relatively free to develop their own cultures without fear of legal liability. But, let's consider the path of least risk for an institution covered under a rights-to-difference regime. Even an innocent policy (such as integrated dorms) might conflict with the desires of some members of a protected group and hence potentially be actionable as "cultural discrimination." In this context, the only bullet-proof policy would be one that was strictly *necessary* to the institutional mission, narrowly defined. The risk averse institution would adopt only policies that focused exclusively on objectively defensible goals such as technocratic expertise, efficiency and the bottom line. By way of rights-to-difference we arrive at the epitome of capitalist alienation as described by leftists since Karl Marx. In effect, the rights-to-difference project may encourage the bland institutional monoculture that it fears.

Institutions, Culture and Intergroup Conflict

One of multiculturalism's central insights is that racial, cultural and ethnic differences matter. People are invested in their identities, they experience group affinities as authentic and self given and they often act according to the demands of group solidarity, for better and for worse. Because group identity matters, the symbols and stylistic conventions of group membership matter. These insights lead many to advocate some form of rights-to-difference.

These are valid insights. But legal rights-to-difference don't follow from them. In fact, precisely because the symbols of group affiliation matter, they may at times be dangerous and subversive of legitimate institutional goals. If group difference and affiliation matter, they can do harm as well as good. Even more vexing: group difference might be both good and harmful in the same instance. A source of group affiliation and pride for insiders can be a powerful message of exclusion and hostility for outsiders. Institutions charged with the evenhanded management of diverse multicultural groups will at times have good reasons *on inclusive, pluralist grounds* to discourage or forbid overt expressions of group affiliation.

To illustrate this point, I've chosen to examine a case that has become a standard citation for advocates of cultural rights: *Garcia v. Spun Steak*.[19] *Spun Steak* looks like a good case for cultural rights because it involves an attribute of culture that is unambiguously central to an unambiguously subordinated minority group. The case involves the right (lack thereof as it turns out) of Latinos to speak Spanish:

> Spun Steak employs thirty-three workers, twenty-four of whom are Spanish-speaking. Virtually all of the Spanish-speaking employees are Hispanic. While two employees speak no English, the others have varying degrees of proficiency in English. . . . Appellees Garcia and Buitrago are production line workers. . . . Both Garcia and Buitrago are fully bilingual, speaking both English and Spanish. . . . Prior to September 1990, these Spun Steak employees spoke Spanish freely to their co-workers during work hours.

> [Then] the following rule was adopted:

> It is hereafter the policy of this Company that only English will be spoken in connection with work. During lunch, breaks, and employees' own time, they are obviously free to speak Spanish if they wish. . . .

> Garcia, Buitrago, and Local 115, on behalf of all Spanish-speaking employees of Spun Steak, filed suit, alleging that the English-only policy violated Title VII [the federal employment discrimination law]. . . . The district court . . . granted the Spanish-speaking employees' motion for summary judgment, concluding that the English-only policy disparately impacted Hispanic workers without sufficient business justification, and thus violated Title VII.[20]

The plaintiffs had reason to be optimistic; an Equal Employment Opportunities Commission (EEOC) guideline provided that "an employee makes the *prima facie* case . . . merely by proving the existence of an English only policy. . . . [b]ecause . . . English-only rules may 'create an atmosphere of inferiority, isolation and intimidation based on national origin which could result in a discriminatory working environment'."[21]

However, the Ninth Circuit Court of Appeals reversed, holding that "the bilingual employees have not made out a *prima facie* case and that Spun Steak has not violated Title VII as to them."[22] The court held that the policy did not discriminate against bilingual Spanish speakers "[b]ecause . . . the bilingual employee can readily comply with the English-only rule. . . . There is no . . . [discrimination] with respect to a privilege of employment if the rule is one that the affected employee can readily observe and nonobservance is a matter of individual preference."[23]

Numerous law review articles criticize the decision in *Spun Steak* as a betrayal of sound anti-discrimination principles.[24] But few of the critics mention several salient details of the factual context of the dispute. It bears noting in passing that twenty-four of Spun Steak's thirty-three employees were Spanish-speaking Latinos.[25] This fact alone suggests that the English-only policy was not intended as a proxy for illicit racial or national origin discrimination. Even more striking, the policy was adopted in response to complaints that the *plaintiffs in the case*, Garcia and Buitrago, "made derogatory, racist comments in Spanish about two other co-workers, one of whom is African-American and the other Chinese-American."[26] The company's president "concluded that an English-only rule would promote racial harmony in the workplace."[27]

Although Latinos are a minority in society at large, they were not a minority on the Spun Steak production line. Given that twenty-four of thirty-three Spun Steak employees were Spanish speakers, it is understandable that management would have been concerned about the social isolation of the other nine employees and especially concerned about the solitary black and lonesome Asian employee. In light of the complaints of these employees, it is plausible that the *Spun Steak* plaintiffs were not helpless minority victims of a English-speaking hegemony, but rather members of a belligerent *majority* who used their common language as a means of isolating and harassing employees who were minorities both in society at large *and* at work.

One might complain that the management could have forbidden racial harassment without an English-only rule. But disparaging a fellow employee in a language that she does not entirely understand (but can no doubt partially decipher) may be an especially effective isolation tactic, much like whispering or passing notes among a racially exclusive clique. It's not obvious that anti-discrimination law should prohibit management from dealing with racial tensions by depriving potential harassers of an effective tool.

Suppose, for instance, that a hypothetical "Son of Spun Steak" workplace is one of tense race relations, one in which the members of each racial group exhibit some animus towards coworkers of other races. Suppose that over time each group develops tactics to harass the other groups and to establish in-group solidarity (the two could become hard to disentangle): whites begin to wear confederate flags and whistle "Dixie"; blacks wear braids, *kente* cloth and greet each other with the clenched fist of black power; Chinese-Americans make disparaging racial jokes in Cantonese, Latinos do so in Spanish. The Son of Spun Steak management responds to escalating racial tensions with a set of workplace rules: no singing or whistling, no flags, no *kente* cloth, no raised fists, no language other than English.

The English-only, no *kente* cloth and no raised fists rules in this context are no more discriminatory than the "no flags and no whistling" rule. Many southern whites feel that the confederate flag is an important—indeed indispensable—symbol of their heritage. They would undoubtedly feel burdened, perhaps even stripped of their identity, by the workplace rule. They would insist that the confederate flag is not a symbol of racism, but instead a symbol of southern pride and that the management can prohibit racial slurs without burdening innocent forms of cultural expression. They might even claim that the rule discriminates against whites, especially if Son of Spun Steak was located in, say the southeastern United States, as opposed to northern California.

They would be wrong. By the same token it also is wrong that rules prohibiting expressions of cultural differences should *always* be legally actionable. An employer may have good, non-discriminatory reasons for such rules, not only rules that *incidentally* impede cultural expression (arguably the Spun Steak rule or, say, the effect of a rule prohibiting male employees from wearing long hair on members of certain Native-American tribes) but also those that intentionally impede cultural expression. In the "Son of Spun Steak" hypothetical case, the *purpose* of the rules was to impede expressions of cultural and racial difference. Yet the rule did not reflect racial animus on the part of management. Nor did the rule simply reflect the hegemonic racial animus of another group that the management felt compelled to oblige (as it would have had management prohibited non-English languages simply to placate xenophobic English speakers in its workforce or customer base). Policies prohibiting expressions of difference may serve legitimate functions, especially in a society of relatively insular and mutually suspicious groups. Such policies at times may be the best means to ensure that intergroup friction does not ignite a conflagration. In this sense, the Spun Steak policy reflects a recognition of the salience of cultural difference and an attempt to foster a harmonious multicultural workplace.

Institutions should be allowed to experiment with different responses to cultural pluralism. Just as the desire to foster group separatism and distinctiveness can be, but is not necessarily a form of bigotry and discrimination, so too the desire to promote a cohesive and harmonious institutional culture that, by necessity, excludes certain manifestations of individuality and group difference, is not necessarily a form of bigotry. There are good, culturally sensitive and non-discriminatory arguments both for and against mandatory dormitories for college freshmen, for and against ethnic theme houses and for and against rules prohibiting expressions of group identity. *In context* we may determine that a particular instance of such a policy is motivated by bias or has consequences we find unacceptable, but there is simply no reason to *presume* that any one of these policies is objectionable, much less to support the contention that any of them are objectionable per se.

Of course, Yale's, Cornell's and Spun Steak's policies require or encourage some degree of assimilation. That's enough to condemn them in mind of some. Yoshino, for instance, explicitly argues for a legal right against forced assimilation, a proposal that is in harmony with the vast majority of multiculturalist literature. But some degree of assimilation is a natural and unavoidable part of social integration and a necessary phenomenon in any complex society. Although modern societies and institutions can and do accommodate a great deal of pluralism, there are limits, limits that are difficult to identify even through trial and error and impossible to identify in the abstract or to codify in the form of legal rules. Assimilation is a necessary and desirable phenomenon in complex societies; it is integral to the formation of cohesive social institutions and it is also a part of the process of minority subgroup formation. Most if not all of the "canonical" social groups—those that we presently identify as salient—became cohesive groups and remain so through the assimilation of disparate elements to a common group identity.

Such a partial and ad hoc assimilation need not entail the wholesale destruction of minority group practices and the dominance of a single culture. It rarely does: even the world's most aggressive imperial hegemonds often have been the most aggressive consumers of disparate cultural practices as well. Despite the prevalence of the overused and undertheorized term "cultural genocide," a more prevalent and significant phenomenon has involved the selective appropriation and recombination of minority cultural practices by both the "mainstream" and by the minority groups themselves. This more fluid and varied process of cultural melding can generate the common cultural norms, practices, events, artifacts and customs that bind potentially disparate groups together into an institution or a society.

Such cultural melding is rarely complete or comprehensive. Without rights-to-difference, group identities will remain, ethnic affiliations will continue to exert their gravitation pull on group members and social groups will retain traditional distinctive practices and develop new ones. But at the same time groups and their practices will change in response to social incentives and disincentives; particularly unpopular or maladaptive practices and expressions of group difference will be discouraged by other members of society and in many cases will eventually die out.

Multiculturalists often object to assimilation by insisting that dominant cultural norms are not universally valid or valuable but rather culturally specific. But a partial and contingent acquiescence in assimilation does not depend on a belief in the objective, universal or transcendent nature of the norms to which assimilation takes place. In fact, it is notable that the type of assimilation that takes place in modern cosmopolitan societies often involves no preexisting set of cultural norms to which all assimilate; instead common cultural norms and practices emerge from the collision of a multiplicity of older traditions. It may be that some practices and norms are morally or practically superior to others (the disagreement over "cultural relativism" is one about which I am agnostic), but the ethical acceptability of assimilation does not depend on this. It is enough to observe that institutions and societies often require *some* set of shared norms: it often matters less what the norms are than that they are shared.

Here's the tough sell: it would be unrealistic to imagine that any such process could be entirely voluntary, painless or easy. The rough and tumble of social and economic interaction is such that most people find at least some social demands unwelcome and some individuals and groups find many social norms frankly oppressive. This is inevitable if a society is to develop any common norms; perhaps the best we can hope for is that the sacrifices of present generations will smooth the way for future generations to enjoy the benefits of belonging in a stable, prosperous and mutually supportive society. Legal interventions premised on the false assumption that social cohesion can be achieved without any unwanted change are likely to be ineffectual at best and counterproductive at worst.

Perhaps for no group is this more true than for those urban sociologist William Julius Wilson has dubbed "The Truly Disadvantaged": people raised in impoverished, racially segregated neighborhoods who have, predictably, adopted a cultural style distinctive to their environment. Through a series of interviews Wilson illuminates the attitudes of employers toward such inner city blacks:

> An employer from a computer software firm in Chicago expressed the view "that in many businesses the ability to meet the public is paramount and you do not talk street talk to the buying public." . . . [A] suburban

employer added "They [inner city blacks] don't know how to dress when they come to an interview. They bring fourteen other people with them." . . . [A] black employer in a Chicago insurance company argued that "there is a perception that most of your kids are black and . . . they don't know how to write. They don't know how to speak. They don't act in a business fashion or dress in a business manner[,] . . . in a way the business community would like. And they just don't feel that they're getting a quality employee." When asked whether he thought this was a false impression, the employer responded "I think there's some truth to it."[28]

In connection with these employer attitudes, Wilson notes that

> Given recent shifts in the economy, employers are looking for workers with a broad range of abilities: "hard" skills (literacy, numeracy, basic mechanical ability, and other testable attributes) and "soft" skills (personalities suitable to the work environment, good grooming, group-oriented work behaviors, etc.). While hard skills are the product of education and training[,] . . . soft skills are strongly tied to culture, and are therefore shaped by the harsh environment of the inner city ghetto. If employers are indeed reacting to the difference in skills between white and black applicants, it becomes increasingly difficult to discern the motives of employers: are they rejecting inner-city black applicants out of overt racial discrimination or on the basis of qualifications?[29]

Rights-to-difference and difference discourse would answer Wilson's question by insisting that discrimination on the basis of identity correlated "soft skills" *is* racial discrimination. The inner-city minority race poor are compelling potential beneficiaries of rights-to-difference because they are the most needy— they are the class of potential beneficiaries who in fact benefited least from the civil rights reforms of the 1960s—and because their cultural traits are most likely deeply ingrained and therefore not easily malleable.

But how successful are rights-to-difference likely to be in this context? Rights-to-difference claims are most persuasive where the cultural traits to be protected are not obviously related to the legitimate objectives of the institution that would be required to accommodate them: one reason that Rene Rogers's claim is compelling was that the cornrow hairstyle strikes many people today as unrelated to job qualifications. By contrast, many of the cultural attributes associated with the inner-city poor strike most employers as directly related to qualifications.

Wilson's hypothesis regarding the increasing importance of "soft skills" is echoed by scores of economists and sociologists who note that the

"postindustrial" or "service" economies of today's wealthier nations are bifur-
cated between a well-paid group of skilled culture and information managers
distinguished by their mastery of "soft skills" and a poorly paid group of
menial service laborers, increasingly consigned to part-time, temporary and
seasonal work (without health insurance, retirement benefits or meaningful
job security) and catch-as-catch can in the informal economy.

Even in jobs where soft skills are not of central importance, it is common
practice for employers to treat grooming, dress, demeanor and self-presentation
as signals of job-related traits such as reliability, respect for authority, detail orientation and sociability. In fact, it is commonplace for *everyone* to evaluate
people based on such "cultural" traits as grooming, dress and demeanor:
whether choosing a building contractor or deciding whether you approve of
your daughter's new boyfriend, these "soft" attributes play a crucial role in our
evaluation of others.

If soft skills are of *central* importance in a growing number of the stable
and reasonably well-paid jobs in our economy, it is unlikely that legislatures
would approve, or that courts would apply, an anti-discrimination norm that
forbade employers to consider them. Rather than an intervention designed to
disrupt racial practices that most Americans agree are illegitimate, this would
be a requirement that employers ignore qualifications that almost everyone
agrees are relevant. The social commitment to anti-discrimination could not
bear the weight of such a major reorientation of the economy.

This is not to suggest that we need no antipoverty policy reform. Indeed,
to echo Wilson, the point is that *antipoverty reform* is precisely what we need.
We need vocational training, remedial education to correct for schools that
have failed, substance abuse counseling and government work programs for
those who cannot find employment in the private sector. We need affordable
housing and efficient public transportation. We need vigorous enforcement of
anti-discrimination law to ensure that the vast majority of desperately poor
people who are anxious to improve their lives have the access to opportunity
they deserve. What we don't need is the counter-productive message that difference discourse sends to the disadvantaged: that they need not, indeed
should not, bring their practices into line with the expectations of most of
society, that they have a *right* to persist in socially dysfunctional behavior
and that the way to a better life is not to adapt, but rather to complain and if
possible, to sue. This siren's song reaches a crescendo in rights-to-difference,
which promise what no legal reform can deliver: to remove cultural considerations from the economy by separating the economy from the influence of
culture.

Cosmopolitan Difference

Collective structures, tribal or cultural, reproduce themselves historically by risking themselves in novel conditions. Their wholeness is as much a matter of reinvention and encounter as it is of continuity and survival.[30]

It's rare that an institution is interested in wiping out a minority culture. Generally institutional decision makers are busy pursuing their own goals—transcontinental air travel, higher education, meatpacking, what-have-you—and make some judgment as to whether a particular practice is good, bad or of no moment given their institutional goals. But institutions such as businesses and universities influence the practices of their members. Such influence often takes the form of both subtle and overt pressure to modify or abandon elements of what might be called a group culture. Is such pressure to assimilate a social injustice? Law professor Mari Matsuda makes this argument:

> [T]he right to cultural difference must spread to the full range of culture chosen and defined by *the group*, not by any dominant culture. That is, we cannot say "Thai food, yes, Thai accents no" or "Black music, yes, Black English no." The selective filter that appropriates certain aspects of subordinate cultures and discards others is not pluralism; it is domination. Radical pluralism includes self-determination—the rights to make and promote one's culture and to share it in *whole cloth* with other politically equal cultures. [emphasis mine][31]

Similar arguments are a staple of the multiculturalism literature. Will Kymlicka, for example, defines the societal cultures he would protect with extraordinary group rights as "a full set of social practices and institutions, encompassing all aspects of social life" and insists that "decisions about which particular aspects of one's culture are worth maintaining and developing should be left to the choices of individual members [of the minority group].[32]

In most workplaces and social environments today, a constellation of social norms and cultural influences promotes some group cultural practices and discourages other practices: precisely the "selective filter" Matsuda identifies as domination. If we accept Matsuda's and Kymlicka's accounts, most social institutions promote cultural domination.

The idea that group cultures must be accommodated "whole cloth"—reminds one of an old ethnic joke: in Heaven there are English banks, French cuisine, Italian sociability and German cars. Hell is only slightly different: there are Italian banks, English cuisine, German sociability and French cars.

In a world where group cultures must be taken "whole cloth," if you want to savor coq au vin you've got to drive (or push) a Citroën to the café; if you want the financial stability of the English Pound Sterling you must sate your hunger with Toad in the Hole.

Happily, we aren't faced with a stark choice between accepting the practices of a social group whole cloth and cultural domination. In fact, historically, minority cultural styles have not been systematically rejected. Instead the *culture* often has been embraced and the *people* have been rejected. The profound contributions of racial minorities to what is now mainstream American culture are forgotten or denied even as the cultural contributions themselves are readily adopted by the white majority, at times in a strikingly direct manner (consider Elvis Presley's largely unacknowledged cover of Big Mama Thornton's "Hound Dog," the Rolling Stones's stylistic mimicking of American blues artists or Led Zeppelin's direct quotation of the standard blues double entendre: "squeeze my lemon till the juice runs down my leg"). Rather than worry about the largely made-up phenomenon of "cultural genocide," perhaps we should endeavor to acknowledge the many important contributions of minorities to mainstream culture and institutions.

This is not to say that we should replace the obsession with cultural genocide with an obsession with cultural appropriation. Cultural appropriation, as the examples above suggest, can produce striking and priceless artistic and expressive advances. Of course, the cultural hybrids that emerge from this phenomenon are mutations; they add and subtract from the original cultural forms—Robert Plant is not Junior Wells in whiteface. Unlike Matsuda, I don't think this selective embrace of cultural styles, practices and artifacts is objectionable or preventable. I expect that it is inevitable that people will pick and choose among minority cultural practices: Jazz is more popular than Ebonics; Thai food is more popular than, say, Thai ethnic dance. This is not necessarily domination—indeed it seems to be a necessary stage in the development of the cultural hybrids Matsuda celebrates in the following passage:

> The only center, the only glue, that makes us a nation is our many-centered cultural heritage. Just as our use of language is rich, varied, interactive, and changeable, so is our national culture. We are the only country in which an Okinawan vendor serves Kosher pastrami and stir-fried vegetables wrapped in a tortilla to young white punk rockers at 3:00 a.m. in the morning. . . . From the oversized plaster chickens and donuts that mark our highways to the exquisite wisps of nouvelle Franco-Latin-Japanese cuisine set before our expense-account diners, we are a nation fantastic and wide-ranging in our vernacular and our juxtapositions. From the Grand Ole Opry to neo-metal,

from zydeco to the Met, we are a range of tastes and sounds wider than ever before known to the nations of this planet.[33]

Here Matsuda's account of American society is distinctly cosmopolitan; she celebrates the emergence of novel cultural forms, multi-cultural hybrids and the complication of the loyalties that might bind people to cultural practices and artifacts in the form of nations, races or ethnicities. But in stark contrast to this compelling affirmation of cultural pluralism and hybridity, Matsuda concludes that we need "rights to make and promote one's culture and to share it in *whole cloth*." At this point the dizzying swarm of cultural styles is forced into a rigid organizational schema suitable for judicial enforcement. Where in the former account we had cultural artifacts circulating free of the restrictions of pedigree or membership, here we have tightly compacted groups that determine "their" culture. Where before we had a story of cultural fragments, recombined to become parts of a multitude of novel expressions, here we have an insistence on cultures that can be conceived of and promoted "whole cloth." Where before we had individuals building and teetering on top of decentered identities in the frenetic intersection of national customs, popular culture and commercial capitalism, here we get the fantasy of a placid reorientation around the trope of "self-determination," as if the self that would determine the content of its culture is self-evident and the process of determination is the cognitive process of a single-minded consciousness.

Matsuda's powerful celebration of cultural cosmopolitanism suggests why the project of preserving cultural difference "whole cloth" is misguided. The prevalence of cultural appropriation and the popularity of its cultural products casts some doubt on the widespread fear that mainstream society is opposed to minority cultural *practices* and seeks to eliminate them without a trace. It suggests that the preoccupation with cultural genocide overstates the dangers to cultural practices (and distracts attention from the still very real evil of status prejudice.) Viewed sympathetically, cultural appropriation could be renamed cultural syncresis: a process of melding and recombination through which new cultural forms are produced.

Cultural syncresis provides an alternative model of cultural pluralism and of social identity; one that is not assimilation to a preexisting and rigid norm but is also not preservation of a group-culture in an isolated stasis, one that is not colorblindness or monolithic humanism but is instead a pluralist humanism that embraces social identities in an anti-canonical, flexible way.

Consider Paul Gilroy's discussion of black cultural practices that reach across oceans, blend traditions, arise and mutate according to the politics of the day and even cross the color line. On pan-Africanism, Gilroy writes:

The sense of inter-connectedness felt by blacks to which [pan-Africanism] refers, has in some recent manifestations, become partially detached from any primary affiliation to Africa and the aspiration to a homogenous African culture. Young blacks in Britain . . . stimulated to riotous protest by the sight of black "South Africans" stoning apartheid police and moved by the sense of brutality transmitted from that country by satellite, may not feel that shared Africanness is at the root of the empathy they experience. It may be that a common experience of powerlessness somehow transcending history and experience in racial categories; in the antagonism between white and black rather than European and African, is enough to secure affinity between these divergent patterns of subordination.[34]

Notice that Gilroy's black Britons are intensely race conscious, but embrace racial identity as a response to their lived experiences as the objects of racial categorization, not as a narrative of pedigree, historical continuity or tradition. These socially contingent and explicitly cosmopolitan expressions of racial identity are the source of some of the most exciting artistic and creative expressions in the contemporary developed West. Gilroy's account of racial identity and its cultural products in the book *There Ain't No Black in the Union Jack* includes discussions of the writers of Harlem Renaissance, the proto-funk of James Brown, the "mothership" funk of Bootsy Collins and George Clinton, the pioneering reggae of Bob Marley, the early hip-hop of Grandmaster Flash and the Furious Five, the British hip–hop of Afrika Bambaataa, Jamaican "dancehall" and its London clubland offshoots. In each case, the artistic expression was a hybrid of "local culture" and affiliations and influences from Africa and other sites of the African diaspora. For instance, "Bob Marley's reggae was, like all reggae, a hybrid marked as much by its ties to American rhythm and blues as by its roots in Mento and calypso. One of the best known songs of Marley's middle period 'Three O'Clock Road Block,' is for an example, extrapolated from Cole Porter's "Don't Fence Me In."[35] And Marley's diasporic identifications are evident from his references to the Rastafarian's Ethiopian Zion and his ambiguously critical identification with the American "Buffalo Soldier." American hip-hop borrowed African motifs and psuedonyms while British hip-hop borrowed as heavily from the South Bronx as from Brixton.

These racial identities are at times multi racial (or perhaps they define race as a contingency and practice rather than reify it as an essence.) People from Pakistan and the Indian subcontinent identified as "black" in British antiracist youth culture. The interracial "Two Tone" movement of the 1970s and 1980s grafted a subcultural style of 1960s working-class white British youth (the Mods—for an example see the film *Quadraphenia*) onto an amalgamation of the popular music of late 1970s urban England (punk), of late 1960s urban America (soul) and of 1970s Jamaica (the reggae precursor "ska"). As Gilroy writes:

> the "two-tone" cult . . . [included] racially mixed groups . . . [who] sought to display the contradictory politics of "race" openly in their work. The best efforts acknowledged the destructive power of racism and simultaneously invited their audience to share in its overcoming, a possibility that was made concrete in the co-operation of blacks and whites in producing the music.[36]

In the 1990s London's "electronica" style met traditional Indian musical styles in, for example, Talvin Singh's aptly titled "Soundz of the Asian Underground" (the spelling of "soundz" itself a nod to African-American hip-hop slang).

Most of what we think of as ethnic or group culture is *already* a syncresis of disparate elements: as philosopher and cultural critic Cornel West notes, "what is distinctive about black religion and black music [is] their cultural hybrid character in which the complex mixture of African, European, and American elements are constitutive of something that is new."[37] Hip-hop godfather Run DMC's biggest hit was a cover of "Walk This Way," penned and first made famous by the kings of New England white trash rock, Aerosmith. Kid Rock took the white trash/hip-hop hybrid to its latest extreme: for instance, in a nod to hip-hop's now defunct group Niggas with Attitude's milestone album *Straight Outta Compton*, Rock quips: "I'm not straight outta Compton; I'm straight out the trailer." Meanwhile the pantheon of "black" hip-hop's most respected artists includes three Jews from Long Island (the Beastie Boys) and a blond from Michigan (Eminem) even as African-American rapper Will Smith is seen as a mainstream pop star, lacking "street cred." (In one song Eminem mimicks a schoolmarm's voice and chides: "Will Smith don't gotta curse in his raps to sell records" and then retorts in his own voice "Well *I* do, so fuck him and fuck you too!")

These cultural styles are or were all, in various ways, both "authentic" cultural artifacts and political expressions of racial identity. Their politics lies, not only in a reaction to institutionalized racial subordination—the whip hand of the overlord or the jackboot of the police—but also in their rejection or determined redescription of the traditional culture of the white and non-white mainstream. London's Two Tone movement was an attack on conservative politics and the mainstream culture of the New Britian (as expresssed in the Specials's grimly melodramatic "Rat Race," and the wickedly ludic anti-Thatcher anthem "Maggie's Farm") but also a reformulation of racial identity with ideological stakes that were quite independent of anti-Thacherism. Hip-hop is unthinkable except as an angry reaction to the racism of white mainstream America (there are examples too numerous to mention, perhaps the archetype is Public Enemy's "It Takes a Nation of Millions to Hold Us Back"), but it is also unreadable except as an attack on mainstream *black* America (witness, for instance, Public Enemy's declaration of "war on black radio": their reaction to mainstream black radio's rap-free playlists).

As these examples suggest, cultural syncresis produces expressions of group affiliation, overt and subtle: the "soul" handshake, the gay community insider's earring and bandana during the early 1980s (quickly adopted by straight hipsters worldwide), ethnic street festivals and parades and other appeals to solidarity for political causes or social activities. These types of group identification are responses to the subjugations of social hierarchy and also have the significant merit of being fun and at times deliciously subversive of otherwise purposely alienated environments.

"Fun" and "subversive" are two qualities that difference discourse has in very short supply. Among the most depressing aspects of contemporary identity politics are its single chord of sanctimonious earnestness, obligation and indignation and its unrequited faith in top-down authoritarian fixes to complex social ills. By contrast, the cultural practices shared by groups and adopted, altered and adapted by individuals are vibrant and dare I say authentic expressions of the maelstrom of culture, politics, economy, art, philosophy and passion that are our (multi)cultural world. They are not only fun and subversive; they are usually quite resilient. There's a reason that suburban high school kids blast hip-hop from Mom's SUV and cop an African-American style of speech and dress (often much to Mom's chagrin). It's no fluke that Latin-American inspired music, *performed in Spanish* is the hottest ticket from Los Angeles to New York. And it's not even news that "gay" cultural affectations are the lingua franca of urbane sophisticates everywhere (and have been at least since Noel Coward, maybe since Oscar Wilde).

Racial cultures? You bet, but not canonized social groups queuing up neatly to present their culture whole cloth to other rights-bearing cultures. Instead we have the rough and tumble of street culture, the rock-and-roll of who gets on MTV, the *strum und drang* of new poetry being created even as you read these words, the warp and weave of the clothes you're wearing as you read them.

Of course, these underground and about-to-be-mainstream cultural styles and expressions are varied and mixed: some produce art of great value and others produce ephemeral doggerel, some generate profound social critique and others generate derivative and reactionary cant. Too many participate in the most destructive versions of the difference fetishism I have attacked in this book: social critic Stanely Crouch, criticizes "the ganster-rap wing of hip-hop for reiterating a kind of minstrelsy in which black youth was defined as truly 'authentic' in the most illiterate, vulgar, anarchic and ignorant manifestations. . . . [S]uch material [is] popular among whites because such 'authentic' Negroes, however hip hopped up, [are] aggressively reinstituting the folklore of white supremacy."[38] Still, for better or for worse these new social identities and expressive frameworks are the future of any society, culture or subculture. The subcultural hybrids of today will give birth to the canonical genres and political and social identifications of tomorrow. This is why the authoritarian discourse of difference and regulatory proposals for rights-to-difference should be met with apprehension and resistance by anyone who cares about either social identities or culture.

The Cosmopolitan and the Province: An Ideological Reorientation

My argument in this chapter presupposes certain normative commitments that may not be universally shared. It presupposes that at least some of the projects of private institutions (a certain liberal vision of higher education, harmonious relations among a multiracial workforce, fostering of an esprit de corps among workers in high-stress occupations) are often more important than the exhibition of group difference. It presupposes that cultural pluralism that takes the form of new hybrids is an acceptable alterative to the canonization of distinctive group cultures. It presumes that individual freedom is better realized through the ability to negotiate a multiplicity of social styles and influences than as an exclusive option on the one associated with one's ascribed identity. It presupposes that social integration of minority groups is an important social goal, more important in a great many cases than the attachment of some individuals to the social practices associated with group difference.

These are debatable points. One might plausibly insist that recognition of difference is a fundamental human right, which always trumps any competing consideration. A difference advocate might argue that what I object to about difference discourse—its tendency to *produce* the correlation of behavior and ascribed identity it claims to describe and its tendency to discredit those group members who don't play along—is not a *problem* of the discourse but rather central to its charm. The whole point, he might rejoin, is to foster the solidarity of minority groups, not as a means to some crass political end or to the redistribution of the white man's filthy lucre, but as an end in itself. Solidarity of this kind requires discipline, especially in the context of the shallow seductiveness of cosmopolitan society and the tempting privilege of the *assimilado*. He might argue that conventions that help to preserve and consolidate minority cultures are to be celebrated despite, or even because of their detrimental effect on individual mobility. Where I see "protective custody," he may see a nurturing safe haven; conversely where I see opportunities for growth, freedom and creativity, he may see the potential for betrayal, dissolution of group ties and anomie.

To such a person I can only respond that I disagree. My normative vision is simply incompatible with this one. I wish to convince as many people as I can to reject the priorities and commitments of difference discourse in favor of different priorities and commitments. My approach in this regard will be, not so much to argue for my foundational convictions, as to describe them in terms of an ideological opposition. This opposition is not the familiar one of left versus right; instead it cuts across the left/right division.

We might identify this less-familiar ideological division with the caption *Cosmopolitanism v. Provincialism* in order to suggest a reorientation of the ideological stakes, one in which my own commitments will be more clear, and I hope, more compelling. It's my hope that naming and organizing these inchoate commitments will help to uncover the ideological stakes of difference discourse and my critique of it. Once the stakes are unearthed and dusted off it should be clear that rights-to-difference implicate ideological commitments that are largely distinct from those underlying established anti-discrimination law.

Put casually, cosmopolitanism entails an embrace of fluidity and movement through and between social distinctions and cultural practices; cosmopolitanism celebrates cultural mixing and hybridization, it revels in the shock of the new, it values the innovation that comes from the interaction of various traditions, the freedom that comes from the ability to exit close knit communities and to pick and choose among the practices, customs and artifacts of social groups. It finds even the violence of clashes between cultural practices and norms potentially productive. It worries little about the erosion of cultural continuity or the destruction of traditional ways; indeed, the cosmopolitan is suspicious of claims of tradition and of group solidarity and loyalty. Philosopher Jeremy Waldron describes the cosmopolitan ideal:

> The practitioner of the [cosmopolitan] ethos . . . may live all his life in one city and maintain the same citizenship throughout. But he refuses to think of himself as defined by his location or his ancestry or his citizenship or his language. . . . He is a creature of modernity, conscious of living in a mixed up world and having a mixed up self. . . . [A] world in which deracinated cosmopolitanism flourishes is not a safe place for minority communities. Our experience has been that they wither and die in the harsh glare of modern life.[39]

It's easy to dismiss cosmopolitanism as faddish and shallow: the damming (and simultaneously seductive) image of the cosmopolitan is of an elite globe-trotter who jets from place to place, sampling the food, savoring the local culture, enjoying an exotic sexual encounter and then, without making bothersome attachments or being changed in any significant way, moves on the next experience. Ian Fleming's James Bond is the personification of a certain cosmopolitan ideal, one that for many is dammed by association with cold war imperialism and chauvinism.

But cosmopolitanism is also the ideal underlying the profound humanism and internationalism of the postwar era: the United Nations, the World Court, the International Monetary Fund and Amnesty International. Cosmopolitan ideals have inspired aid to the needy overseas, have helped to eliminate foreign injustices and have underwritten asylum for political dissidents. Cosmopolitan sensibilities have given us cubism, surrealism, jazz and reggae, the writings of Italo Calvino, Toni Morrison, Salmon Rushdie and Gabriel Garcia Marquez; the art of Henri Matisse and Paul Gaugin, the music of Duke Ellington and Philip Glass. Cosmopolitanism is, almost by definition, varied and complex: it underlies international human rights, Esperanto and the much-celebrated and much-maligned global economy; it's McDonald's on the Champs Elysee and haute cuisine on the Las Vegas strip; it's KFC in New Delhi and Bollywood at a theater near you; it's MTV Asia and Hong Kong's John Woo as the next Stephen Speilberg; it's American troops in Somalia, and a war crimes tribunal in the Hague; it's foreign aid from the industrialized West and it's Argentina catching pneumonia when Wall Street gets the sniffles.

Provincialism respects traditions and reveres communities of fate; it is deep seated and cares about roots and pedigree. It identifies authenticity with the patina of age. It understands the desire for homogeneity within communities. Provincialism seems to stay at home and tend the garden while cosmopolitanism goes on a safari. But provincialism is secretly ambitious: it wants to preserve native cultures and foster group difference and it has to hit the road in order to do it. The provincial agenda is as global and as proactive in its aspirations as cosmopolitanism. Provincialism is legal prohibitions against the introduction of English terms into the French vocabulary and British resistance to the Euro (notice the ambiguous provincial valence of these goals: the preservation of a high imperial language and of a currency that remains a global financial standard); it's Pat Buchanan's critique of the "New World Order" and the refusal of Congress to pay membership dues to the United Nations; it's the "English-only" laws adopted by small suburbs in reaction to immigrant owned businesses; and the Supreme Court's embrace of the Village of Belle Terre, New York's ordinance prohibiting college rooming houses and hippie communes. It's the seclusion of Amish, land rights for Native Hawaiians and ethnic theme houses on college campuses. It's Jean Marie Le Pen's "France for the French," "neighborhood schools" as a defense against racial integration and Iran prohibiting Western influences. It's Santa Monica passing rent control to avoid becoming California's Miami Beach.

Describing cosmopolitanism and provincialism as opposed pairs is not entirely satisfactory. They are actually mutually constitutive, both in the strictly semiotic sense that the idea of cosmopolitanism is meaningless unless we can oppose it to something like provincialism and in a more practical sense: much of cosmopolitanism involves recombining elements of provincial cultures. For instance, Picasso's *Demoiselles d'Avignon* borrowed motifs from African sculpture; the composition relies on them and is unreadable without reference to them.

We can say something similar about provincialism: what we understand today as provincial cultural traditions participate in and are reactions to globalization, urbanization, the mass media—in short, cosmopolitanism. Kwanzaa, the "traditional" African-American winter solstice celebration, was invented in Los Angeles in the 1960s by black nationalist Ron Karenga for strictly contemporary ideological purposes. The historian Hugh Trevor-Roper makes a compelling case that the traditional Scottish kilt and clan Tartans were invented, from whole cloth as it were, in late-eighteenth-century *London*:

> [In 1745] the only way in which a highlander's loyalty could be discerned was not by his tartan but by the cockade in his bonnet. Tartans were a matter of private tastes. . . . [W]hen the great rebellion of 1745 broke out, the kilt as we know it, was a recent English invention and the "clan" tartan did not exist. . . . The kilt which, having been invented by an English Quaker industrialist, was saved from extinction by an English imperialist statesman.[40]

The original Indian Arts and Crafts Act, passed in 1935, recognized that "traditional" Native-American handicrafts were in fact designed for a cosmopolitan marketplace:

> Only to a limited extent are any of these products produced today primarily for the use of their producers. The Navajos . . . do not use their own rugs. . . . the Pueblo woman is likely to prefer a lard pail or tin pan to her

> pottery. . . . by and large, shoes and machine goods have replaced [traditional handicrafts] for everyday wear. . . . These products are vestiges or adaptations of products originally made for Indians' use, they are produced today primarily for the market. . . . They represent an attempt to capitalize native material and old skills for the purposes of trade.[41]

In this sense cosmopolitanism is not an alternative to provincialism in the sense that we could choose one over the other. Instead the difference between them is one of interpretation, emphasis and priority, and any policy that promotes one always already reinforces its "opposite": more tradition means more raw material for cosmopolitan hybrids; cosmopolitanism means a market and vital material support for tradition.

But in another sense cosmopolitanism and provincialism are antagonists. Cosmopolitanism seeks to supplant provincial tradition and vice versa in many arenas of social life. Esperanto sought to *replace* national languages, at least in overtly international forums. Modern art tore traditional motifs from their traditional contexts and presented them *as motifs*, as evocative elements in a larger whole. Cosmopolitanism selectively appropriates—to use Matsuda's terminology—or discriminates, to use a terminology even more loaded with meaning—with a vengeance. While defenders of provincial cultures insist that deep seated tradition is necessary to live a decent life, cosmopolitanism seduces us with the possibility that as rich and rewarding a life is available free of the constraints of tradition, as Waldron argues:

> Suppose first, that a freewheeling cosmopolitan life, lived in a kaleidoscope of cultures, is both possible and fulfilling . . . rich and creative, and with no more unhappiness than one expects to find anywhere in human existence. Immediately, one argument for the protection of minority cultures is undercut. It can no longer be said that people need rootedness in the particular culture in which they and their ancestors were raised in the way they need food, clothing and shelter. . . . [I]mmersion in the culture of a particular community . . . may be something that particular people like and enjoy. But they no longer can claim that it is something that they need.[42]

Cosmopolitanism does not threaten to eradicate provincial cultures, but it does threaten to reduce them in status to a quaint luxury or an expensive taste. At the same time provincial traditionalism makes demands on individuals that are inconsistent with cosmopolitan commitments: as Waldron points out, Salman Rushdie was sentenced *to death* by the traditionalist clerics of

Iran for the crime of apostasy, despite the fact that he never accepted the faith as his own. This book has been full of much milder examples of a similar impulse to require adherence to the customs of one's ascribed identity.

So although cosmopolitanism and provincialism are mutually constitutive, they are nevertheless antagonistic positions. We can figure them as ideological positions to which one might feel an affinity or commitment, if not in an absolute sense, then at least in a given context.

Difference discourse is by and large provincialist on this account. It insists that groups should preserve a canonical set of traits and practices in the face of cosmopolitan influences and pressures to change at least some of those traits and practices. It is inspired by a vision of univocal and hermetic social groups each of which must be encouraged to preserve its culture "whole cloth" and to share it on "it's own terms" (and is confident in the assumption that the group is united in what those terms might be).

Of course, because provincialism needs cosmopolitanism to some degree, it is also somewhat ambivalent. Difference discourse does envision that groups will share their culture with others, and it insists on rights-to-difference in order to ensure that such groups have access to the institutions of cosmopolitan society. Difference discourse offers a vision of a society in which cultural difference coexists with equality, where citizens can enjoy both the security of insular communities-of-fate and the freedom of uninhibited access to the voluntary associations of the market and civil society. It's an attractive vision because, unless you look at the fine print, it seems as if we can have it all: subgroup cultural autonomy and seamless integration into a common culture, tradition and modernity, the tribal council and a republican form of government, the ancestral hearth and central heating.

But when push comes to a shove (as it has whenever we must resort to formal legal rules) difference discourse will fall back to provincialism. For difference discourse, the institutions of cosmopolitan society are not themselves envisioned as sites of cultural production; instead they are seen as instrumentally necessary and therefore properly confined to narrow, technocratic ends (universities should transmit technical and uncontroversial knowledge, but must not seek to impart cultural values or insist on common experiences; employers should produce goods or services defined in terms of technical necessity and the profit motive so as to exclude "cultural" norms which participants might be required to adopt or adhere to.) Even the more integrationist ideal of "sharing" cultural practices with outsiders too often assumes that culture is pre-formed and static, a durable object that can be passed around the room for show and tell and will not change from the interaction.

I've evoked cosmopolitanism and provincialism with lists as well as defining the terms abstractly, in part in order to make the stakes of the critique of difference discourse come alive, and in part because these, like many ideological commitments, escape the boundaries of formal definition. One embraces them through revelation as much as through persuasion; one finds them less often in the debating forum than while on the way to Damascus. I hope you, the reader, recognize cosmopolitanism and provincialism as meaningful ideological positions in our society and have a sense of the stakes of the antagonism between them and the rhetorical tools commonly employed by the combatants.

I would also suggest that the cosmopolitanism/provincialism split doesn't line up neatly with an antiracist, antisexist or antihomophobic agenda or with the more familiar left/right ideological dichotomy. The new map can supplement these more familiar ideological positions by suggesting the possibility of "antiracist cosmopolitans" and "antiracist provincialists" as two antagonistic camps within a loose confederation of antiracists. This suggests that at times the commitments of cosmopolitans and of provincialists as such may overwhelm those defined by anti-racism.

To say that difference discourse is provincialist is not in and of itself a critique; it is simply a description of a set of commitments. My attempt to "out" the latent provincialism of difference discourse only provides us with another criterion of evaluation. A consequence of this revelation is that people who support antiracist, antisexist or antihomophobic projects need not feel obliged by those commitments to support difference discourse. They can and should consider cosmopolitan alternatives to antiracist provincialism and evaluate difference discourse in terms of its provincialism.

For some, such an evaluation will make the discourse all the more attractive. Indeed, difference discourse is likely to attract some people who are indifferent or hostile to the anti-animus agendas but who have sympathy with provincialism. But for others, the provincialism of difference discourse may be troubling. For those of us who are not sanguine about the narratives of social identity we have inherited, difference discourse is a clear and present danger. Those of us with cosmopolitan leanings should resist the equation of rights-to-difference with civil rights and policies designed to eliminate illegitimate hierarchy.

4. The Ends of Anti-Discrimination Law

Many perfectly just claims—as well as any number of claims that are either intrinsically unworthy or must be balanced against competing concerns—are *not* civil rights claims, . . . claim hopping on the (ideological) backs of instances of genuine victimization . . . threatens the real battles against social caste at the same time that it threatens chaotic and irrational distributive policies.[1]

In the first two chapters of this book, I advanced the somewhat counterintuitive idea that the lived experience of group difference is a consequence, rather than a cause, of stories, beliefs and rituals of group difference. I argued that the day-to-day manifestations of group difference—folk beliefs, stories and narratives, subjective identifications, outward expressions of group affiliation and performances of "group culture"—are not reflections of intrinsic human difference but rather are effects of social, political and legal institutions that produce and enforce group difference. I argued that this social production of group difference often limits freedom, stifles creativity and forces individuals into preordained social roles. I argued that the law has participated and continues to participate in the production of group difference and that official legal "recognition" of group difference would augment this pernicious form of social power. Finally, the most obvious victims of this form of group chauvinism are often also among its most effective agents; like a virus that compels an organism's own antibodies to attack the organism, difference discourse does some of its most destructive work from within.

In chapter 3 I argued that "cultural discrimination" is inevitable and often desirable. I argued that formal institutions—precisely those subject to the restrictions of anti-discrimination law—have cultures that are as vital

169

and profound as those of the canonical social groups and that protection of minority group cultures through rights will deprive these institutions of the ability to perpetuate their cultures, often to the detriment of minority group members and society at large. Finally, I argued that minority cultural practices will survive without legal protection, albeit often in an altered, fragmented and recombined form, and that such survival in an admittedly Hobbesian social competition is preferable to the distorted and blinkered version of group difference we should expect cultural rights to produce. This chapter expands on the more general prescriptions for anti-discrimination law suggested by my arguments above.

Civil Rights as a Limited Mechanism of Social Justice

Flushed with the enthusiasm generated by the Supreme Court's 1954 holding that segregated public schools are unconstitutional, [civil rights leaders] pledged publicly that the progeny of American's slaves would be "Free by 1963," the centennial of the Emancipation Proclamation. The pledge become the motto for the National Association for the Advancement of Colored People's 1959 convention . . . where were gathered, in jubilant euphoria, veterans of racial bias and society's hostility who believed that they had finally, and permanently, achieved the reform of the laws that had been for a century vehicles for the oppression of black men, women and children.[2]

To say that blacks never fully believed in rights is true. Yet it is also true that blacks believed in them so much and so hard that we gave them life where there was none before; we held onto them, put the hope of them into our wombs. . . . This was the resurrection of life from ashes four hundred years old.[3]

If we have poured our hearts and souls into legal rights then it's not surprising that we expect a great deal from them in return. In fact, many Americans, of all races, expected nothing less than the end of racial injustice. This dashed expectation has led many to become disillusioned with civil rights and critical of the institutions charged with enforcing them. For others, it is a driving force behind rights-to-difference proposals.

In *And We Are Not Saved*, law professor Derrick Bell convincingly argues that civil rights have not come close to achieving racial justice. He argues that civil rights were the result of a Faustian bargain that required blacks to renounce radical activism in exchange for legal protections. He insists that many political elites supported the civil rights movement not primarily because of their opposition to racial injustice, but instead because American racism stood between them and the moral high ground they wished to occupy in foreign affairs. This account was seen as blasphemous by some in the civil rights establishment and as damning by many others.

But if, as I suggested in chapter 2, we think of rights as a form of public policy, Bell's account is neither blasphemous nor damning. It is not even surprising. We should not be dismayed to find that a *policy* victory required compromises and we shouldn't think the victory hollow as long as it was worth the compromises required to obtain it.

Similarly, the ulterior motivations of lawmakers who passed civil rights legislation are a scandal if rights are supposed to be the pure incarnation of timeless principles of justice. Bell's hypothesis that cynical foreign policy considerations partially drove civil rights legislation is a harsh accusation given the common set of beliefs about rights. But it is also typical of how laws are passed in a representative democracy. Ulterior motives and self-interest, while not exactly milk and honey, are the steak and martinis that fuel beltway politics.

If we thought of rights as policy we would have more realistic expectations. We would not expect that one public policy approach could eliminate racial injustice. We would measure the efficacy of civil rights, not against such a Herculean metewand, but by the human yardstick that applies to other public policies: did they make the problem less severe at a reasonable cost? By this earthly standard, civil rights are among the most successful policy initiatives in American history.

Thinking of rights as a form of public policy may be deflating given our customary epics of lawyers and judges who speak as the mediums of Justice and act as the midwives of History. But this more modest view of civil rights in no way diminishes the heroism of those men and women who sacrificed and fought to secure civil rights legislation and courtroom victories. Indeed, in a sense their achievements are all the more impressive: civil rights were not latent in the logic of the Constitution or the nature of Man, simply waiting to be discovered; they were forged of the rough materials of mortal experience, human intelligence and earthly judgment and established, not by Destiny, but by the labor of political compromise and moral suasion. Thinking of rights as public policy with inherent limitations does not mean that our aspirations for social justice must be similarly limited. But only by recognizing both the potential and the limitations of rights can we ensure that rights live up to their potential. And liberated from the idea that civil rights alone can secure social justice, we are better able to evaluate other approaches to the same end.

Anti-discrimination Law and Joint Costs

As a general matter, my prescriptions for anti-discrimination doctrine follow the suggestion of law professor Robert Post to reject what he calls the dominant approach to anti-discrimination law:

> [which] typically requires employers . . . to make decisions as if their employees did not exhibit forbidden characteristics, as if, for example, employees had no race or sex . . . [and] requires employers to base their judgments instead on the deeper and more fundamental ground of "individual merit" or "intrinsic worth."[4]

I have already suggested that anti-discrimination law does not and should not mandate "fairness" generally nor should it require employers to judge employees based on some abstract idea of "intrinsic worth." My comments to follow take up Post's suggestion to adopt instead a "sociological account, in which antidiscrimination law is understood as a social practice that acts on other social practices . . . [and] must be seen as transforming preexisting social practices, such as race and gender."[5] Accordingly I am concerned less with preventing subjectively experienced injury to individual plaintiffs than with the social consequences of anti-discrimination law for the social practices that reinforce ascribed statuses generally. With Post, I would endorse the late Supreme Court Justice Brennan's opinion that the purpose of anti-discrimination law is "to break down old *patterns* of . . . segregation and hierarchy."[6]

If, as a sociological account would suggest, anti-discrimination law regulates social practices, it, like most governmental regulation, will do so at some cost. Any such cost will be borne by both members of majority and to members of protected minority groups. The dominant conception obscures these costs, implying that anti-discrimination law simply requires us to judge others based on their "intrinsic worth" and therefore does nothing more than prevent identity-specific injuries. But in some cases the costs associated with anti-discrimination law will outweigh the benefits to be derived from its application. Because they restrict the liberty of group-members and undermine legitimate institutional cultures, rights-to-difference especially would be likely to result in such cases. This would be a bad thing both in and of itself and also because it would threaten to undermine the legitimacy of anti-discrimination law generally, which properly applied, offers benefits that far outweigh its costs.

A cost/benefit approach to the analysis of legal regulation and social conflicts has been widely recognized as superior in private law since the mid-twentieth century. For instance, in nuisance law, the now-discredited jurisprudence of cause-and-effect, victim-and-perpetrator, has given way to the conceptions of nuisance "injuries" as problems of joint costs arising from mutually incompatible activities. The central insight of this "joint costs" analysis, developed by the economist Ronald Coase, is that a victim and injury focused approach is incoherent because we can't determine who the "victim" (the party who will bear the costs of a social conflict) in a conflict is until we determine who has the legal entitlement to either continue or enjoin the challenged activity—precisely what is at stake in the dispute.[7]

A classic example: if a railroad company operates a train that throws off sparks that regularly ignite fires in a wheat field bordering the railroad tracks, the older view, based on a theory of objective causation, was that the railroad was the perpetrator who had *caused harm* to the victimized (and passive) owner of the wheat fields. This was thought to imply that the perpetrator should be forced either to stop causing the harm under the common law doctrine sic utere tuo ut alienum non laedes ("use your property only so as not to harm your neighbor") or at least that the perpetrator should be forced to "internalize the costs of his activity" by paying money damages to the victim.

Coase rejected this approach to the problem, pointing out that, viewed without preconceptions, we were faced with two potentially "injurious" activities—operating a train and growing wheat (if the wheat farmer can enjoin the railroad from operating, wheat farming effectively injures the railroad)—not one. The problem was not well described in terms of causation and harm but rather in terms of incompatibility. And the question to be answered was therefore not an objective, formal one—how shall we prevent harm or force perpetrators to internalize the costs of their activity?—but rather a subjective, policy question— which activity should society privilege? As Coase noted, this reformulation does not help us to answer the policy question but it does clear away the metaphysical chaparral that hinders our view of the underlying policy landscape.

We could consider anti-discrimination doctrine in terms of Coasian "joint costs" as well. In Coase's terms the conflict involves two actors who wish to engage in incompatible activities. In an employment dispute, the employer/defendant wants to implement a policy that would exclude the potential employee/plaintiff (and/or wants the plaintiff to conform to a particular workplace rule) while the plaintiff wants the job (and/or wants it without having to conform to the rule.)

Coase's important insight is that it biases our analysis to begin by describing the situation in terms of victims and perpetrators or harm and injury ("the employer's policy harms minority applicants.") Instead, the clash of these conflicting desires gives rise to what Coase would call "joint costs." Someone will suffer injury regardless of how the case is decided: if the employer prevails, she will be free to exclude the job applicant from a job the applicant wants. But if the applicant prevails, he will be able to force the employer to suspend a policy that employer wants to implement. Either way, someone suffers an "injury," or, in Coase's terms, is forced to internalize a cost of the clash of incompatible activities. In this sense anti-discrimination law does not prevent injuries from occurring; instead it shifts the costs of social conflicts from one group of actors to another.

This isn't a critique of anti-discrimination law; in fact one could argue that this type of cost shifting is the *goal* of anti-discrimination law. Take the paradigm case of a racist employer who simply doesn't want to work with blacks. A Coasian analysis suggests that anti-discrimination law doesn't simply prevent the racist from harming blacks; it requires the racist to bear the cost of an incompatibility between his desire to exclude blacks and the desire of blacks for gainful employment. Framing it in this way does not, I hope, change anyone's mind about how the case should be decided. We *should* require the racist to bear this cost. We should do so because social justice demands that resources be distributed to help a long-suffering group get a foothold in the economy rather than to support its oppressors, because it demands that the cause of racial exclusion be starved of resources and because the desire of an individual to earn a living deserves respect while the desire of a racist to avoid contact with blacks deserves contempt.

The Coasian insight might make a difference, however, as one moves away from the paradigm case. Most importantly, while the typical "harm/injury" formulation casts one party as an active perpetrator and the other as a helpless vicitim, the Coasian analysis reminds us that both parties are actors. By looking at the problem as one of joint costs, we can see that both parties are potentially empowered to affect the outcome. In the paradigm case I offered above this is true only in an academic sense: the black applicant who doesn't get the job from a racist could *in theory* "bribe" the racist employer to hire him by taking a pay cut so the employer would prefer him to the best white candidate for the job (sans bribe). But the "bribe" would strike most people (I think properly) as impractical (would a racist hire a black at *any* wage?), degrading and unjust, so we properly forbid discrimination instead.

But if a hiring policy or term of employment prohibits a voluntarily adopted style, behavior or trait, the joint cost analysis changes in two potentially significant ways. One, behavior is more likely to be *objectively* costly to the employer—take for example a decision to speak a non-English language that makes monitoring of employee behavior on the job (for example, potential harassment of coworkers, as was alleged in *Spun Steak*) objectively more difficult, thereby requiring the assignment of extra supervisors. Two: the plaintiff could avoid the conflict by changing his behavior while at work. There may be very real costs to doing so in terms of personal identity and emotional comfort, but these costs are "soft" in the sense that they are subjective and nonmonetary. There are good reasons to credit even these "soft" costs more than the (equally soft) cost to a racist of having to work with people she simply doesn't care for. But if there are real costs to the employer that are not a function of bias then the relevant normative balance is between the cost to the plaintiff of changing the behavior and the cost to the employer of accommodating it. Such a case is different than one in which an employee is powerless to change a trait, such as a physical characteristic or even a low score on a test for which studying has little effect. The "mutability" of the trait weighs against rights protection because behavior is precisely what people are legitimately expected to alter in exchange for wages or other benefits of membership in an exclusive institution.

One might insist that anti-discrimination law imposes analogous "objective" costs in the paradigm case as well. Take Walter Williams's example of the "Intelligent Bayesian" (so-named in honor of Sir Thomas Bayes, the father of statistics.) Faced with uncertainty about the likely performance or behavior of a given individual, the intelligent Bayesian economizes on costly information-gathering (trial and error) by acting on the basis of statistical probabilities about the type of person he confronts. One readily available source of cheap, if not particularly refined, information about an individual comes in the form of race and sex. If, say, a jewelry store owner has statistical data, personal experience or even word-of-mouth hearsay that indicates that a particular group is more likely to rob him, it may be rational for him to refuse to hire members of that group, implement additional security measures when members of the group enter the store or exclude all members of that group from the premises. Therefore, "[a] white jeweler who does not open his door to young black males cannot be labeled a racist" according to Williams "[because] in this world of imperfect information . . . jewelers play the odds. To ask them to behave differently is to disarm them."[8]

If anti-discrimination law requires the jeweler to open up on a racially non-discriminatory basis, it imposes on him an objective cost: the jeweler will either have to invest more in security measures that may not otherwise have been cost justified, suffer high losses from theft, or invest in more costly race-neutral individual screening. Similarly, if statistics suggest that some groups are more likely than others to be good employees, anti-discrimination law may impose a cost on employers by requiring them to eschew racial screening and use more costly evaluation methods. We encounter similar concerns in the politically charged context of "profiling" by law enforcement. If statistical data collected in good faith indicate that members of particular groups are more likely to commit certain crimes, is it acceptable for law enforcement to target those groups in the use of prophylactic measures such as checkpoints and "stop and frisk" street searches and traffic stops?

Anti-discrimination law does not simply prevent injury in these contexts; it allocates social costs. But it is appropriate to require potential discriminators to bear these costs. Because of the widespread social animus that makes anti-discrimination law necessary, judgments about the probability that minority groups will engage in socially destructive or criminal behavior are particularly likely to be in error. No doubt there are some true "intelligent Bayesians," but it is fair to presume that there are also many less-intelligent racists who radically overestimate the probability that racial minorities will commit crimes or engage in otherwise destructive behavior. In short, what Williams might imagine is a reasoned and objective assessment of racial probabilities will be in many cases a crude stereotype. A core purpose of anti-discrimination law is to prevent social actors from acting on the basis of stereotypes (I'll emphasize in passing that this core purpose is radically at odds with rights-to-difference, which effectively would promote group stereotypes under the rubric of group culture). Admittedly, anti-discrimination law forbids not only unjustified stereotypes but also statistically accurate generalizations. It therefore imposes a cost on social actors by depriving them of cost-effective, if crude, screening criteria. But again, the fact that anti-discrimination law allocates social costs is not an indictment. We should require social institutions to bear reasonable costs in order to prevent widespread and unjustified discrimination.

The costs borne by the putative plaintiff forced to comply with a culturally burdensome institutional policy may be hard to distinguish in principle from the costs that the institution would bear if required to change its policy. Often, these costs will be "soft" for both the potential plaintiff and the institution in the sense that no expenditure of real social resources is required to comply with or suspend the policy. An employee can, in most cases, comply with, say, a grooming rule without spending money, taking a pay cut or working longer hours; the institution can in most cases accommodate unconventional grooming without suffering a loss in productivity. But either party may incur a "soft" loss if the other has the legal entitlement: the employee will suffer emotional distress if required to change his grooming or dress while on the job; the institution may suffer the dilution of a business image if required to accommodate employees with unconventional appearances. And in both cases the "soft" cost can be converted into hard currency: the employee would presumably pay some amount of cash for the privilege of retaining his cultural style while at work while the employer's loss of business image if required to accommodate the cultural style may well result in fewer sales and lower profits.

Again, if we think that the employer's aversion to a group-correlated behavior is simply a manifestation of aversion to the group (whether his own or that of his customers), the employer should bear the cost of accommodation for social justice reasons. But if the aversion to the behavior is truly the result of "cultural difference," it is not obvious that the cultural norms that dominate in the market should yield to those held by the individual employee.

To decide which should yield we would need to make some educated guesses about the extent of entrenched and unjustified cultural hegemony (as opposed to the dominance of practices and norms that are in fact better suited to a particular enterprise), the malleability of cultural traits and the costs of cultural pluralism. Over time, will people lose their aversion to the cultural traits at issue? Will it take more time and cause more suffering to change the hegemonic cultural norm or for the class of potential plaintiffs to accommodate themselves to it? We would also need a normative theory of the inherent value of cultural diversity. Finally we would need a sharp account of the goals of anti-discrimination law. If a central goal is (as I believe it is) to ensure the inclusion and integration of currently underrepresented groups in the institutions of the market economy, then the question in these cases is whether we will get more inclusion in the long run by requiring employers to accommodate cultural differences (with the risk that pervasive aversion remains, isolationist tendencies are reinforced, workplace tensions increase or customers stay home) or by requiring employees to change their "culturally related" behavior (with the risk that they simply take jobs in culturally homogenous enclaves rather than bear the cost of changing deeply valued and embedded traits).

Finally, the analysis of joint costs must consider not only employers as a group and employees as a group but also potential divisions *within* the classes. At times, rights-to-difference will distribute costs among differently situated groups of employees *within* the class of potential plaintiffs. Rights-to-difference will function to regulate members of the group they purport to protect, effectively requiring them to bear some of the costs of rights assertion whether they like it or not. This problem is often overlooked because difference discourse tends to treat the social groups it describes as monolithic, with naturally aligned interests, at least in relationship to outsiders. For instance, Will Kymlicka places a great deal of weight on the distinction between regulations internal to a group (which he believes are problematic) and controls on outsiders designed to protect "the group" (which he believes usually are just):

[W]e need to distinguish two types of claims that an ethnic or national group might make. The first involves the claim of a group against its own members; the second involves the claim of a group against the larger society. . . . The first kind is intended to protect the group from the destabilizing impact of *internal dissent* (e.g. the decision of individual members not to follow traditional practice or customs), whereas the second is intended to protect the group from the impact of external decisions (e.g. the economic or political decisions of the larger society). . . . Internal restrictions . . . raise . . . the danger of individual oppression [whereas] [e]xternal protections . . . raise . . . dangers—not of individual oppression but of unfairness between groups.[9]

But restrictions on outsiders can become effective restrictions on insiders as well, raising the possibility of the individual oppression that Kymlicka associates exclusively with internal restrictions. For instance, law professors William Bratton and Drucilla Cornell defend a right to speak Spanish in the workplace as a logical extension of anti-discrimination protection for Latinos (precisely the type of equation I have attacked in this book). Their defense is elaborate, using economic, psychological and philosophical arguments and I will not engage it in detail here. I wish only to focus on one tension in their argument. Echoing Kymlicka, Bratton and Cornell present their rights proposal as a restriction on outsiders—employers—that will provide greater freedom for Latinos by offering a "legally provided psychic space to incorporate . . . to re-evaluate . . . or to contest . . . [the primordial relationships and identifications through which we pattern a self and become a person]."[10]

But they also admit that "bilingual Latino/as themselves . . . would pay for special Title VII protection in the form of lower wages."[11] This admission reflects a common economic argument that nonwaivable and objectively costly legal entitlements that attach only to select and identifiable groups make those groups less competitive in the marketplace. Employers will either avoid the employees who enjoy or are likely to enjoy the objectively costly entitlement, or attempt to pass its costs on to the employees in the form of lower wages. Here a classic argument involves maternity leave: the claim is that employers will be less likely to hire women of child-bearing age or will attempt to reduce their wages in order to compensate for the costs of mandatory maternity leave. Assuming language rights are objectively costly, the argument applies with equal force there.

I am only partially convinced by this argument as a general matter (a lot depends on the specifics of the labor market and of the anti-discrimination regime), but Bratton and Cornell accept it and concede that Spanish-language rights will be paid for by Latinos themselves. If so, it seems to me that the right-to-Spanish will be, on balance, a raw deal for at least some Latinos (those who would prefer the higher wage to the entitlement to speak Spanish). Yet Bratton and Cornell brush this problem aside by fiat: "choices respecting language implicate an individual's right to treatment as an equal. . . . [W]e must make sacrifices to secure those freedoms. We have no doubt that Latinos/as stand as ready as other Americans to incur this cost."[12]

Here what Kymlicka would call an external protection (a requirement that *employers* accommodate Spanish but not a requirement that any Latino speak it) is in effect also an internal restriction (*all Latinos* will bear the cost of a right-to-Spanish, whether they want it or not). Group rights assertion—even when on its face it burdens only "outsiders"—may restrict, as much as expand, the liberty of group members. Given this, we have, not a simple case of respect for minority rights, but a difficult case of distributive justice; if Bratton's and Cornell's assumptions about the labor market are correct, a right to Spanish is a proposal to privilege those who would prefer an entitlement to speak Spanish on the job to higher wages *at the expense* of those who would prefer the higher wages to the right to speak Spanish on the job.

Joint costs analysis suggests that we must confront issues of culture, cultural difference, cultural assimilation and cultural solidarity on their own merits, as questions of policy that involve conflicting goals, the allocation of social costs and inevitable trade offs. Assuming a central goal of anti-discrimination law is to promote the social and economic integration of stigmatized groups, cultural rights proposals raise thorny factual and normative questions. In the face of social and economic pressure to assimilate, when will cultural minorities do so, when will they retreat to isolated enclaves and when will they suffer the cost of retaining difference in mainstream institutions? Is cultural diversity desirable in and of itself, or only as a means to the end of social integration? How should the costs of accommodating insular cultural minorities or of achieving a more unified culture be borne? If cultural assimilation could be achieved at some significant emotional and psychological cost to one generation of cultural minorities, but at dramatically and constantly lessening costs to each successive generation until "full assimilation" had been achieved (and future costs were zero), would such a policy be morally acceptable? Would it affect our evaluation of such a "tough" policy if we knew that the alternative was an intractable social fragmentation with high and enduring costs for both cultural minorities and the majority?

Doctrinal Reform

American anti-discrimination law prohibits two distinct types of discrimination: *disparate treatment*—facially discriminatory policies ("no blacks allowed") and facially neutral intentional discrimination (a formally neutral rule implemented for the purpose of excluding or segregating blacks)—and *disparate impact*—facially neutral policies that may not be intentionally discriminatory, but nevertheless have a disproportionate impact on the protected group and are not sufficiently justified by some legitimate purpose.

Rights-to-difference could fall under either broad category of prohibition. As a *disparate treatment* cause of action, a right-to-difference might entail a claim that certain traits or behavior are *elements* of the protected group's status, such that a workplace rule prohibiting the behavior or trait would be illicit discrimination per se, just as a rule requiring that all employees have fair skin would be racial discrimination per se. It could also entail a claim that a rule prohibiting the behavior or trait is a proxy for the prohibited discrimination.

The former argument (per se discrimination) dominates the rights-to-difference literature, perhaps for the simple, tactical reason that, if accepted, it would make the claim of discrimination irrefutable (although not indefensible: except in the case of race, disparate treatment claims are subject to some affirmative defenses). By contrast the second argument (discrimination by proxy) necessarily allows the defendant to respond that the challenged rule was not a proxy for illegal discrimination but in fact reflected legitimate motivations.

The per se claim is, however, problematic as a general matter. As I have argued above, the claim that a given behavior or trait is an element of a protected group status is ultimately conceptual. As a doctrinal matter, the per se argument therefore is conclusory: the claim that a behavior or trait is an element of a "protected identity" is nothing more than a surreptitious way of saying that discrimination against the behavior or trait should be actionable. The proxy claim, by contrast, asks a potentially judiciable question and *should* be a valid cause of action (its current status in American employment discrimination law is somewhat doubtful, as I will discuss below.)

As a *disparate impact* cause of action, rights-to-difference entail an assertion that because certain behavior or traits disproportionately appear in protected groups, policies that prohibit or burden them effectively discriminate against those groups. As a doctrinal matter, any disparate impact claim is vulnerable to an affirmative defense: the policy is not illegal despite its disparate impact if it is sufficiently "job related," or necessary to the conduct of the business or to the institutional mission.

Because they would protect volitional behavior, expression and self-presentation, rights-to-difference would appear to be precluded by the well-established requirement that actionable discrimination be based on "immutable characteristics." The immutability requirement has received a great deal of scholarly criticism, much of it, not surprisingly, from the advocates of rights-to-difference. In the context of disparate treatment, I agree with the proponents of rights-to-difference that immutability should not be a strict requirement. But, immutability—understood as the inability to change or avoid the disadvantage attendant to a stigmatized status—is an appropriate criterion for a disparate *impact* claim.

Below, I will explore these concerns in more detail, offering some admittedly incomplete suggestions for doctrinal reforms consistent with my analysis above.

Disparate Treatment

The legality of discrimination on the basis of characteristics or behavior that are statistically correlated with minority group identity is somewhat ambiguous under contemporary American anti-discrimination law. Characteristics that are outside the immediate control of the plaintiff ("immutable") and very highly correlated with protected group statuses are treated as manifestations or elements of the status; discrimination on the basis of such characteristics is presumed to be discrimination on the basis of the status. For instance, a Federal Court of Appeals held that proof of discrimination on the basis of a foreign accent established a prima facie case of disparate treatment based on national origin.[13]

Discrimination against group-correlated characteristics may also be prohibited as a *proxy* for illicit discrimination, sufficient in and of itself or along with other evidence to establish a prima facie case of discrimination. For instance, several courts have held that proof of a policy of hiring based on the "word of mouth" of present employees or acquaintances was circumstantial evidence of disparate treatment on the basis of race because the policy predictably resulted in a racially exclusive workforce.[14] Although semantically awkward, we could describe word-of-mouth hiring as discriminating based on the "characteristic" of familiarity with certain informal social networks, thereby analogizing these cases to cases involving group-correlated characteristics generally.

It is doubtful, however, that discrimination on the basis of cultural traits is actionable disparate treatment under existing law. The proxy cases send mixed signals: for instance the Supreme Court held that factors highly, but not precisely, correlated with age, such as pension status and years of service, are not proxies for age discrimination.[15] Moreover, all the proxy cases involved "characteristics" that were not within the immediate control of the plaintiff. Policies regulating volitional behavior generally survive disparate treatment challenges.

There are exceptions: sex-specific grooming standards that go beyond "commonly accepted social norms" have been found to be "demeaning," based on "offensive stereotypes" and therefore unlawfully discriminatory. But a sex-specific policy is facially discrimatory whereas "cultural discrimination" requires *all* employees to comply with a common rule or prohibition.[16] And courts have generally upheld even explicitly sex-specific grooming standards that required adherence to *conventional* gender norms: women can be required to wear out-fits with "feminine touches"[17] or to wear skirts rather than pants.[18]

So it's unlikely that formally neutral policies that prohibit or discourage group-correlated practices can be successfully challenged as disparate treatment under existing law. Because the policies regulate volitional behavior, the cases involving accents and word-of-mouth hiring are arguably inapplicable. And because they do not involve explicitly discriminatory classifications, the cases prohibiting "demeaning" grooming standards likewise do not apply. Under existing law, the potential plaintiff will never get the chance to prove that such policies are motivated by discriminatory intent; that the policies are formally neutral and regulate volitional behavior effectively insulates them from further scrutiny.

This is a serious gap in needed legal protection. An effective anti-discrimination policy must prohibit policies that are proxies for racial discrimination, *including policies that regulate behavior*. Although she should not prevail because of the centrality of braids to black identity, if Rene Rogers could demonstrate the airline adopted its no-braids policy in order to screen black women from its workforce, she should prevail on that basis. Under this proposal, the plaintiff could show through direct or circumstantial evidence that the policy was the result of animus or bias: for instance, if American Airlines had forbidden braids but allowed other unconventional hairstyles, this should raise a suspicion of bias.

Obviously this leaves important evidentiary questions unanswered. How high a correlation between the characteristic and group status must there be? Is evidence of a high correlation alone sufficient or must the plaintiff offer additional evidence of illicit intent? Brief and incomplete answers will have to suffice. If correlation is the only evidence of discriminatory intent, the correlation should be quite high indeed, otherwise the case is more properly handled under disparate *impact* doctrine, which deals with policies for which discriminatory intent cannot be proven. Somewhat lower correlations might still be circumstantial evidence of discriminatory intent, which, combined with other evidence, could be sufficient to establish a prima facie case of disparate treatment.

This may appear to be an endorsement of the proposals I have criticized as rights-to-difference, but there is a crucial distinction: the usual shibboleths of difference discourse—"culture," "identity," and the plaintiff's subjective attachment to the trait—are irrelevant to this prohibition. Instead, the attempt is to root out the illicit intent underlying the challenged policy. If the no-braids policy is a proxy for forbidden discrimination, it is illegal, whether braids are deeply and historically important or merely a fleeting fashion trend.

This approach to disparate treatment doctrine corrects some disturbing implications of existing doctrine. In the *Rogers* case for instance, the court strained to distinguish Rene Rogers's unprotected all-braided hairstyle from the Afro or Bush style: "Banning a natural hairstyle would implicate the policies underlying the prohibition of discrimination on the basis of immutable characteristics . . . [A]n all braided hairstyle is a different matter . . . as it is not the product of natural hair growth but of artifice."[19] Nice try, but this can't be the reason to distinguish the two hairstyles. There is no doubt that an employer legally can require an employee to cut unusually long hair, whether it is long and straight or in an Afro, despite the fact that both are the product of "natural hair growth." What the court may have meant is that an employer could not ban *every* type of Afro/Bush style, requiring employees with naturally curly hair to straighten it artificially. But why not? After all, if they can straighten it, it's not an immutable characteristic.

The answer lies in the reasonable inference of prejudice and resonates with the cases prohibiting "demeaning" sex specific dress codes. The law allows employers to establish sex-specific dress codes,[20] reflecting a pragmatic acquiescence in social conventions of gender, but it forbids employers to require only women to wear a uniform while men wear simple business attire, condemning such a rule as "demeaning" to women.[21] As law professor Robert Post points out, these disparate results cannot be explained with the typical idea of a norm prohibiting sex discrimination: both policies discriminate yet only one is actionable.[22] Instead, the inquiry seeks to determine whether the challenged policy is demeaning: "skirts for the ladies and pants for the gents" is a conventional norm and, at least in today's environment, not demeaning to women, whereas a requirement that women wear uniforms is demeaning. Similarly, a grooming policy that bans cornrows, along with many other unconventional hairstyles, is not demeaning despite the correlation of cornrows with race because cornrows are a relatively unconventional hairstyle; however, a rule requiring employees to straighten their conventional "natural" curly hairstyles would be demeaning.

Disparate Impact

Anti-discrimination law also prohibits policies that may not be intentionally discriminatory but nevertheless have a disproportionate impact on a protected group and are not sufficiently justified by some legitimate purpose. Although, as I have noted, many rights-to-difference arguments are figured as disparate treatment challenges, they are probably better analyzed under disparate impact doctrine. Disparate impact could prohibit policies that disfavor practices that are arguably part of the culture of a distinctive group. Indeed, Brian Barry, for the most part a severe critic of multiculturalism, endorses such an interpretation of an analogous doctrine in Great Britain's Race Relations Act: "culturally derived characteristics that do not demonstrably interfere with ability to do the job cannot be accepted as a basis for job discrimination."[23]

Here I will argue that a disparate impact action should not lie for policies that regulate volitional behavior (I would thereby eliminate disparate impact claims for "cultural discrimination"). Given my support for disparate *treatment* claims challenging policies that regulate behavior, this may seem inconsistent. But it follows from the distinction between disparate treatment and disparate impact. The essence of a disparate treatment claim is some form of manifest bias against the protected group. This bias may take the form of an overt classification or distinction, or it may take a more covert form, such as a proxy. It may be a bias that is consciously held by the decision maker, a subconscious bias that reveals itself through her behavior or a reflection of the bias of her customers. But in any case, it's *manifest bias* that is prohibited. It shouldn't matter *how* the bias is manifested. The word-of-mouth cases established that it doesn't matter whether the policy targets the group directly or indirectly—if the employer adopts a requirement that it knows is likely to screen out minority applicants, and adopts it *because* it is likely to screen them out, that employer is guilty of discrimination. Likewise it shouldn't matter whether the reason the employer thinks that the requirement will screen out the minorities is that she thinks that they can't conform to its terms (as in the word-of-mouth cases) or because she thinks they will refuse to conform. Here, the mutability of the characteristic is irrelevant because the touchstone of the cause of action is the motivation of the employer.

Disparate impact is different. It's useful to think of disparate impact doctrine as two doctrines in one. To understand the first function of disparate, impact, it's helpful to note that disparate impact doctrine was developed in reaction to employment criteria that looked suspiciously like proxies for racial status. In many disparate impact cases, it is fair to suspect that a hidden, underlying racist motivation animates the challenged policies. Here, the conception of discrimination is the same as that underlying a disparate treatment claim. The practical significance of disparate impact is that it gives rise to a presumption that the challenged policy is motivated by bias or animus. The plaintiff need not *prove* bias, she need only establish that the challenged policy has a disparate impact; then, practically speaking, the defendant must prove that the policy is *not* motivated by animus in order to avoid liability.

The second function of disparate impact is to attack a different social evil. Here the doctrine is not concerned with animus or intent at all; instead *any* decision that has a disparate impact, regardless of motivation, requires independent justification. Here the underlying policy objective is not rooting out illicit motivations but rather avoiding group specific disadvantage.

In many instances, this distinction makes little difference: we want to root out illicit intent that may be hard to prove *and* we want to force employers and other decision makers to eliminate policies that unjustifiably disadvantage historically subordinated groups. In practice it is somewhat unclear whether disparate impact is essentially an individually focused doctrine—like disparate treatment—designed to protect individuals from policies motivated by animus, or whether it is primarily a group-focused policy designed to protect historically subordinated groups from the cumulative effects of disadvantaging policies.

Under the individualist conception of disparate impact—wherein disparate impact gives rise to a presumption of underlying group-based animus—the mutability of the behavior, traits or characteristics disfavored by the policy would seem to be irrelevant, just as it is in the case of disparate treatment: if the policy is motivated by animus, it should be actionable. The question is whether or not this presumption and the consequent requirement that the defendant rebut the presumption by demonstrating that the challenged policy is "job related" are warranted.

In the case of cultural discrimination, it is not warranted. A requirement that airline employees conform to conventional grooming norms cannot be defended as objectively related to the tasks they must perform, yet if a rule requiring, say, all male employees to trim hair that falls below the collar had a disparate impact on some ethnic group, few would infer from this fact alone that the rule was motivated by animus against that group.

Whether or not motivated by animus, we should not allow an employer's subjective whim to deprive members of a disadvantaged group of employment opportunities. This is precisely why policies that disfavor *immutable* characteristics and have a disparate impact on disadvantaged groups are and should presumptively be actionable. But policies that disfavor "mutable characteristics" (read: "behavior") do not *deprive* anyone of job opportunities. Instead they condition the opportunities on a willingness to comply with workplace rules. Unlike discrimination that disfavors immutable characteristics, "cultural discrimination" does not, properly speaking, disfavor the *characteristics* of potential employees at all; rather it hinders the satisfaction of their preferences. The conflict generated by a policy that disfavors an immutable characteristic pits the subjective preferences of the employer against the ability of the potential plaintiff to gain or keep her job. By contrast, in the case of mutable "characteristics," the conflict pits the subjective preferences of the employer against the equally subjective preferences of the employee. *Neither* can justify their preferences *objectively* (there is no objective reason that Rene Rogers must wear cornrows or that bilingual Latinos must speak Spanish on the job.) The commitments underlying anti-discrimination law give us no warrant for privileging the subjective preferences of the individual employee over those of the employer.

On the second type of disparate impact analysis, when disparate impact is not concerned with rooting out illicit intent but instead is designed to remedy widespread segregation or exclusion of historically disadvantaged groups, we would want to ask whether invalidating policies that may or may not be motivated by animus is a justifiable means of improving the lot of those groups. Here again, the mutability of the characteristic matters because the number of policies that might have a disparate impact on mutable "characteristics" (potentially any policy that regulates behavior) is extremely large *and the impact of such policies will vary depending on the choices of members of protected groups*. Will a no-braids rule in fact have a disparate impact on African-American representation in the workplace? That depends on whether African-Americans generally comply with the rule or not. If a significant number of potential African-American applicants (or current members of the workforce) refuse to comply with the rule, it will have a disparate impact, but if most comply, it will not.

An economist might describe this situation as a "moral hazard": a disparate impact claim for policies that disfavor volitional behavior essentially provides a perverse incentive for noncompliance with the workplace rule. The availability of a disparate impact claim will reduce the effective cost of refusing to comply with a workplace rule (because noncompliance may result, not, in discharge, but in a successful lawsuit). Put in Coasian terms, it will redistribute the joint costs of the clash between the employer's desire for the rule and the desires of some subset of employees to engage in the behavior that the rule prohibits. And again, since, by hypothesis, we don't know that the rule is motivated by illegitimate bias (else, under my reform proposed above the plaintiff would have a valid disparate treatment claim) it is not clear that we should favor the subjective desires of the class of potential plaintiffs over the (only loosely business-related and therefore) subjective desires of potential employers. The "moral hazard" severely complicates traditional disparate impact analysis, which assumes that the impact of a challenged policy on a group will not be affected by the potential availability of the disparate impact remedy itself. (Admittedly, one could argue that even a policy with which most members of the group comply has a disparate impact if the group members *suffer* more than others by complying. But how can we know that group members who comply with the rule suffer more than nonmembers—that for instance, Rogers, would suffer more than her white, Bo Derek–emulating colleagues, from changing her all-braided hairstyle? We can't unless we *presuppose* the link between group membership and the hairstyle: precisely what is at issue in the dispute.)

So, as a matter of prediction, we can't be sure whether or not rules against group-correlated styles, practices and traits will result in workplace segregation or under representation because we can't know in advance how many group members will comply with the rules and how many will resist them. Perhaps if almost no group members would accept employment that was conditioned on suspending a given practice or trait (as might be, for instance, in the case of a requirement that blacks straighten their hair), then the overarching purpose of disparate impact doctrine would require something that looks like a right-to-difference. But of course, none of the proponents of rights-to-difference condition their proposals on such an extraordinary circumstance. This is so, one suspects, for the simple reason that the practices and traits they wish to protect do not enjoy such unanimous prestige among the members of any given social group. Only some group members have the desire to exhibit the behavior in question and among those who do even fewer would forgo an otherwise attractive job opportunity that was conditioned on refraining from the behavior.

The Bottom Line

My argument above has been that disparate impact doctrine can be thought of in two ways. One, a policy that has a statistical disparate impact may give rise to a presumption of bias or animus, which the defendant may rebut my demonstrating that the challenged policy is objectively job related. Here disparate impact doctrine is designed to safeguard individual rights against status-based discrimination. But if the challenged policy disfavors "culture," we face a conflict of mutually incompatible subjective preferences: the employer's preference for the policy versus the employee's preference for the cultural traits or behavior. Because anti-discrimination law gives us no warrant to privilege the subjective preference of plaintiffs over those of defendants, a disparate impact action should not lie in such cases.

Two, a policy that has a disparate impact may be objectionable in and of itself because of its exclusionary effect on a disadvantaged group. I have argued that when group members themselves can affect the severity of the impact by complying or refusing to comply with the policy's requirement, it is difficult, if not impossible, to know which policies will or do in fact impact a group as a whole.

Rights-to-difference advocates would be right to insist that some policies that regulate behavior *are* motivated by bias and/or *will* have exclusionary or segregative effects. But because these policies cannot be identified with confidence, I would attack them only indirectly, by focusing on the ultimate or "bottom line" segregative or exclusive effect of an institution's potentially actionable policies. Disparate impact challenges should be limited to workplace rules that discriminate on the basis of immutable characteristics. A disparate impact action should lie whenever the plaintiff can identify any such policy or combination of policies that contribute to demonstrated segregation or exclusion. Likewise, employers whose workforces are *not* in fact segregated or exclusive with respect to the plaintiff's group should be immune from disparate impact liability, even if the challenged policy, evaluated in isolation, might have a disparate impact on that group.

Rights-to-difference advocates complain that this would allow an employer to prefer an "assimilated" group member over other "less-assimilated" members of the same group. For instance, legal scholar Stephen Cutler argues:

> [A] selection process, or even a single selection criterion, that results in group parity may still have an adverse impact on the *least assimilated* individuals in that group. . . . A proportional outcome should not be allowed to mask the discriminatory impact of even one selection criterion upon a subgroup of individuals defined by their possession of group-linked characteristics.[24]

Cutler insists that a selection process may discriminate against nonassimilated group members on the basis of group characteristics of which they are in "possession." This implies a spectrum on which more and less-assimilated group members can be located according to the intensity and extent of their possession of group cultural characteristics. This far into our journey I hope the drawbacks of this type of analysis are obvious.

By defining the traits or behavior disfavored by the hypothetical selection process as group characteristics, Cutler leads us to the conclusion that a policy with no disparate impact and that, by hypothesis, is not racially motivated is nevertheless discriminatory. Consider an employer who prohibits cornrows but nevertheless hires as many black women as one would expect a non-discriminating employer to hire given the pool of qualified black female applicants (including those ruled out by the no-cornrows rule) by selecting from the pool of black female applicants who don't prefer cornrows or are willing to sacrifice them in order to get the job. This could easily occur despite the *potential* impact of the cornrows rule on black women, either because the employer's other rules have an equal impact on other groups (suppose the rule is one part of a broad grooming code, the other elements of which also screen out an equal percentage of men and of women of other races) or because the employer compliments the rule with targeted outreach or affirmative action. Under Cutler's approach, this employer is nevertheless guilty of racial or sex discrimination because the challenged policy discriminates against individuals on the basis of "group characteristics."

Cutler's approach echoes the Supreme Court opinion in *Connecticut v. Teal*,[25] which held that an employer cannot avoid liability for a single rule or policy that has a disparate impact on a protected group by demonstrating that, "at the bottom line" his work force is racially balanced, because the central focus of anti-discrimination law is the protection of individual rights rather than the impact on the minority group as a whole. Those individuals harmed by the policy have a right to redress, even if the employer offsets its disparate impact by implementing policies that favor other members of the group. This approach superficially may appear to offer an especially robust anti-discrimination guarantee. But rejecting an ultimate focus on the "bottom line" invites confusion as to the underlying purpose and practical application of disparate impact doctrine and ultimately ill serves the broader social goals of reducing underrepresentation and segregation of workplaces.

Like a poorly trained attack dog, the disparate impact theory of *Connecticut v. Teal* turned against civil rights plaintiffs, its demeanor worse for wear, in *Ward's Cove Packing Company v. Atonio*.[26] There, citing *Teal*, the Court insisted that just as an employer cannot *defend* its practices by reference to a racially integrated "bottom line," so too "a Title VII plaintiff cannot *attack* an employer's practice by showing that "at the bottom line" there is a racial imbalance in the work force." For the Court in *Ward's Cove*, even an extreme group-based statistical disparity most probably caused by the cumulative effect of a collection of practices and policies was insufficient: the plaintiff had to show that the disparity was caused by a specific practice. Although Title VII was amended in 1991 in response to other aspects of *Ward's Cove*, *Teal's* and *Ward's Cove's* rejection of the "bottom line" still governs disparate impact doctrine.

Here I would propose a modest but significant reform. Unless the disparate impact of the challenged policy gives rise to a reasonable presumption of bias, we should not think of disparate impact doctrine as protecting *individuals* from discrimination at all; instead we should ask whether the employer's practices as a whole contribute to exclusion or segregation, an inquiry that would focus on the employer's "bottom line"—the approach rejected by *Teal* and *Ward's Cove*.

If disparate impact is conceived of as evidence giving rise to a presumption of illicit motivation, it makes sense to say that an *individual* may suffer its effects: here we mean that the individual suffers *intentional discrimination* of which the disparate impact is evidence. But when the presumption that a disparate impact is a consequence of underlying animus is not warranted (as it is not in most cases of "cultural discrimination"), then it's unclear that any individual plaintiff has suffered a status-based injury at all. To say, for instance, that an *individual* suffers discrimination based on race because he is disfavored pursuant to a race-neutral policy that has a coincidental disparate impact on a racial *group* is sophistry: the individual suffers precisely the same injury that anyone who is disfavored by the policy suffers (it may still be that the individual, along with *everyone* disfavored by the policy, unjustly suffers because the policy, though race-neutral, is unjust for some other reason).

Against *Ward's Cove* we should invalidate policies that, in concert, disparately impact minority groups, even if no one policy alone can be shown to be directly responsible. Conversely, and against *Teal*, we should not penalize employers whose policies, as a whole, do not have a disparate impact. Potential immunity from disparate impact liability would be a powerful incentive for employers to achieve representative and integrated workplaces. And an employer with a representative and nonstratified workforce *should* be exempt from disparate impact liability because, taken as a whole, his polices do not have a disparate impact.

This leaves some important questions dangling. Whether or not an employer's workforce is exclusive, segregated or stratified is as much a conceptual as a practical question. The appropriate definition of "nonexclusive" and "desegregated" must be, to a significant degree, a context specific inquiry. Another book of this length would not adequately address the complexities of this aspect of disparate impact doctrine; I'm afraid I must raise such questions only to leave them.

As a general prescription, I would sacrifice conceptual elegance for the sake of practical effect and define the "bottom line" pragmatically, with an eye to pushing employers to do better with respect to desegregation and inclusion. Rights-to-difference advocates' best arguments concern the subtle discriminatory practices that are difficult or impossible to prove in court; I would argue that policies that focus explicitly on group parity and group disadvantage will address them more effectively (albeit indirectly) and with far fewer deleterious side effects than the expansion of individual anti-discrimination rights reflected in rights-to-difference.

For instance, as a conceptual and as an evidentiary matter, it will be difficult at times to distinguish cultural discrimination that is genuinely free of the taint of racially or other status-based animus from cultural discrimination that is at least in part motivated by such animus. An employer who considers cornrows to be an unconventional and unprofessional hairstyle may truthfully insist that this judgment is unrelated to the identity or status of the individual employee or potential employee who wears them; he would require the white Bo Derek clone to change her hair style just as surely as he would a black Cicely Tyson wanna-be, and for the same reasons. But we may still suspect, with justification, that the judgment that cornrows are unconventional or unprofessional is related to the relative popularity of cornrows among African-American women. At least some of the distaste for racially identified or correlated traits will indeed be the "but-for" result of racial animus: we can justifiably presume that at least *some* of the people who dislike cornrow hairstyles dislike them because they associate them with black women.

What some commentators have called "subconscious racism" further complicates matters. Law professor Charles Lawrence writes:

> The culture . . . transmits certain [racist] beliefs and preferences. Because these beliefs are so much a part of the culture, they are not experienced as explicit lessons. . . . The individual is unaware, for example, that a ubiquitous stereotype has influenced her perception that blacks are lazy or unintelligent. Because racism is so deeply ingrained in our culture, it is likely to be transmitted by tacit understandings. . . . These tacit understandings . . . are less likely to be experienced at a conscious level.[27]

In our society, in which racism is expressly and consistently condemned and yet which also is saturated with subtle and implicit racism and racist ideology, it is likely that many people will absorb, accept and act on racist ideology without consciously acknowledging it. As the Southern Poverty Law Center asserts, "people can be consciously committed to egalitarianism, and deliberately work to behave without prejudice, yet still possess hidden negative prejudices or stereotypes."[28] Indeed there is now a significant literature and field of study devoted to uncovering the phenomenon of subconscious bias.[29]

Here, evidentiary problems merge with conceptual questions. What does it mean to say that a policy is or is not motivated by racial animus? Is it enough that the decision maker honestly and consciously believes that her policies are not biased? To what extent should courts infer bias from circumstantial evidence? When should the defendant be required to *prove* that questionable policies are not motivated by animus, for instance by offering some other justification for the policies? And how can we be sure that the alternative explanation is not a mere alibi, masking some underlying, perhaps unconscious bias? When we leave the domain of objective and technical job qualifications and enter the vast and murky realm of "soft skills," generic professionalism, attitude, demeanor and aesthetics, many facially neutral criteria of evaluation are susceptible to attack as secretly or subconsciously biased.

Yet such "soft" criteria are legitimate bases of evaluation and discrimination. Almost everyone treats grooming, demeanor and self-presentation as indicative of more objectively relevant and less immediately apparent virtues such as diligence, attention to detail and intelligence. And almost everyone considers physical appearance, attitude and demeanor to be salient in and of themselves.

In the subset of "soft" subjective preferences that disfavor arguably group-linked traits we face a policy question: is social justice (along with other, potentially conflicting, legitimate ends such as social cohesion, efficient and cost-effective evaluation of individual merit, and the emotional and aesthetic satisfaction of employers, customers, institutional members and bystanders) best served in the long term by the attempt to eliminate such preferences or by the attempt to encourage the members of the stigmatized groups to adapt to them? This question is in my view, impossible to answer in the abstract and extremely difficult to answer even in any given case. Because it is impossible to answer in the more abstract manner that would justify a legal right and because (as I have devoted much of this volume to arguing) presuming an answer that favors legal protection of "group culture" flirts with perils best shunned, I would default to a policy of guided laissez faire in such cases.

We can think of a disparate impact doctrine that is guided by a focus on the bottom line as a policy of guided laissez faire. Viewed from a pragmatic sociological perspective, a focus on the "bottom line" of institutional segregation and stratification is the most practical means of achieving a pragmatic anti-discrimination goal: to break down patterns of segregation and hierarchy. Here the goal of disparate impact doctrine is to encourage employers to reconsider policies that might effectively screen out members of socially disadvantaged groups and generally to encourage employers to be as inclusive as sound business practices permit. Rather than micromanage, insisting on an elusive "job relatedness" for every potentially culturally discriminatory policy, this approach minimizes joint costs by allowing employers—the parties best situated to evaluate the costs and benefits of various policies—to decide *how* best to avoid workplace segregation, while providing them with a powerful incentive (the threat of litigation) to avoid it somehow. And by refusing to invalidate rules that regulate employee behavior, it also avoids joint costs by placing these conflicts—conflicts that both employers and employees potentially can influence—in the domain of collective bargaining and management/labor relations, where all of the costs—to both employers and employees—can be evaluated and efficiently allocated.

It bears emphasis that laissez faire—more or less the policy we currently employ for cultural traits—has not led to the melodrama of "cultural genocide"; instead it has and will continue to allow for a variety of approaches to culturally distinctive traits. Employers today are free to prohibit arguably ethnic hairstyles, free to forbid their bilingual employees from speaking non-English languages on the job and, even in jurisdictions that prohibit discrimination on the basis of sexual orientation, free to require their gay employees to avoid stereotypically gay sartorial affectations. Many employers fail to avail themselves of these liberties because they, like many multiculturalists, believe it would be unjust or oppressive to do so and/or because it simply doesn't make good business sense. In many markets the typical customer prefers or is indifferent to overt racial, ethnic and cultural affectations. And as society becomes more culturally hybrid and pluralistic, some of the practices once exclusively associated with a particular group will be more widely adopted; previously unconventional traits will become commonplace, the once off-putting style will become chic and eventually mundane. Of course, some practices and traits will continue to be quite unpopular and people who cling to them will suffer for it. This is an inevitable consequence of cultural pluralism. If people and groups are culturally distinctive, they often will reject those traits that clash with their own subjective cultural commitments, styles and predilections: to demand otherwise is to insist that culture should not matter—an odd proposition for those who would also seek to protect culture with legal rights.

The primary reason a focus on the "bottom line" has not been adopted in disparate impact doctrine does not involve concern for individual plaintiffs. Instead it is the concern that it would lead institutions to adopt "quotas." The majority in *Ward's Cove* for instance was explicit that it rejected the bottom-line interpretation of employment discrimination law because it would, in effect, require employers to use quotas in order to avoid statistical imbalances or stratification.[30]

This quota-phobia is overblown. In fact, an employer under a bottom-line disparate impact regime would not be *forced* to adopt quotas: it would have several options. It could review its employment practices and eliminate those likely to have a disparate impact; it could adopt outreach or other affirmative action policies to counteract any policies that had a disparate impact but that it wished to retain (remember, the "bottom line" would also be a defense); finally, if it were confident that its practices were legitimate, it could defend them as sufficiently "job related."

The neoconservative obsession with "quotas" echoes the left's obsession with cultural assimilation. Like the fear of forced assimilation, the conservative phobia of "quota systems" and "proportional representation" is largely a conceptually driven obsession that is dramatically out of proportion to any practical risks. Whether in the context of affirmative action, electoral reapportionment or anti-discrimination law, a reflexive aversion to "quotas" has undermined the use of numerical benchmarks and probabilistic statistical data to help set realistic goals and identify potential sites of discriminatory practices. Quota-phobia has ensured that anti-discrimination law—including the logically group-focused notion of disparate impact—retains an exclusively individualist orientation that is ill suited to the compelling policy imperative to dismantle social practices of segregation and hierarchy—practices best understood and addressed at a societal level.

Ironically, a result of quota-phobia has been to speed the popular embrace of difference discourse. Just as Justice Powell's quota-phobic *Bakke* opinion drove universities and students ultimately to emphasize diversity rhetoric, so quota phobia in the context of anti-discrimination law has led to the popularity of rights-to-difference. Unable to address obvious and pressing social injustices by identifying and redressing suspicious statistical imbalances and forced to articulate what are essentially social grievances in terms of individual injury, many civil rights advocates have been forced to develop ever more expansive theories of individual injury, the apotheosis of which is the infinitely elastic concept of "cultural discrimination."

To be sure, the rights-to-difference approach avoids the implication of "quotas" (and in so doing offers no guarantee of socially effective results), but it replaces them with a potentially infinite expansion of judicial intervention into the day-to-day operations of businesses and other institutions. It is unlikely that the regulated institutions would prefer a regime of individualized scrutiny that potentially involves courts in micromanaging almost every business practice to ensure that it is "job related" to one that leaves it to employers to devise their own means of avoiding workplace segregation and stratification.

Nor does the marriage of difference discourse and quota-phobia serve the groups commonly thought to benefit from difference assertion. Contrast the practices at issue in *Ward's Cove*—where no individual right-to-difference could be evoked—to those at issue in cases attacked by right-to-difference proponents such as *Rogers, Chambers* and *Spun Steak*. Ward's Cove cannery presided over a racially stratified workforce in which menial and lower-paying "cannery" jobs were predominantly staffed by non-whites while higher paying noncannery jobs were predominantly staffed by whites. The racially divergent cannery and noncannery staff lived in separate dormitories and ate in separate mess halls. The *Ward's Cove* plaintiffs alleged that a variety of practices led to and maintained this racial stratification: nepotism, rehire preferences, separate hiring channels for the cannery and noncannery positions and a practice of filling the more desirable positions from outside rather than promoting from within. Ward's Cove had established a set of practices that ensured in effect that racial minorities would be concentrated in the lower-paid cannery jobs, that eliminated the possibility of upward mobility from those jobs to the better paid noncannery jobs and that physically segregated employees in a manner that mirrored Jim Crow segregation. These policies not only effectively produced racial stratification, but an inference of underlying racial animus is, if not unavoidable, at least reasonable. But it was difficult to establish that any *individual* person was mistreated because of his or her race or even evaluated based on criteria that were racially linked.

By contrast, in *Rogers, Chambers* and *Spun Steak* no one alleged that the employers' workforces were racially stratified or that the racial group was under represented. In each case there was a plausible rationale for the offending rule that did not involve race and that was related, if not necessary, to the functioning of the institution: in *Rogers* the employer's no-braids rule was consistent with other practices in an industry that was famous for its obsession with business image; in *Chambers* the "role model" rule served the employer's central mission, which was that of helping young, predominantly black women improve their lives—not conclusive, but highly suggestive of an absence of racial animus; and in *Spun Steak* the employer's English-only rule was adopted in order to thwart race harassment in the workplace. Finally, in each of these cases the plaintiff had the option of complying with the workplace rule and avoiding censure or discharge (except arguably Crystal Chambers—whether we consider her pregnancy a decision—she could have abstained from sexual intercourse, used contraception and or terminated the pregnancy—involves questions of time framing, morality and individual freedom that are beyond the scope of our discussion). Although each of the plaintiffs in these putative right-to-difference cases could claim individual discrimination based on a plausible but contestable conceptual definition of race, none could plausibly claim that the challenged workplace policy perpetuated segregation or hierarchy. And an inference of racial animus is speculative at best in *Rogers* and barely plausible in *Spun Steak* and in *Chambers*.

Rogers Redux: Toward a Pragmatic Approach to Difference

Let's consider the implications of a pragmatic, sociological approach to group difference in the context of the *Rogers* case. We should not ask whether cornrows are or are not fundamental to racial identity; instead we should ask whether or not anti-discrimination law should intervene in the practice of racial identity by prohibiting policies that disfavor a hairstyle that is correlated with certain conceptions of racial identity (and by implying that the hairstyle indeed is fundamental to racial identity). If we decided that cornrows, or any other racially correlated but voluntarily adopted traits and behavior did not merit rights protection, we would not need to insist that the behavior in question was "not fundamental to" the racial identity in question. Instead we would simply insist that extending anti-discrimination law to cover it would regulate the practice of the identity in a way that hindered or failed to advance our policy objectives.

A rights-to-difference approach, driven by a conceptual—almost theological—inquiry into the nature of racial identity, collapses a number of distinct concerns raised by the extension of anti-discrimination protection to volitional behavior. Notice how many distinct issues are implicated in Rene Rogers's claim:

1. *Workplace rules that prohibit or burden "Identity linked" practices or traits are* disparate treatment *based on status.*

Rogers might claim that the grooming policy constitutes what civil rights lawyers call *disparate treatment* on the basis of race. Disparate treatment is what most laypeople think of when they think of illegal discrimination: it means that the plaintiff was treated differently because of a classification or status that the relevant anti-discrimination law disallows. "No Blacks Allowed" or "Colored's Restrooms in Back" are classic examples of disparate treatment. In order for a disparate treatment claim to lie in the *Rogers* case, we would have to determine that the hairstyle *is* race or is a proxy for race in the same way that we intuitively understand that skin color and certain morphological features "are" race.

This is to be distinguished from a *disparate impact* claim, which would argue that the trait in question is statistically correlated with the protected group such that the policy would affect members of the group to a greater degree than nonmembers. Under current federal anti-discrimination law a disparate impact claim requires the plaintiff first to prove that the policy in question did in fact have a disparate impact and then would allow the employer to defend against the claim by showing that the policy was sufficiently related to a legitimate business objective. By contrast a disparate treatment claim involves no proof of statistical disparate impact on a group and there is often no defense once it is established (in certain cases—notably not racial discrimination—a disparate treatment claim is subject to a defense similar to the "business necessity" defense: the employer can claim that the status is a Bona Fide Occupational Qualification (BFOQ)—for instance, sex may be a BFOQ for hospital or nursing home attendants who must help change or bathe disabled or elderly patients.)

Many of the rights-to-difference proposals seem to envision a disparate treatment claim in which certain traits would be defined as elements of a protected identity: For instance Juan Perea argues that discrimination against "ethnic traits" should be prohibited as disparate treatment because of the difficulty of proving such discrimination in terms of its disparate impact on a racial or national origin group[31]; similarly Barbara Flagg's proposal to prohibit discrimination against racially correlated traits is designed to avoid the necessity of demonstrating a statistically disparate impact.[32]

The disparate treatment approach to difference claims may have one of two underlying rationales. The first rationale insists that discrimination against identity-linked traits *is* discrimination on the basis of status because the traits are "part of" the status. So barring cornrows isn't a proxy for racial discrimination, it *is* racial discrimination, every bit as much as discrimination against people with dark skins or full lips is racial discrimination. Without defining the various "protected identities"—something I've spent some time arguing is a bad idea—we can't dismiss the premise of this claim as incorrect. But this rationale rests on a "factual" premise that can't be verified, falsified or even evaluated empirically. As I have suggested, this factual claim is really a conceptual and ultimately a normative one in drag. To say that a trait is fundamental to, central to, or an element of a protected status is just a less direct way of saying that we should extend civil rights protection to the trait. The "factual" claim adds nothing to the analysis.

The second rationale argues that discrimination against identity-linked traits is a *proxy* for discrimination based on status. Here the relevant inquiry is psychological and the focus is ultimately on the intent underlying the policy under review. This rationale insists that any employer who prohibits certain traits or characteristics in fact must be *motivated* by the prohibited bias and therefore we should remove the often insurmountable burden of proof from the plaintiff. Here Rogers's claim would be: "the only reason American Airlines would prohibit cornrows is that management is biased against black women"; and an analogous claim would be "the only reason Spun Steak would prohibit Spanish is that management is biased against Latinos."

This suspicion is often well founded. Juan Perea and Mari Matsuda are right to insist that racism against Latinos and Asians can take the form of discrimination on the basis of accent and language. Paulette Caldwell is right to suggest that a hostility to cornrow hairstyles is sometimes simply a reflection of an underlying hostility to black women.

Sometimes, but not always. Airlines, more than most businesses, historically have worked hard to develop specific business images and have tended those images meticulously. The primary means by which the airlines have communicated their corporate image to the public has been through flight attendants and other personnel serving the public. The images have changed over time—from professional nurse to surrogate wife to sexy "fly me" girl, but the strict control the airlines maintained over those images has been a constant. And hair has been a central concern. In the 1972 book *Flying High: What It's Like to Be an Airline Stewardess*, the author advises the potential stewardess:

> Don't let your hopes soar about keeping your waist length hair. Count on its being cut to perhaps an inch or two below your collar, and then later, if you are lucky enough to conceal longer hair in a chignon or knot, you can be happy. Many training schools offer hairpieces at a discount price, and the instructors will show you how to manage them.[33]

Nor did the regulations end with hairstyles: in the late 1960s Delta airlines required flight attendants to be "between 20 and 26 years of age, between 5'2" and 5'8", weight in proportion to height but not over 135 lbs., never married and in radiant good health."[34] Some of these requirements were later invalidated by courts or rejected by the flight attendants labor union, but many—along with the concern in the airline industry for business image—survived.

Given the likelihood that American Airlines, like its competitors, sought to promote a business image that excluded any unconventional grooming, we cannot presume that a policy that forbade cornrows as part of such a general prohibition was motivated by racial bias. Courts should make a pragmatic determination based on the available evidence: policies most likely motivated by bias should be actionable, but those well justified by nonbiased (even if not strictly necessary or tightly job related) purposes should not subject defendants to liability.

In summary, viewed as a claim of disparate treatment rights-to-difference make two distinct inquiries: a conceptual inquiry as to whether a social identity is inseparable from traits that are stereotypically associated with it and a more pragmatic inquiry as to whether discrimination against certain traits is often a proxy for illicit discrimination based on status. The former inquiry is metaphysical in nature and courts should reject any claim that depends on it; the latter inquiry is an appropriate focus of anti-discrimination law and can be resolved by the type of pragmatic factual inquiry courts routinely and competently engage in.

2. We should protect group-linked traits because institutional policies burdening such traits have a disparate impact *on the group.*

Another idea latent in the *Rogers* claim is a variation of a traditional *disparate impact* claim. Here the analysis is statistical: if the cornrow hairstyle disproportionately is worn by blacks, then a rule against it has a disparate impact on blacks. As a threshold matter, the strength of the claim will depend on how the disputed rule is framed: the plaintiff will want to frame the rule narrowly as a prohibition against cornrows, but the employer will want to frame it broadly as a rule against "non-traditional grooming" thereby including prohibitions against styles favored by white men and women (and will draft it accordingly if its lawyers have anything to do with it).

One significant merit of disparate impact analysis is that it is likely to expose hidden illegitimate bias: as law professor Paul Brest notes "[t]he accumulation of suspected but unproved race-dependent conduct . . . may systematically deprive minorities of important benefits. And the existence of a state of affairs which 'everyone knows' is based on racial discrimination but no one will remedy is demoralizing and stigmatic."[35] This returns us to the proxy rationale that I identified in the context of disparate treatment. We may think that some employers would impose a no-cornrows rule, knowing that blacks disproportionately wear the style, in the hope that the rule will discourage black applicants and provide an excuse to terminate current black employees. Here the grooming rule is a strict proxy for prohibited discrimination: if the underlying intent reasonably can be established, this should be actionable as disparate treatment.

But a disparate impact claim, by definition, need not rely on underlying discriminatory intent. If we have a social commitment to the integration of subordinated and marginalized subgroups, policies that have the effect of excluding members of these groups demand extraordinary justification. Here the impact claim raises an empirical question that will in some cases have an answer that we can discover. If we *know* that the policy will reduce the number of minority group members because the group members will by and large prefer to take less remunerative employment elsewhere rather than comply with the policy, then we face a straightforward conflict between the interest of the employer in the policy and the interest of society in the integration of that workplace. This is true regardless of what we think of the practices that the employer's policy prohibits: it's conceivable that a rational policymaker would want to force an employer to accommodate even silly or repugnant practices if the alternative were the prolonged isolation of an important social group.

But the fact that the employee readily can comply with the rule raises additional conceptual problems that frustrate traditional disparate impact analysis. For instance, when evaluating the effect of the American Airlines rule on blacks we cannot assume that the rule will exclude every black person with cornrows. Presumably some will change their hairstyle in order to get or keep the job or will comply in some other fashion (for instance, the American

Airlines grooming rule allowed Rogers to cover her cornrows with a hair-piece). Conversely we can't know how many African-Americans who do not currently wear their hair in cornrows will adopt the style and, having done so, refuse to comply with the grooming rule.

Moreover, as I have suggested above, the behavior of the protected group may respond to legal decisions. A decision to allow a disparate impact claim for grooming rules might encourage the types of grooming likely to be protected simply by removing potential disincentives; it might also politicize the grooming and create the identifications that underlie the statistical disparity.

This dynamism raises the *possibility* that the workplace rule will not reduce the number of employees from the protected group (it will not serve as a proxy for discrimination against the group), but rather will reduce the number of people engaging in the prohibited practices while on the job. In other words, it will do precisely and only what it purports to do on its face: discriminate against the prohibited *practices*. At this point we would need an account of why we should protect the *practices* in the given workplace in order to justify the application of a legal right to engage in them.

If the disputed workplace policy is likely to reduce the prevalence of the *practices*, but not reduce the integration of the institution then we face a different set of policy questions that have to do with cultural preservation itself. Do we think that the group *practices* are valuable in and of themselves? Do we have reason to value group distinctiveness (of which the contested characteristic is an instance) in and of itself? If so, must the practices be accommodated in the institution in question in order to thrive, or can the minority group members comply with the disputed policy and still maintain the practices outside the institution?

On the other side of the scale: does the institution have a compelling reason to prohibit the practices? Can the institutional goals served by the workplace rule be achieved in some other fashion at a reasonable cost? Finally, do we have reason to worry that the plaintiff's association of the practices with the group identity is itself an effect of subordination. If Rene Rogers experiences her identity as dependent on a *hairstyle*, this may be a symptom of racial oppression, not racial liberation, and accordingly something we should wish to overcome, not to reinforce.

3. *The employer (or university or social club or other social institution regulated by anti-discrimination law) should not regulate* any *employee conduct that is not sufficiently related to a legitimate core institutional objective.*

A related claim is that the business should not be allowed to prohibit the hairstyle because it doesn't affect workplace productivity. Doctrinally, this argument is a preemptive refutation of the defendant's potential defense that the disputed policy serves a legitimate business objective.

If we take this claim standing alone, we could develop a general theory of labor regulation that limited businesses to employment criteria that were rationally related to a legitimate business objective. Under such a rationale, both Rene Rogers and the dreadlocked blonde would have a cause of action. So would, to borrow law professor Mark Kelman's example, someone who was fired because he reminded the boss of a hated stepfather.[36] But the devil is in the distinctions implied by words such as "rationally" and "legitimate." Is it "legitimate" for a business to want to project a conservative image that precludes all unconventional grooming practices? It might depend on the business: a grooming code that is justified for a bank manager might be unreasonable for a data entry clerk working in an isolated cubicle.

We could run with this approach, drafting or waiting for courts to develop a canon of legitimate criteria for various jobs: weight is a legitimate criterion for a fashion model but not for a law professor (what about an aerobics instructor, assuming she can perform the physical aspects of the job?); hairstyle regulations are okay for waiters in fancy restaurants but not in greasy spoons; women hired as cocktail waitresses in "gentleman's clubs" can be required to wear make-up and dress provocatively but airline stewardesses cannot. This approach is the logical extension of the argument that employers should not be able to prohibit "culturally linked" practices except for reasons of business necessity. Courts have already adopted this approach in the limited context of defenses to anti-discrimination claims, but they are understandably reluctant to expand the approach. This inquiry involves courts in the micro-management of businesses; this alone is probably enough of a reason to reject it as a widespread approach to anti-discrimination law.

4. *We should protect the traits and conduct that are especially important to the individual.*

Another possible rationale is that we should protect culturally linked practices because they are especially important to the individual. Standing alone, this claim covers any nonconformist, not only members of the canonical groups. It would apply equally to our dreadlocked blonde or to an individual with multiple and visible body piercings or tattoos. The fact that Rene Rogers's hairstyle is favored by many blacks would be merely evidentiary under this rationale. It might help us evaluate her claim that the hairstyle is important to her, but it is neither necessary nor sufficient: anyone could put forth evidence supporting the claim that the disputed grooming is especially important to them (for instance the physical discomfort associated with piercing and tattooing would also be evidence of subjective value to the plaintiff.) Conversely, a link to a social subgroup alone should be insufficient to carry the plaintiff's burden. (Suppose for instance we find that Rene Rogers was a trendy follower of fashion who changed hairstyles on a seasonal basis.)

Here we will face severe conflicts between a policy that protects behavior and traits because of their subjective importance to individuals and many compelling institutional and business objectives.

5. *We should protect the traits themselves in the name of promoting cultural pluralism.*

Here we'd need an account of why and in what circumstances cultural pluralism is a good thing. In at least some instances uniformity and standardization have clear advantages over pluralism—language is an obvious example but far from a lonely one. It is inevitable that some conduct that is important to an individual (and arguably part of a group's culture) will also be very destructive to an institution. As imminent a sociologist as Orlando Patterson argued that explicit sexual banter is a part of African-American culture, yet most institutions explicitly discourage such conduct (and federal sex harassment law makes the *institution* liable if the sexual banter creates a hostile work environment for women—an inherently subjective determination—unless the institution takes action to stop it.) Finally, rights-to-difference may *undermine* cultural pluralism by forcing social institutions, including those controlled by minority groups, to adopt a sterile culture of profit seeking or technocratic mastery.

I suspect that many readers will find some, but not all, of the above rationales for a rights-to-difference claim compelling. I also suspect that the superficial appeal of the rights-to-difference approach depends on this imprecise super-justification: there are so many reasons to support a right-to-difference that one need not examine any one of them with rigor. The conceptualism of rights-to-difference collapses this diversity of distinct arguments by substituting what looks like a single empirical question—What is race?—for the numerous normative and practical questions that identity assertion and cultural difference actually implicate. The wealth of potential justifications for rights-to-difference also insures them a reasonably large contingent of supporters, and the supporters will find strength in numbers—so many people with a similar idea can't be wrong! This confederation of believers has allowed rights-to-difference to grow into a legal zeitgeist.

But if I am right that the supporters of rights-to-difference support them for disparate reasons—in other words if the supporters agree *that* they support rights-to-difference but not about *why* they support them—then it's likely that if the approach were actually implemented there would be no consensus about how it should be implemented or which situations it should cover. Moreover it's possible that alternative reforms might satisfy many of the concrete concerns of many of the supporters of rights-to-difference. It is with this possibility in mind that I offer the following tentative gestures towards an alternative approach to reform.

Alternative Approaches to Group Conflict and Social Injustice

Almost any policy to which a disproportionate number of minority group members object could be defined as "biased" against that group given a sufficiently generous definition of bias. But as a practical matter anti-discrimination law is best at attacking practices and policies that can be attributed to animus or bias with some confidence. We need classical anti-discrimination law to combat manifest and demonstrable or reasonably inferred bias and animus (and if my proposed "bottom-line" approach to disparate impact doctrine were adopted, we would have a combination of classical anti-discrimination law and a broader public policy to fight group disadvantage.) But anti-discrimination law alone will not eliminate racism or other types of status-based social animus.

Even if it could, it would not eliminate status hierarchies which are interlaced with other social institutions and practices in complex ways. Lawyers and legal scholars have long recognized that some of the most damaging aspects of status hierarchies are not the result of bias or animus in the conventional sense of those terms. Some of our most destructive and intractable racial problems, for instance, are not the result of contemporary racism at all but rather of the present day effects of racism and racist policies of the past.

Here's an example, drawn in part from my own work elsewhere. Most American cities fund public services primarily through property taxes. They also are entitled to and with very rare exceptions do limit access to local services to residents of the city. This means that cities have an overwhelming incentive to encourage in-movers with resources who will invest in real estate and thereby increase the value of property (and tax revenues) and who will require relatively little in terms of public services. They will have an equally compelling incentive to discourage in-movers without resources whose presence will tend to depress property values and who will need a lot of public services. It scarcely needs to be said that the heavily minority race urban poor fit the latter description. And although American local governments do not have explicit immigration policies, they do have quite broad powers to restrict land uses. By excluding all or most high-density or multifamily housing, middle-class and wealthy suburbs can and do effectively screen out low-income (again, disproportionately minority race) potential residents by prohibiting the housing that they can afford. Moreover, suburban local governments can and do resist services that many low-income people require, such as intercity public transportation, halfway houses, group living arrangements and rehabilitation centers.

Nowhere in this description of racial disadvantage need racism or racial animus appear. It is quite plausible that a community without a racist bone in the body politic could, acting from motivations of financial interest alone, implement policies that do more to further racial division and hierarchy than do the deliberate acts of a committed racist employer. Residential segregation—one of the most destructive elements of contemporary American racial hierarchy—does not require ongoing racial animus to function; therefore, even a policy that could somehow root out all racism—conscious and subconscious, overt and subtle—would not eliminate the evils of racial injustice. Urban sociologist William Julius Wilson makes a related point in arguing against the thesis that the plight of the black underclass can be explained by contemporary racism:

> No serious student of American race relations can deny the relationship between the disproportionate concentration of blacks in impoverished urban ghettos and historic racial subjugation in American society. But . . . the recent rise in social dislocation [in the ghetto is] . . . difficult to explain with a race-specific thesis. It is not readily apparent how the deepening economic class divisions between the haves and have-nots in the black community can be accounted for . . . especially when it is argued that . . . racism is directed with equal force across class boundaries in the black community. Nor is it apparent how racism can result in a more rapid social and economic deterioration in the inner city in the post civil rights period than in the period that immediately preceded the notable civil rights victories.[37]

The conceptual and practical obstacles to rooting out discriminatory impulses *entout*, and the likelihood that racial injustice would endure even if these obstacles were surmounted suggest that other, more programmatic, approaches to social justice are required. To take just one example: if one believes, as I do, that desegregation is vitally necessary to a racially just and harmonious society, then one should advance policies most likely to effectively promote meaningful and durable desegregation, whether they do so by eliminating and countering racism or by some other means. Law professor Owen Fiss offers observations along these lines, which have the considerable merit of slicing cleanly through conceptual fat to the sinew of the issue: "The ghetto is . . . a means by which a group is prevented from sharing in society's successes and kept far beneath others in terms of wealth, power and living standards. This structure must be dismantled . . . [W]e must provide those who now live . . . [in the ghetto] with the economic means to move into middle and upper-class neighborhoods."[38]

We have good reasons to address group specific social injustices that aren't well described in terms of discrimination or bias; we can and should make the case for such programmatic policy interventions on their own merits. I think we should combat residential and workplace segregation, *even when we can't attribute it to ongoing bias*, because racial segregation is intrinsically socially destructive and effectively unjust. I think we should insist on workplace accommodations for pregnant women, *even when the lack of such accommodations is not attributable to sexism* because pregnancy is hard enough even when people do accommodate it (the willingness to go through nine months of weight gain, hormonal imbalance and dietary restrictions qualifies as a type of national service.) I think we should eschew laws and policies that regulate the sexual indulgences of consenting adults, not because such regulation is biased against certain naturally defined and stigmatized groups, but because sexual regulation *creates* stigmatized groups (which we don't need any more of) and because sexual indulgence between consenting adults is, on the whole, a good thing and is not in need of regulation.

At the same time, some of the issues that rights-to-difference claims involve do not implicate disadvantaged or stigmatized groups as such but instead raise questions that apply to individuals regardless of group identity or status. In the absence of racial animus, cultural difference claims, such as Rene Rogers's claim to her cornrows are much like the claim of a white male counterpart to long hair and beard, or like the claim of a male counterpart to wear earrings—in each case we confront a mainstream distaste for an unconventional or countercultural personal style. It is a mistake to conceive of and argue for these claims in the uniquely charged language of racial discrimination.

Many industries strictly control the personal grooming of their employees. For instance, such businesses as Disneyland, the South Coast Plaza shopping mall in California and the Ritz Carlton hotel chain make no apologies for their strict grooming requirements. According to the *Los Angeles Times*:

[E]mployees find that if they want to keep their jobs, they have to check their personal style at the door of their workplace. Everything about their appearance . . . is often preordained by a . . . corporate personnel or human resources department. [At the Ritz-Carlton] guidelines require that hair be a "natural color," . . . other forbidden looks: beards and goatees, "mutton chop" sideburns, dreadlocks, big hair (buns, twists or bangs higher than 3 inches from the top of the head), earrings larger than . . . a quarter, more than two rings on each hand, skirt lengths higher than 2 inches above the top of the knee and long fingernails.[39]

Whether or not such practices should be legal is a complex question, requiring us to weigh the interests of a business and its customers in a particular business image against the expressive interest of employees. What should be obvious is that it is not a question of racial discrimination but instead involves distinct stakes that require analysis on their distinctive merits.

My own impulse is one of sympathy for people who wish—for reasons of sincere belief in an authentic cultural identity, self-fashioned biography, newly minted persona or adventurous aesthetic taste—to assert themselves in a nonmainstream style. We might seek to promote individual autonomy through legal rights that apply regardless of identity or group affiliation. We have ample precedent for rights to engage in specified behavior that do not take the form of anti-discrimination law, such as the First Amendment rights to freedom of expression, assembly, association and religion, and the "penumbral" right to privacy that prevents the several states from outlawing contraception and abortion. We don't think of these rights as prohibiting discrimination based on status—rather we think of them as substantive commitments to protect specific types of *activity*. We *could* imagine the First Amendment right to expression as an anti-discrimination protection for loquacious people or the right to privacy as protecting sexual libertines, but we don't. Instead, we think of them as protecting everyone in so far as they engage in a specific type of activity. It is undoubtedly true that political minorities and countercultural artists benefit more from First Amendment protections than people who only advance popular causes or artists who avoid controversy. But the right applies equally to all of them and public support for the right is largely the result of the efforts of those who need it least (the *New York Times* will support both a socialist newspaper and a gay pornographer.) We have freedom of expression, not because we are concerned about bias against the talkative but because we believe in the value of expression.

Similarly, it seems to me that if we were to protect cornrows, languages or other cultural practices, we should do so because we think these *activities* merit protection, not because of solicitude towards the type of people likely to want to engage in them. Imagine if it had been possible for Rene Rogers's to articulate her complaint against American Airlines in terms of a generally applicable right to control one's personal grooming, rather than as an cultural claim on behalf of black women. Suddenly problematic facts for Rogers are transformed into arguments in her favor. The fact that people of all races and genders (such as Bo Derek) wore the cornrow hairstyle and were potentially regulated under American Airlines' grooming rules would not undercut her claim; instead it would contribute to its urgency. The fact that the airline industry at the time had grooming policies that forbade all sorts of even mildly countercultural styles would not undercut a potential disparate impact argument, instead it would inspire a powerful coalition of support: men with long hair or facial hair, women with short hair, people with body piercings or tattoos, people of all races with braided hairstyles, people with hair dyed in unnatural colors. In each of these cases we could describe the grooming choice as a part of identity (what grooming decision isn't?): hippies, beatniks, punks, urban primitives, bikers. But by using a generic claim we leave open the possibility of coalition building among groups and the cross identification and cultural syncresis such political interaction might foster.

Or consider Drucilla Cornell and William Bratton's proposal to advance Spanish language rights as an extension of racial or national origin anti-discrimination rights for Latinos. The underlying issue—fairly widespread hostility to non-English speakers, especially perhaps, but not exclusively, Spanish-speaking Latinos—suggests at least two alternative approaches. One is a generic expressive right to speak a chosen language at work. It would apply to everyone—Russian émigrés, seasonal workers from Central America, Latino-Americans who simply prefer Spanish, fourth-generation Americans trying to learn French. The other is to promote bilingualism for everyone in regions of the country where there is a significant second language. Such "regional bilingualism" is not unheard of: Switzerland consists of officially Italian-, German- and French-speaking Cantons. Just as the history and contemporary demographics of Switzerland support such an arrangement so too perhaps the history of the American Southwest supports official bilingualism in English and Spanish. Both of these approaches have the merit of highlighting a specific practical aspect of the language diversity issue. Should people be free to speak foreign languages on the job over the objections of their employers? Should we recognize the existence of a significant language minority with long and deep-seated ties to a region and its culture? Advancing these approaches to language diversity may seem more arduous than a "simple" discrimination claim but both seem to me as politically feasible and probably more durable and more dignified if successful.

Viewed as questions of public policy, many of the practical concerns raised by rights-to-difference may be better understood as questions of labor/management relations and the regulation of markets for goods and services.

For instance, "discrimination" against overweight passengers by the airline industry (in the form of requiring very obese passengers to purchase two seats on crowded flights) should be seen as symptomatic, not of the industry's hostility to difference, but of the increasingly thin profit margins on which deregulated airlines operate. Deregulation has brought some benefits to the flying public—mainly dramatically lower airfares. But it has also produced overbooked flights, circuitous routes, underserved cities and smaller airline seats. A discrimination claim is a particularly bad fix for these problems—whatever one thinks the solution should be.

Similarly, some cases of what many aggrieved parties now call discrimination may be better understood as wrongful termination. Most states have very weak wrongful termination laws; several have none at all.[40] Because wrongful termination is difficult to establish even when available as a cause of action and lacks rhetorical firepower, people have an incentive to look for a more muscular complaint; if they can appropriately reframe their grievance they find strength in anti-discrimination law. There are good arguments for strengthening wrongful termination laws and passing them in states where they do not exist. But the creeping tendency to redescribe garden variety labor/management conflicts as the more rarified phenomenon of discrimination not only dilutes the rhetorical and practical force of anti-discrimination discourse for historically subordinated groups, it also siphons energy away from any political movement to reform the excesses of our increasingly harsh market economy.

As to group pluralism proper, I think we should experiment with multiple approaches. The rights-to-difference proponents make some decent arguments (along with some bad ones) that it would be an improvement if employers, universities, social clubs and local governments accommodated many things that might be described as group cultural practices or identity-linked traits. But, rights-to-difference also promote other highly questionable ends and begin from questionable premises. Therefore I'd rather let these institutions experiment with other approaches to group pluralism, too.

I suspect that these practical observations will fail to move many of the advocates and converts to difference discourse. Difference discourse reflects a deep psychological need for group recognition. I suspect that much of the appeal of extraordinary legal protection of group traits stems from the potential validation of a *particular* narrative of group culture. Explicitly group-based rights that incorporate a substantive account of group distinctiveness would give a governmental, occasionally even a constitutional, imprimatur to that account of the group in question. More than the recognition of a pre-existing sociological fact, such rights would canonize the protected practices as the norm for the social group. Traditional anti-discrimination law coupled with an array of social welfare programs and generally applicable rights would not provide such an imprimatur; hence no matter how successful at achieving its goals, such an alternative program would fail utterly to provide the recognition that I believe is the aspiration at the very heart of difference discourse. I question difference discourse generally and reject rights-to-difference in particular because I believe such explicit canonization of substantive group difference is precisely what the law should withhold.

Postscript: Beyond Difference

I am suggesting that these walls—these artificial walls—which have been up for so long to protect us from something we fear, must come down. I think that what we really have to do is to create a country in which there are no minorities—for the first time in the history of the world . . . the majority for which everyone is seeking which must reassess and release us from our past and deal with the present and create standards worthy of what a man can be—this majority is you. No one else can do it.[1]

Racial Cultures has, for most part, been critical in analysis and corrosive in tone. I've debunked the presuppositions and lampooned the utopianism of group difference advocates and put up signposts labeled "Next Exit: Hell" on the path paved with their good intentions. I imagine the breezy iconoclasm that has characterized this book will annoy some readers: these are serious issues and they deserve serious treatment. But humor and irreverence have their place in serious argument. It strikes me that one of the most effectively spellbinding aspects of difference discourse has been its somber and weighty sanctimoniousness, which has intimidated those who might puncture its pretensions and deterred deserved critique. What Brian Barry says of religious fanaticism is as true of the quasi-religious commitment to group difference: "few people have ever been converted . . . by a process of 'examining beliefs critically' . . . [instead such commitment] is whipped up by non-rational means, and the only way in which it is ever likely to be counteracted is by making people ashamed of it . . . the core of [such a] deflationary strategy [must include] mocking, ridiculing and lampooning."[2]

Behind this book's deliberately light touch lies a serious concern. Difference discourse has the potential to stall egalitarian and humanist reforms and deprive us of much of the exciting potential of cosmopolitan society. Despite setbacks, disappointments and retrenchment this is a far better society than the one into which I was born in 1966. The primary

211

reason that it is better is that the people who believed in profound and intrinsic differences between the races and other groups defined by ascribed statuses are being pushed to margins of social respectability. We should keep pushing and reject the segregationist's creed of intrinsic difference in favor of a more noble and more difficult ideal, what Randall Kennedy has called a: "cosmopolitan ethos . . . that does not mean we should blind ourselves to racial realities . . . [but does insist that] [t]he prominence of race in our society does not mean that individuals must or should continue to use race as a factor in choosing their intimate affiliations. We are free to restructure and improve the society we have inherited."³

If difference discourse were put on hiatus we might have more frequent and more meaningful relationships between people of different races, ethnicities and sexualities and better relations between the sexes. Free of the superstition of intrinsic and implacable group difference and the corresponding moral obligation to preserve group differences and cultures "whole cloth," we might find it easier to connect across the canonical identity categories because we would be open to finding and building commonalities rather than seeing shared institutions, values and norms as the mechanisms of "cultural genocide." We would be open to the potential experience of other group affinities that, at times, could overshadow the canonical divisions of race, gender and sexuality, just as for most people, other affinities often overshadow, say, religious and ethnic differences. Such affinities would go a long way towards establishing the trust and social capital that will be necessary in order to confront the social conflicts raised both by cultural difference and by America's ongoing tawdry affair with status hierarchy.

Difference discourse, with its "standpoint epistemology" presupposition that "only we can understand" deprives social justice struggles of the dialogue that might stimulate viable solutions and convincing arguments. Difference discourse provides an easy alibi when disagreement or conflict emerges in a relationship: if outsiders just can't understand, what's the use of trying to explain our positions diplomatically, much less of listening to differing opinions? Having learned the lessons of difference discourse all too well, most people rarely venture to comment on any of the social issues where they can be cast as the insensitive oppressor—and if they do they're careful to parrot the politically correct position to a fault. Many whites are content to cede the field of race relations to people of color, straights are willing to leave sexuality discourse to the gays, lesbians and bisexuals and men are satisfied to leave gender studies to women, all in the name of respect for difference—at least so long as not much is at stake. The problem is that a lot is at stake: correcting centuries of socially pervasive bias will cost society something and it's up to those of us who think it's worth the costs to make the strongest possible case as to why.

To make real progress on any of these issues we need people from outside the canonical groups of identity politics; we need their ideas and we need their cooperation. Ethnic enclaves and exclusive organizations might provide a save haven in a heartless world, but if one wants to change society, ultimately one must engage it, "outsiders" and all. Antiracists, feminists and antihomophobes with new ideas (or even good if out of vogue old ones) should run the risk of being called insensitive and speak up when they disagree with the difference agenda. Otherwise, when the antibias position—deprived of the rigor of challenge and dissent and poisoned by the difference agenda—emerges, flabby and unpersuasive, into the arena of public debate, bigots and those simply indifferent to socially pervasive bias, more than happy to voice *their* contrary opinions, will be well poised to deliver the knockout punch.

This has been a critique. To the extent that it is a proposal, it is first and foremost a proposal that we question some ideas that many people in our society have come to accept as common knowledge. Although I have offered suggestions and analysis that I believe would help us more effectively to negotiate the tensions occasioned by the production and punishment of difference, they would do only that: *negotiate* the tension. I don't think law is capable of resolving or banishing this tension. In that sense law is incapable of guaranteeing social justice. Social justice for people of color and for other stigmatized social groups will require a revolutionary social and cultural transformation—one more sweeping and more penetrating perhaps than any this nation has seen. One more profound perhaps than any society can achieve while remaining the same society.

Some of the radicals of the civil rights movement opined that racial justice could never be secured in American society. The conviction that inspires this book is that in a profound sense they were right: an America without racism, without sexism, without homophobia would be a society none of us alive today would recognize. And—this is the truly thrilling and terrifying part—it would be a society that could not produce or sustain people like us. It may be that the price of providing future generations with a world free of the social stigma and oppression of statuses like race—a world we could be proud to call more just—is that they would not share *our* identities, that they would be our heirs but *not* our descendants.

Suppose you could make a deal with the angel that Faust never got to meet. The angel offers you this: a world free of racism, of sexism, of homophobia, of all of the illegitimate hierarchies and oppressive aspects of ascribed identities. And no, this is not a world of sterile colorblindness or lockstep uniformity;

instead it is world of diversity without stigma, of social justice that reaches every corner of the globe and nourishes every human heart. But there's a catch. You can't go there. You're too far gone, too fallen, too conflicted, too much a part of what makes your own wretched world so far from the world the angel has described. For you, this just world would be a kind of hell in which you could never find a comfortable place. The angel offers a ticket for your unborn children, or perhaps their children; this is a pass good for all and only those still supple enough to adapt to the good society. And it's a one-way ticket: if your children or grandchildren and future generations take this ticket, they can't come back to you. It's is not an arbitrary restriction, the angel explains, it's inherent in the nature of the journey they will have to make. If they go, they will be just as alienated from this world as you would be from the good society. And—here's the rub—they will be just as alienated from you. Of course they will love and respect you, but they will also fear and pity you. They will be repelled by the petty bigotries you harbor, the dangerous little myths you cling to, your alibis, your short cuts past Truth, the golden calves you worship when you think Moses and God aren't watching. Train's leaving, all aboard who's coming aboard. Would you let them go?

NOTES

PREAMBLE

1. Randall Kennedy, *Interracial Intimacies* (2003) at 34.

2. Chadran Kukathas, *Are There Any Cultural Rights?* 20 Political Theory, 1992 at 105.

3. Kwame Anthony Appiah, *Multicultural Misunderstanding*, 44 New York Review of Books, October 9, 1997, at 36.

4. William Kymlicka, *Multicultural Citizenship* (1995) at 60.

5. Id. at 96.

6. Id. at 99.

7. Id. at 75, 84.

8. Id. at 75.

9. Id. at 84.

10. Id. at 85.

11. Steven M. Cutler, *A Trait Based Approach to National Origin Claims Under Title VII*, 94 Yale L.J. 1164 (1984).

12. Mari Matsuda, *Voices of America, Accent, Antidiscrimination Law, and a Jurisprudence for the Last Reconstruction*, 100 Yale L.J. 1329 (1991).

13. Barbara Flagg, *Fashioning a Title VII Remedy for Transparently White Subjective Decisionmaking*, 104 Yale L.J. 2009, 2012 (1995).

14. Kenji Yoshino, *Covering*, 111 Yale L.J. 769 (2002).

15. Paulette Caldwell, *A Hair Piece: Perspectives on the Intersection of Race and Gender*, 1991 Duke L.J. 365 (1991).

16. Juan Perea, *Ethnicity And Prejudice: Reevaluating "National Origin" Discrimination Under Title VII*, 35 Wm and Mary L. Rev. 805, 866–67 (1994).

17. Bratton and Cornell, *Deadweight Costs and Intrinsic Costs of Nativism: Economics, Freedom and Legal suppression of Spanish*, 84 Cornell L. Rev. 595 (1999).

18. See Peter Wood, *Diversity* (2003).

19. Of course, one might insist that all three positions do derive from the same generic set of commitment and beliefs: all three distrust governmental intervention in a certain sphere based on a pair of complementary beliefs: one, that government is too clumsy to regulate delicate human relations competently and two, that regulation of any sort violates an individual liberty interest to decide certain things for oneself. But at this point the argument proves far too much. We might as well say that the libertarian, the civil libertarian and the sexual libertine are ideological kin because their titles share a common root "liberty." Ayn, Nadine, Ellen and I dare say everyone reading these words share certain beliefs and commitments simply by virtue of living in a Western post-Enlightenment society. A commitment to some idea of liberty as freedom from intervention by government (perhaps any sufficiently powerful and centrally controlled institu-

tion) unites virtually every political thinker of the modern era. The relevant ideological distinctions all take place within this very broad but significant sphere of agreement.

20. Brian Barry, *Culture and Equality* (2001) at 11–12.

21. See Michael Warner, *The Trouble with Normal* (1999).

22. See Wendy Brown and Janet Halley eds., Left Legalism, Left Critique (2002).

CHAPTER 1

1. *Renee Rogers, et al. v. American Airlines, Inc.*, 527 F. Supp. 229 (1981).

2. Caldwell, *A Hair Piece*, text following note 5.

3. *Martinez v. Santa Clara Pueblo*, 402 F. Supp. 5 (1975).

4. *Ferrill v. The Parker Group*, 168 F. 3d 468 (1999).

5. Immanuel Wallerstein, *Geopolitics and Geoculture: Essays on the Changing World System* (1991) at 173–75.

6. Dorothy Roberts, *Why Culture Matters to Law*, in *Cultural Pluralism, Identity Politics and the Law*, A. Sarat and T. Kearns eds. (1999) at 88–89.

7. Alex Johnson, *Bid Whist, Tonk and United States v. Fordice: Why Integrationism Fails African-Americans Again*, 81 Cal L. Rev. 1401, 1450 (1993).

8. Id.

9. Roberts at 91.

10. Johnson at 1456.

11. Harold Cruse, *The Crisis of the Negro Intellectual* (1967) at 564.

12. Gary Peller, *Race Consciousness*, in *Critical Race Theory: The Key Writings that Formed the Movement* (1995) at 150.

13. Ward Connerly, *The Racial Privacy Initiative: Why I Support it and Why You Should Too*, http://www.racialprivacy.org/miscellaneous.htm#misc3 (July 2003).

14. *Outrageous LA*, San Francisco Chronicle Books. (1984); 8–9 reprinted in *Leave any Information at the Signal* (2002).

15. Clayborne Carson, *In Struggle: SNCC and the Black Awakening of the 1960s* (1981) at 77.

16. E. David Cronon, Black Moses: The Story of Marcus Garvey and the Universal Negro Improvement Association (1955, 1969) at 188–89.

17. "[I]f there is substantial agreement in law, language and religion; if there is a satisfactory adjustment of economic life, then there is no reason why, in the same country and on the same street, two or three great national ideals might not thrive and develop, that men of different races might not strive together for their race ideal as well, perhaps even better, than in isolation." Du Bois, On the Conservation of Races, (1897) at 257.

18. International Commission of Inquiry into the Existence of Slavery and Forced Labor in the Republic of Liberia and Cuthbert Christy, *Report of the International Commission of Inquiry into the Existence of Slavery and Forced Labor in the Republic of Liberia. September 8, 1930.* Washington, DC: U.S. Government Printing Office, 1931.

19. Peter Applebome, *Keeping Tabs on Jim Crow*, New York Times, April 23, 1995 at Sec 6, 34.

20. Michel Foucault, *The History of Sexuality Volume One: An Introduction* (1978) at 9.

21. Eric Hobsbawm and Terrance Ranger eds., *The Invention of Tradition* (1983).

22. Barbara Jeanne Fields, *Slavery, Race and Ideology in the United States of America*, New Left Review 95 (1990) at 181.

23. See generally, Stokley Carmichael and Charles V. Hamilton, *Black Power: The Politics of Liberation in America* (1967); Gary Peller, *Race Consciousness* in *Critical Race Theory: The Key Writing That Formed the Movement*, Crenshaw et al. eds. (1995) at 127.

24. *Regents of the University of California v. Bakke*, 438 U.S. 265 (1978).

25. *A Program for Minority Students*, Stanford University School of Medicine (1969).

26. *Minorities: The Talent Search is On!* In Stanford M.D (Summer 1969) at 5.

27. Kaplan, Graduate School Admissions Advisor, 4th Ed. (2001) at 139.

28. Ruth Lammert-Reeves/Kaplan, *Get Into Law School: A Strategic Approach* (2003) at 164.

29. Willie J. Epps, Jr., *How to Get Into Harvard Law School* (1996) at 273.

30. Id. at 292.

31. Id. at 297.

32. Id. at 298.

33. Id. at 300.

34. Id. at 310.

35. Id. at 312.

36. Id. at 318.

37. Id. at 333.

38. Id. at 365–66.

39. Id. at 333.

40. Claude Steele, *Thin Ice: "Stereotype Threat" and Black College Students*, Atlantic Monthly, August 1999.

41. Janice E. Hale-Benson, *Black Children: Their Roots, Culture and Learning Styles* (1982) at 42.

42. Id. at 16.

43. Steele.

44. Id.

45. *Grutter v. Bollinger*, 539 U.S slip op. (2003) at 3.

46. 539 U.S ____(slip op. 2003).

47. Id., slip op. at 11.

48. Id. at 26.

49. Slip op. at 11.

50. Slip op. at 26.

51. Press release, "Leading Constitutional Scholars Analyze Supreme Court's Affirmative Actions Decisions; Civil Rights Leaders Applaud Ruling's Upholding Use of Race to Promote Diversity," The Civil Rights Project, Harvard University, June 23, 2003.

52. This is epitomized by Charles Taylor's discussion of the Quebecois Separatism and First Nations groups in Canada; Jürgen Habermas's discussion of German immi-

gration and naturalization, and Anthony Appiah's exploration of American (the two continents, not the United States), European and African versions of pan Africanism. See Gutmann and Taylor eds., Multiculturalism (1994).

53. Todd Gitlin, *The Twilight of Common Dreams: Why America is Wracked by Culture Wars* (1995) 149, 154.

54. See Anthony Appiah, *Race, Culture, Identity, Color Conscious* (1996) at 99.

CHAPTER 2

1. Audre Lorde, *Age, Race, Class and Sex: Redefining Difference*, in *Out There: Marginalization and Contemporary Cultures 285* (1990) (emphasis mine).

2. Yoshino at 934.

3. Flagg at 2012.

4. Perea criticizes an approach that would limit anti-discrimination protection to those cases where "ethnic traits . . . serve as [statistical] proxies for national origin or race" Perea at 851. [both prohibited bases for discrimination under existing law] as insufficiently inclusive. He worries that a requirement of statistical correlation will leave plaintiffs vulnerable to a judicial determination of the degree of statistical correlation required to establish that a given trait is a proxy for prohibited classification. Perea at 851–853. But in absence of such an objective criterion, what would serve to establish that a trait is ethnic? Perea seems to think that ethnicity has a sufficiently self evident meaning as to overcome this problem; hence his proposal to expand federal anti-discrimination statutes to include "ethnicity and ethnic traits." Id. at 860–861.

5. Yoshino at 938.

6. I owe this line of analysis regarding gender to Judith Butler. See generally Judith Butler, *Gender Trouble* (1990). Note that it is not necessary to deny the existence of biological differences between the sexes in order to question the thoughtless conflation of these biological differences with a host of *social* differences.

7. *Price Waterhouse v. Hopkins*, 490 U.S. 228, 235 (1989).

8. Ann Hopkins, *So Ordered: Making Partner the Hard Way* (1996) at 148

9. Id. at 202.

10. See *Craft v. Metromedia, Inc.*, 766 F.2d 1205, 1207 (8th Cir. 1985).

11. *Willingham v. Macon Tel. Pub. Co.*, 507 F.2d 1084 (5th Cir 1975).

12. *Devine v. Lonschein*, 621 F. Supp. 894 (S.D.N.Y. 1985).

13. 813 F.2d 1406 (1987).

14. Frederic Jameson, *Postmodernism: The Cultural Logic of Late Capitalism* (1992) at 322.

15. Yoshino at 844.

16. Yoshino at 846-7.

17. John McWhorter, *The Power of Babel: A Natural History of Language* (2003) at 169.

18. Orlando Patterson, *Thomas hearings can help us reassess views of race and sex*, St. Petersburg Times, October 22, 1991, 11A.

19. Id.

20. Id.

21. Id.

22. Id.

23. Regina Austin, *Sapphire Unbound*! In *Critical Race Theory: The Key Writings That Formed the Movement*, Crenshaw et al. eds. (1994) at 426.

24. Id. at 428.

25. Id. at 429.

26. Id. at 429 (emphasis mine).

27. Id. at 432.

28. Id. at 433.

29. Id. at 430.

30. Id. at 432.

31. Id. at 430.

32. Id.

33. Charles Taylor, *The Politics of Recognition* in Charles Taylor and Amy Gutman eds., *Multiculturalism* (1994) at 25–26.

34. Juan Perea, *Ethnicity And Prejudice: Reevaluating "National Origin" Discrimination Under Title VII*, 35 Wm and Mary L. Rev. 805, 866–67 (1994).

35. Id.

36. Kwame Anthony Appiah, *Identity, Authenticity, Survival* in Charles Taylor and Amy Gutmann eds., *Multiculturalism* (1994) at 157.

37. 25 U.S.C.A. 1915 (a).

38. Kennedy, INTERRACIAL INTIMACIES (2003) 498–99.

39. 49 Cal. Rptr. 2d 507 (1996).

40. 849 P. 2d 925 (Idaho 1993).

41. 92 Cal. Rptr. 2d 692 (2001).

42. 490 U.S. 30 (1989).

43. Id. at 37.

44. Id. at 50, 54 (emphasis mine).

45. 92 Cal. Rptr. 2d at 697.

46. Cited in Social Work 44, 5 at 444 (Sept 1999).

47. Elizabeth Bartholet, *Nobody's Children* (1999) at 123–24, 125.

48. Bartholet at 125, 127.

49. Barry, *Culture and Equality* at 260 (quoting Dennis Wrong).

50. See Rudolph Alexander, Jr. & Carla M. Curtis, *A Review of Empirical Research Involving the Transracial Adoption of African-American Children*, Journal of Black Psychology, 22, 2: 223 (1996).

51. See. e.g., Ruth Arlene W. Howe, *Redefining the Trans-racial Adoption Controversy*, Duke J. Gender L. & Policy 2, 131 (1995).

52. See generally, Alexander and Curtis.

53. Eugene Genovese, *Black Studies: Trouble Ahead* in *Basic Black* (1970) at 40.

54. Lawford L. Goddard, *Transracial Adoption: Unanswered Theoretical and Conceptual Issues*, Journal of Black Psychology, 22, 2: 273, 278 (1996).

55. Id. at 279; Leslie Doty Hollingsworth, *Symbolic Interactionism, African American Families, and the Transracial Adoption Controversy*, Social Work, 44, 5: 443, 444 (Sept. 1999).

56. Kennedy at 499.

57. Joseph Westermeyer, *The Apple Syndrome in Minnesota: A Complication of Racial-Ethnic Discontinuity, Journal of Operational Psychiatry* 10 (1979).

58. Kennedy at 502.

59. See Kennedy at 502 (describing such claims at "junk science" and noting the lack of evidence to support them).

60. Kennedy at 489.

61. Bartholet at 133.

62. Jesse Hamlin, *Something Else: Indian Artists Need ID*, San Francisco Chronicle, July 7, 1991, E2.

63. Editorial, *Rubber Tomahawks*, Wall Street Journal, November 4, 1992, A14.

64. Steve Mannheimer, *Latest Indian War, This Time in the Arts, Come Because of Good Intentions Leading to Hell*, Indianapolis Star, May 9, 1993, G6.

65. Connie Laurenman, *What Do They Have to Prove? Native American Artists Grapple with Questions of Culture, Identity and Seeing Beyond Stereotypes*, Chicago Tribune, December 24, 1995.

66. D. R. Fusfield and Timothy Bates, *The Political Economy of the Urban Ghetto* (1984) at 12.

67. Apologies to Dr. Seuss. See Dr. Seuss, The Sneetches (1961).

68. Herbert Ashbury, *The Barbary Coast: An Informal History of the San Francisco Underworld* (1922) at 38.

69. Id. at 53.

70. Id. at 146.

71. See, e.g., Paulette Thomas, *Blacks Can Face a Host of Trying Conditions in Getting Mortgages*, Wall St. Journal, November 30, 1992, A1, A8–A9 (empirical studies reveal consistent racial bias in lending, regardless of the income, credit history or geographic location of the prospective borrower).

72. For this compacted account of the history of American racism I consulted the following works: C. Vann Woodward, *The Strange Career of Jim Crow* (1901); D. R. Fusfield and Timothy Bates, *The Political Economy of the Urban Ghetto* (1984); Douglas Massey and Nancy Denton, *American Apartheid*; Arnold R. Hirsch, *The Causes of Residential Segregation: A Historical Perspective*" in Issues in Housing Discrimination: A Consultation/Hearing of the United States Commission of Civil Rights, Washington, DC, November 12–13, 1985.

73. Fusfield & Bates at 28.

74. Perea at 863.

75. Flagg at 2025

76. Yoshino at 844.

77. Janice E. Hale-Benson, *Black Children: Their Roots, Culture and Learning Styles* (1982) at 42.

78. Morton Horowitz, *The Transformation of American Law 1870–1960: The Crisis of Legal Orthodoxy (1994)* at 155.

79. Yoshino at 938.

80. Yoshino at 905.

81. *Garcia v. Gloor*, 618 F. 2d 264, 269 (1980).

82. Kenji Yoshino, *Assimilationist Bias in Equal Protection: The Visibility Presumption and the Case of "Don't Ask, Don't Tell"* 108 Yale L.J. 485, 518 (1998).

83. Donald Braman, *Of Race and Immutability*, 46 U.C.L.A Law Review 1375, 1449, 1462 (1999).

84. Gregory Hoard Williams, *In Living Color*, Cleveland Plain Dealer, April 16, 1995 at 6.

85. 163 U.S. 537 (1896).

86. Kwame Anthony Appiah, *In My Father's House: Africa in the Philosophy of Culture* (1993) at 38.

87. Yoshino, *Covering* at 873.

88. Halley, *Don't* (1999) at 126.

89. See generally id.

90. Georgia Code Ann. ß 16-6-2 (1984)

91. Tex. Penal Code Ann. Sec 21.06 (a), 21.01(1) (2003).

92. Lawrence at 17.

93. Halley at 130.

94. *Lawrence v. Texas*, 539 U.S. at 6 (2003).

95. *Romer v. Evans*, 517 U.S. at 641.

96. David A. J. Richards, *Identity and the Case for Gay Rights: Race, Gender, Religion as Analogies* (1999).

97. Neil Gotanda, *A Critique of "Our Constitutional is Color Blind"* 44 Stan L. Rev. 1, 66 (1991).

98. *Trans World Airlines v. Hardison.*

99. See, e.g., *Smith v. Pyro Mining Co.*, 827 F. 2d 1081, 1086 (6th Cir. 1987); *Carter v. Bruce Oakley, Inc.* 849 f Supp, 673, 675 (E.D Ark 1993).

100. Yoshino, *Covering* at 929.

101. Anthony Appiah, *Gender, Race Ethnicity*, The Journal of Philosophy, October 1990 at 499.

102. Clarence Page, *A Credit to his Races*, Newshour wth Jim Leher Transcript, http://www.pbs.org/newshour/essays/page_5-1.html (as of July 2003).

103. http://www.projectrace.com/aboutprojectrace/.

104. Julie C. Lythcott-Haims, *Note, Where Do Mixed Babies Belong? Racial Classification in America and its Implications for Transracial Adoption*, 29 Harv. C.R.-C.L. L. Rev. 531, 539–40 (1994).

105. Kim Cobb, *Racial Revisions to Census Forms Comfort Some, Concern Others*, Houston Chronicle, February 4, 2000.

106. Cindy Rodriquez, *Civil Rights Groups Wary of Census Data on Race*, Boston Globe, December 8, 2000, A1.

107. Soraya Sarhaddi Nelson, *An Ethnic Strategy on the Census Population: Campaign Urges African-Americans to retain clout by defining themselves only as black, even if heritage is mixed*, Los Angeles Times April 17, 2000.

108. Southern Poverty Law Project, *A New Way to Measure America*, http://tolerance. org/news/article_tol.jsp?id=140 (as of July 2003).

109. *Guidance on Aggregation and Allocation of Multiple Race Responses for Use in Civil Rights Monitoring and Enforcement*, Office of Management and Budget, Executive Office of the President, http://www.whitehouse.gov/omb/bulletins/b00-02.html (July 2003).

110. Editorial: *Multiracial Checkoff Is a Vote for Accuracy*, San Francisco Chronicle, June 8, 1997, p. 10.

111. Solomon Moore, *Milestone for Those of Mixed Race For the first time, a person can check two or more ethnicities on the census form*, Los Angeles Times, March 16, 2000.

112. Werner Sollars, "What Race Are You?" In *The New Race Question* at 260, Joe Perlmann and Mary C. Waters eds. (2002).

CHAPTER 3

1. Barry, *Culture and Equality* at 58.

2. Horowitz, *The Transformation of American Law* at 196.

3. Barry at 306.

4. David Rieff, *Multiculturalism's Silent Partner*, Harper's, August 1993 at 52.

5. Robert Allen, *Black Awakening in Capitalist America: An Analytic History* (1969) at 142.

6. Elizabeth Fernandez, *Exercising Her Right To Work, Fitness instructor wins weight-bias fight*, San Francisco Chronicle, Tuesday, May 7, 2002.

7. Kelly St. John and Jim Herron Zamora, *Southwest to Make Overweight Buy Two Seats*, San Francisco Chronicle, June 20, 2002 at A17, 24.

8. Fernandez, *Exercising Her Right to Work*.

9. Daniel S. Hammermesh and Jeff E. Biddle, *Beauty and the Labor Market*, 84 Amer. Econ, Review 1174 (1994).

10. Mark Kelman, *Market Discrimination and Groups*, 53 Stan. L.Rev 833, 864 (2001).

11. Id.

12. G. A. Cohen, *Multiculturalism and Expensive Tastes* in Multiculturalism, Liberalism and Democracy, Bhargava et al., eds. at 85.

13. Some may dislike such institutions and their goals: for instance, one might think that the atmosphere of hushed and muted subservience cultivated by posh restaurants and their staff is itself a form of class oppression. Similarly, there are

reasonable arguments that the uniformity of the armed services are sources of social control and entrenched hierarchy as unjust within the organization as they are difficult to quarantine there. Still, it should be obvious that these are distinct ideological positions from anti racism and should thus be treated separately from antidiscrimination law.

14. William Glaberson, *Five Orthodox Jews Spur Moral Debate Over Housing Rules at Yale*, The New York Times, Section 1, p. 45, Column 2, September 7, 1997.

15. Id.

16. Nick Goldin, *Cornell Battle Anew Over Ethnic Dormitories*, The New York Times, Section B, p. 5, May 6, 1996.

17. Id.

18. Johnson, *Bid Whist* at 1419.

19. 998 F. 2d 1480 (1993).

20. Id. at 1483–1484.

21. Id. at 1490.

22. Id. at 1489.

23. Id. at 1487.

24. See, e.g., Perea, *Ethncity and Prejudice*; Cornell and Bratton, *Deadweight costs and Intrinsic Wrongs*; Christopher David Ruiz Cameron, *How the Garcia Cousins Lost Their Accents: Understanding the Language of Title VII Decisions Approving English-Only Rules As The Product of Racial Dualism, Latino Invisibility, and Legal Indeterminacy, 85 Calif. L. Rev. 1347 (1997)*, 10 La Raza L.J. 261 (1997).

25. 998 F. 2d. at 1483.

26. Id.

27. Id.

28. William Julius Wilson, *When Work Disappears* (1997) at 117, 120, 131.

29. Id. at 136.

30. James Clifford, *The Predicament of Culture: Twentieth Century Ethnography, Literature and Art* (1988) at 341.

31. Matsuda, *Voices of America*.

32. Kymlicka, *Multicultural Citizenship* at 79, 113.

33. Matsuda, *Voices of America*.

34. Paul Gilroy, *There Ain't No Black in the Union Jack: The Cultural Politics of Race and Nation* (1991) at 158–59.

35. Gilroy at 172.

36. Gilroy at 170.

37. Cornel West, *Race Matters* (1993) at 101.

38. Stanley Crouch, *The Problem With Jazz Criticism: A noted critic and social commentator on why he was let go by the JazzTimes*, Newsweek, June 3, 2003.

39. Jeremy Waldron, *Minority Cultures and The Cosmopolitan Alternative*, 25 University of Michigan Journal of Law Reform 751, 754, 761 (1992).

40. Hugh Trevor-Roper, *The Highland Tradition of Scotland*, in *The Invention of Tradition*, Eric Hobsbawm and Terence Ranger, eds. (1993) at 23, 26.

41. Rep. of the Committee on Indian Arts and Crafts, 1934, Senate Reporter 900 at 5.

42. Waldron, *The Cosmopolitan Alternative* at 762.

CHAPTER 4

1. Mark Kelman and Jillian Lester, *Jumping the Queue* (1998) at 226.

2. Derrick Bell, And We Are Not Saved (1987) at 3.

3. Patricia Williams, The Alchemy of Race and Rights (1992) at 163.

4. Robert Post, Prejudicial Appearances (2001) at 11.

5. Id. at 42.

6. *United Steelworkers v. Weber* 433 U.S. 193, 208 (emphasis mine).

7. Ronald Coase, *The Problem of Social Cost*, 3 J. Law & Econ. 1 (1960).

8. Walter E. Williams, *The Intelligent Bayesian*, The New Republic, November 10, 1986 at 18.

9. Multicultural Citizenship at 35–36.

10. Bratton and Cornell, *Deadweight Costs* at 674.

11. Bratton and Cornell at 657.

12. Bratton and Cornell at 658.

13. *Fragante v. City and County of Honolulu*, 888 F. 2d. 591 (9ᵗʰ Cir. 1989).

14. *EEOC v. Metal Service Co.*, 892 F2d. 341, 350351 (3d Cir 1990); *Barnett v. W.T. Grant Co.*, 518 F.2d 543, 549 (4ᵗʰ Cir. 1975); *Parham v. Southwestern Bell Tel. Co.*, 433 F.2d 421, 426–427 (8ᵗʰ Cir. 1970) (word-of-mouth hiring that perpetuated racial imbalance circumstantial evidence of disparate treatment.)

15. *Hazen Paper Co. v. Biggins*, 507 U.S. 604 (1993).

16. *Carroll v. Talman Fed. Sav. & Loan Ass'n*, 604 F.2d 1028, 1033 (7ᵗʰ Cir. 1979).

17. *Craft v. Metromedia, Inc.*, 766 F.2d 1205, 1214 (8ᵗʰ Cir. 1985).

18. *Lanigan v. Barlett & Co. Grain*, 466 F. Supp 1388.

19. *Rogers* at 232.

20. See *Willingham v. Macon Tel. Pub. Co.*, 507 F. 2d 1084 (5ᵗʰ Cir. 1975).

21. See *Carroll v. Talman Fed. Sav. & Loan Ass'n*, 604 F.2d 1028, 1033 & th Cir. 1979).

22. See generally Post, *Prejudicial Appearances* (2001).

23. Barry, *Culture and Equality* at 60.

24. Steven M. Cutler, *A Trait Based Approach to National Origin Claims Under Title VII*, 94 Yale L. J. 1164 (1984) at 1172 (emphasis mine).

25. 457 U.S. 440 (1982).

26. 490 U.S. 642 (1989).

27. Charles Lawrence III, *The Id, the Ego and equal Protection: Reckoning With Unconscious Racism*, in Critical Race Theory: The Key Writings that Formed the Movement, 235, 238 (1995).

28. http://www.tolerance.org/hidden_bias/tutorials/02.html (Sept. 2003).

29. See, e.g., J. A. Bargh, *The Cognitive Monster: The Case against the Controllabil-*

ity of Automatic Stereotype Effects in *Dual Process Theories in Social Psychology*, S. Chaiken, Y. Trope, et al. eds. (1999); *Stereotypes as Individual and Collective Representations*, Stangor and Schaller, eds. (2000); P. G. Devine, *Stereotypes and prejudice: Their automatic and controlled components,* 56 Journal of Personality & Social Psychology 1, 5–18 (1989).

30. 490 U.S. at 652.

31. Perea at 863.

32. Flagg at 2025.

33. Elizabeth Rich, *Flying High: What it's like to be an airline stewardess* (1972) at 76.

34. Johanna Omelia and Michael Waldock, *Come Fly with Us: A Global History of the Airline Hostess* (2003) at 90.

35. See Paul Brest, *In Defense of the Anti-Discrimination Principle*, 90 Harv. L. Rev. 1, 29 (1976), *Keyes v. School District No. 1* 413 U.S. 189 (1973); *Washington v. Davis*, but cf., *Palmer v. Thompson*, 403 U.S. 217 (1971).

36. Kelman, *Market Discrimination and Groups* 53 Stan. L. Rev 833 (2001).

37. William Julius Wilson, *The Truly Disadvantaged* at 10 (1987).

38. Owen Fiss, *What Should Be Done for Those Left Behind*? 25 Boston Review 4, 7 (2000).

39. Kathryn Bold, *Corporate Cleanup; that well groomed and manicured look at many Orange County tourist spots is no accident. Dress codes make sure workers' appearances suit the image*, Los Angeles Times, May 9 1996 Part E, p. 1.

40. See David Autor, John Donahue and Stewart Schwab, *The Costs of Wrongful Discharge Laws* (unpublished draft).

POSTSCRIPT

1. James Baldwin, *In Search of a Majority* in *Nobody Knows My Name* at 137 (1961).

2. Barry, *Culture and Equality* at 31.

3. Kennedy, *Interracial Intimacies* at 35.

INDEX